Public Sector Strategy

Public Sector Strategy explores how strategic decisions are developed and implemented in the public sector, and examines the psychology underpinning strategic decision-making.

Combining knowledge from traditional perspectives with contemporary insights on strategic management, this book considers how managers make their decisions and provides key concepts and practical tools to aid delivery of strategy within highly institutionalised settings. This book provides theoretical grounding, real-life global cases, and practical examples of strategic decisions in an international public-sector context by working through the underpinnings of strategy, the influencing factors of strategic decision-making, strategic implementation, and strategic tools in practice.

It should be a core textbook for advanced undergraduate and postgraduate students studying public sector strategy and strategic management more broadly. It will also be of benefit for public sector managers, consultants, and private sector organisations who wish to interact with the public sector.

Mark Crowder is Senior Lecturer in Strategy, Programme Leader, and the Education Lead Officer for the Department of Strategy, Enterprise, and Sustainability at Manchester Metropolitan University, UK.

Mohammad Roohanifar is Senior Lecturer in Strategy and Subject Lead for Strategy and Sustainability within the Department of Strategy, Enterprise, and Sustainability at Manchester Metropolitan University, UK.

Trevor A. Brown is Senior Lecturer in Strategy and Apprenticeships Lead within the Department of Strategy, Enterprise, and Sustainability at Manchester Metropolitan University, UK, teaching professionals within education, health, and the public sector.

Public Sector Strategy

Concepts, Cases and Tools

Mark Crowder, Mohammad Roohanifar and Trevor A. Brown

Routledge
Taylor & Francis Group
LONDON AND NEW YORK

First published 2022
by Routledge
2 Park Square, Milton Park, Abingdon, Oxon OX14 4RN

and by Routledge
605 Third Avenue, New York, NY 10158

Routledge is an imprint of the Taylor & Francis Group, an informa business

British Library Cataloguing-in-Publication Data
A catalogue record for this book is available from the British Library

Library of Congress Cataloging-in-Publication Data
Names: Crowder, Mark, author. | Roohanifar, Mohammad, author. |
Brown, Trevor A. (Senior lecturer), author.
Title: Public sector strategy : concepts, cases and tools /
Mark Crowder, Mohammad Roohanifar and Trevor A. Brown.
Description: Abingdon, Oxon ; New York, NY: Routledge, 2022. |
Includes bibliographical references and index.
Identifiers: LCCN 2021045688 (print) | LCCN 2021045689 (ebook) |
ISBN 9780367361730 (hardback) | ISBN 9780367361754 (paperback) |
ISBN 9780429344305 (ebook)
Subjects: LCSH: Public administration—Decision making. | Strategic planning.
Classification: LCC JF1525.D4 C76 2022 (print) | LCC JF1525.D4 (ebook) |
DDC 352.3/4—dc23/eng/20211109
LC record available at https://lccn.loc.gov/2021045688
LC ebook record available at https://lccn.loc.gov/2021045689

ISBN: 978-0-367-36173-0 (hbk)
ISBN: 978-0-367-36175-4 (pbk)
ISBN: 978-0-429-34430-5 (ebk)

DOI: 10.4324/9780429344305

Typeset in Bembo
by Apex CoVantage, LLC

Contents

Author details

Mark Crowder

Mark is a senior lecturer in strategy and programme leader at Manchester Metropolitan University, which he joined in September 2013, having previously taught at the University of Chester. He has more than 20 years' management experience in both public and private sectors and studied at Liverpool John Moores University and the University of Liverpool before gaining his PhD in cognitive psychology at the University of Chester. He is a Senior Fellow of the Higher Education Academy and a Fellow of the Chartered Management Institute and is the Education Lead officer for the department of Strategy, Enterprise, and Sustainability.

Mohammad Roohanifar

Mohammad (Moe) Roohanifar is a Senior Lecturer in Strategy and subject lead for Strategy and Sustainability within the department of Strategy, Enterprise and Sustainability (SES) at the Manchester Metropolitan University Business School. Moe has gained considerable experience as an academic and a consultant working across the higher education industry and the private sector specialising in competitive strategy and organisational growth. He has an extensive knowledge of the field of Strategic Management with a PhD specialising in strategy from the University of Liverpool. Moe has been teaching for many years on different undergraduate levels and across variety of executive and specialised postgraduate programmes. He is a member of the Academy of International Business and the British Academy of Management and is a fellow of the Higher Education Academy.

Trevor A. Brown

Trevor is a senior lecturer in strategy and Academic Apprenticeships Director within the Department of Strategy, Enterprise, and Sustainability at Manchester Metropolitan University lecturing to professionals within education, health and the public sector. Trevor is a Fellow of the Higher Education Academy, a Fellow of the Institute for Knowledge Transfer IKT and a Chartered Fellow of the Chartered Management Institute. Much of Trevor's career has involved the management of knowledge transfer between universities and organisations. His research focuses on strategy within different contexts and organisational fields. Trevor has significant experience of developing strategies with organisations and has run numerous strategy-making workshops with a wide range of industries including nuclear decommissioning, education, public sector, health and charities.

Prelude

Introduction to the book

The popular perception of public sector management is that somehow is it less "real" and less "important" than within the private sector. However, the budgets involved dwarf those of many private sector businesses, and the stakes can be at least as important – these can quite literally be life-and-death decisions. Moreover, in many countries, the capacity of governments to deliver value is under attack for reasons that relate to factors such as austerity measures, immigration, and dramatic fractures within nations (see, for example, Brexit, les gilets jaunes, and the Catalan separatist movement). Also, in emerging economies, there are growing expectations from the public sector that relate to the rise of a middle class and the call for better public services.

Given these pressures, why, then, is the public sector so side-lined in the literature? Most strategy textbooks are focused on the private sector, despite the fact that the public sector controls enormous budgets, employs tens of thousands of people, and makes decisions that impact on the lives of each and every person. Indeed, some of these decisions can quite literally be life-and-death decisions.

Most academic strategy texts are focused on theory and high-level strategic planning but there are few that explore how strategy might be "done" and implemented, especially in the public sector. There is an implied assumption that high-level strategy is merely rolled out and implemented by managers. However, the reality is different. This gap is addressed in this book. The book equips readers with key knowledge from the traditional perspectives on strategic management but critically adds the contemporary insights necessary for delivering strategy within a heavily institutionalised setting. By first establishing a strong theoretical underpinning, the book then equips managers with practical tools and insights for use in the workplace.

The book provides students with both theory and practical examples of strategic decisions in an international public sector context and is supported by a wealth of electronic features. It is aimed at business and management students who are employed in the public sector or who are aiming for a career in the public sector, and who are in the final year of their degrees or are undertaking master's level studies. It will also benefit public sector managers, consultants, and private sector organisations who wish to interact with the public sector. By exploring the psychology behind strategic decision-making, this book offers a new approach to textbooks in this field. It explores "how" managers make their decisions and, in this way, it offers guidance that improves clarity by helping managers to refine their thinking. Hence it is designed to improve students' strategic decision-making and give them key knowledge and practical tools that they can apply in their own workplaces.

DOI: 10.4324/9780429344305-1

The book is divided into four key sections, each of which is subdivided into separate chapters. Each chapter builds upon the last, and the nature of public sector strategy unfolds logically and consistently. Theory and practice are interspersed, so that students can become familiar with how concepts are applied in the "real world" and gain an understanding that strategy in the public sector is not some abstract theory that is never used; rather, it has significant practical applications.

Each chapter ends with a summary of the key themes and with questions to allow readers to test their understanding of the topics covered. Further practice questions are interspersed throughout each chapter at key junctures to reinforce learning.

Section 1: introduction to the public sector

Chapter 1 What is the "public sector"?

The public sector is fundamentally different to the private sector, and, therefore, strategy theory needs to be applied differently. This chapter sets the context for the remainder of the book by exploring the public sector in different countries and showing how it is managed. This leads into a discussion of the nature of strategy in this context. The nature of the public sector differs considerably from country to country. In the USA, for instance, health care is largely funded by a system of private insurance, whereas in the UK, the National Health Service is clearly a public function. Some countries, such as France and Greece, have a large public sector, but other countries, such as the UK, have a much smaller public function. These differences are compounded when considering federal and state responsibilities in some countries, and when one takes account of the prevailing political systems which mandate a larger or smaller role for the state. The public sector is, therefore, made up of a range of organisations with a wide remit of functions; but despite the diverse nature of these bodies, public sector organisations have a number of common characteristics and operate according to general rules and procedures.

Section 2: theoretical underpinnings of strategy

Chapter 2 Approaches to strategy development in the public sector

This chapter discusses how public sector strategy has developed over many decades, and demonstrates that there has been a drive towards introducing private sector management techniques into the public sector, despite the fundamental differences between the two sectors. For instance, some concepts that play a central role in business and corporate strategy – such as competition and value appropriation – may bear little relevance in part of the public sector context, where strategy may be more related to collaboration and value (re)distribution. Indeed, it is not always easy to define what "success" looks like in a public sector context. It could be argued that, rather than seeking to make a profit (as in much of the traditional strategy literature), public sector strategy should ultimately deliver public services, and that, therefore, issues arise concerning criteria for the formulation of "sound" strategies and for the appraisal of the results of strategy implementation

The chapter then explores three lenses through which public sector strategy can be viewed – traditional public administration, new public management, and network governance.

Chapter 3 Traditional approaches to strategy and value creation

Value creation is at the heart of strategy. This chapter outlines some of the main theoretical models and frameworks within the area of strategic management focusing on how value is created. Over the past few decades, several theories and frameworks have been developed to answer the "holy grail" of strategic management: why organisations in the same competitive domain outperform one another. In this chapter we review some of the influential frameworks that underpin how value is perceived and captured before focusing on some of the more contemporary approaches about value creation. The objective of this chapter is to draw on key theories within the field of strategy and how they inform value creation within public sector.

This chapter reviews and discusses some of the traditional frameworks that underpin the value creation argument within strategic management. We track the historical development of these frameworks within strategy to provide a better context for understanding public sector strategy. Some of the more contemporary approaches to value creation are discussed. Building on the concept of "shared value" and shareholder and stakeholder perspectives on value, we discuss how value creation within the public sector requires a clear understanding of how value is perceived and captured for different stakeholders. Finally, drawing on earlier discussions and building on key theories of value creation within the field of strategy, we review and discuss the important public value frameworks that take into account the public and the business requirements that many government organisations experience.

Section 3: factors that influence strategic decision-making

Chapter 4 Influences on strategy development: classical models

Strategic decision-making does not simply just "happen". Rather, strategy is the result of a series of decisions, each of which builds upon the last. However, although senior managers like to think that they are immune from influence and always make decisions dispassionately and objectively, this is not the case in reality. This chapter explores how managers are influenced and the impact this has on their decisions. This will, therefore, help practitioners and academics alike to become more aware of these factors, and to factor them into their thought processes and, as a result, improve the quality of their decision-making.

Chapter 5 Influences on strategy development: neo-institutional theory

This chapter continues the exploration of how managers are influenced and the impact this has on their decisions. Here, we dive deeper into the systemic perspective, specifically the neo-institutional drivers that may underpin strategic thinking. The intent is to give the public sector strategist a critical eye when undertaking strategic development and to unmask any unconscious assumptions that may influence or affect strategic thinking.

Chapter 6 The psychology of strategic decision-making

This chapter explores the psychology of strategic decision-making. It explores the nature of decisions and offers a definition of what strategic decisions actually are, and these are distinguished from operational and administrative decisions. We then discuss the various ways in which decisions can be made, and these are grouped into two schools of thought: normative and behavioural decision-making. Normative decision-making uses logical and rational approaches to undertake a series of steps to consider and evaluate the various options that present themselves and, in doing so, produces a final decision that is underpinned by robust analysis. Behavioural decision-making, on the other hand, uses experience and gut instinct to cut through the mass of data that managers are often confronted with, and the resulting decisions are fast but may be skewed by bias or other factors. This is followed by an introduction to cognitive heuristics. These are shortcuts, or rules of thumb, that are inherent within everyone, and they can be used to make decisions. We show that strategy (the long-term big picture) is often based on a series of non-rational steps; these ideas are introduced in this chapter prior to a fuller examination in the next chapter.

Chapter 7 The use of cognitive heuristics in strategic decision-making

This chapter builds upon the previous chapter that explored the psychology of strategic decision-making. In that chapter, we explored different types of decision and were able to identify what we mean by "strategic decisions". We then explored the two main schools of thought in decision-making theory: normative and behavioural approaches. One of the behavioural models is cognitive heuristics, and we closed the previous chapter by introducing them in outline form.

Cognitive heuristics are shortcuts, or rules of thumb, that are inherent within everyone and used to make decisions. In this chapter, we again show that strategy (the long-term big picture) is often based on a series of non-rational steps, and many of these heuristics are examined in detail. Throughout this chapter, we have included illustrative quotes from public sector managers from different countries and disciplines. A total of 11 managers were interviewed for this chapter, and their experiences enrich the discussions and reveal how experienced managers make decisions in real life.

Section 4: strategic tools in practice

Chapter 8 Current debates in strategy as practice, NIT, and workshops

This chapter builds upon Section 2 of the book. Strategy as practice (SAP) is a critical and recent arena of research which addresses the limitations of mechanistic traditional strategy. Within SAP, strategy is something that people do as a social practice which pays attention to how strategy practitioners act and interact. As this field has developed, the definition has widened to incorporate the development and implementation of strategy. SAP aims to move strategy away from being the preserve of the senior manager and incorporates the wider range of actors and influencers. The field has grown to include a range of critical strategic arenas which are explored in this chapter

Chapter 9 Revealed cognitive causal mapping: theoretical underpinning and approaches to analysis

This chapter adds a research-informed depth in underpinning the causal cognitive mapping process detailed in the previous chapter. The guide to undertaking a strategy workshop can be accessed and utilised without the deeper knowledge and underpinning that supported its development. However, strategists may be interested to explore its underpinning processes and justifications. The chapter builds to explore analysis of a developed cognitive map. Again, this is not necessary for undertaking a strategy workshop within an organisation, but it may be of interest for the reader in developing a deeper insight into the focus of strategic attention and any approaches or limitations that may be present within a cognitive map. When undertaking a strategy making workshop, actors, representing their organisations, generate "ideas" (namely, issues, goals, unique capability, and statement of strategic intent) through a cognitive mapping process. The strategy-making process enables participants to express issues, goals, core competence, and a statement of intent that summarises their position and approach to strategy based on "deliberate emergent" strategic principles. The nature of this approach enables organisational actors to express what they perceive as issues of importance from their personal, organizational, and institutional reality. These ideas thus constitute a data set that can be utilised for strategy analysis and that gives the reader an approach to analysis that may scratch below the surface of a strategy workshop, thereby enabling exploration of groups thinking at a far deeper and empirical level.

Chapter 10 Running a strategy workshop – a practical guide

This chapter offers the reader a simple model for undertaking a strategy workshop. It has been adapted from Ackermann and Eden's Strategic Options Development and Analysis model (SODA), with the addition of some classical tools and a modification of some elements. If you find this method appealing, we strongly recommend reading further around Ackermann and Eden's work and exploring the Decision Explorer software designed for the purpose of process mapping. The process shown in this chapter is a simple and straightforward method for eliciting strategy that can work at any level within the organisation, from an organisational team or department through to higher corporate levels.

Chapter 11 Case studies and insights from public sector strategy sessions

This chapter builds upon the previous chapter. In that chapter, we show how workshops might be conducted, but in this chapter we provide worked examples to show what can be achieved in these workshops. This chapter examines three public sector strategy case studies and draws insights and guidance on the type of barriers, thinking, and approaches encountered when exploring strategy. The chapter explores three separate organisations: a profession within the UK National Health Service, a department within local government, and a new form of school.

Section 5: summary

Chapter 12 Summary and conclusions

Public sector management is largely side-lined in the literature. Despite the fact that public sector organisations employ many thousands of people, despite the enormity of public sector budgets and the impact of public sector decisions on all of us, it is still seen by many as less important than the private sector. Nowhere is this more true than in the field of strategy. Public sector strategy is fundamentally different from that of the private sector, focusing on value for its stakeholders rather than on profitability and competitive advantage; and yet, it is neglected by scholars and often overlooked by lecturers in the classroom. This book has been designed to furnish readers with key knowledge from traditional private sector perspectives on strategic management, but we also show how this needs to be modified and adapted for the public sector. By interweaving theory with practical cases, we have sought to equip managers with practical tools and insights for use in the workplace.

Acknowledgements

Mark Crowder:

Thank you Sue, Gemma, and Laura. Thank you for tolerating me when I spent long hours banging away on my keyboards, and for your patience when I disappeared for hours at a time to conduct interviews. Thank you for putting your lives on hold as the book developed. I would also like to thank my colleagues at work – there are too many to list, but you know who you are!

Mohammad (Moe) Roohanifar:

I would like to sincerely thank my mentor, Professor Tom Cannon, who has always guided me throughout my career with his timely advice and support, my parents Ali and Zara for their unwavering love, my family for their care and support, and my friends and colleagues for inspiring me to write this book.

Trevor A. Brown:

I would like to thank Dr Kevin Gallimore for supporting and encouraging me on my research and academic journey; my wife and son, Lisa and Jacob, for their patience and support; and my colleagues Dr Helen Wadham, Dr Lawrence Green, Dr Diane Wright, and Dr Jacqueline McLean.

Trevor and Mohammad (Moe) would also like to express their appreciation and thanks to Dr Mark Crowder for being a consistent and enthusiastic driver in the development of the book.

Section 1

The public sector

Chapter 1

What is the "public sector"?

Learning outcomes

After reading this chapter you should be able to:

- understand the nature of the public sector
- understand the differences between the public and private sectors
- understand why management and strategy are different in the public and private sectors

Pre-chapter questions

- How would you define "the public sector"?
- How many organisations can you think of that are within the public sector?
- Can you think of any organisations that might be part–private sector and part public sector?

Key terms

- Public sector – the part of a country's economy that is controlled by the State (OED, 2021)

1.1 Introduction

This chapter sets the scene for the rest of the book. In this chapter, we outline what the public sector is and show that it is fundamentally different from the private sector in many important ways. It exists for a different purpose; it operates differently; it is subject to different rules and regulations; and it is managed differently. Crucially, and key to this book, its strategy is fundamentally different from that of the private sector.

DOI: 10.4324/9780429344305-3

We begin by defining "the public sector" and, as we will see, this is not as easy as you might think. In broad terms, the public sector is responsible for undertaking tasks that are essential for society. So, government and local councils are public sector,. So far so good. But what about health care? Is this public sector or private sector? Is it both? The boundaries between public and private sector have become increasingly blurred over recent decades, and it is not as easy to differentiate them in broad terms as it once was.

The chapter next looks at the public sector around the world. Obviously, in a book of this length it is impossible to explore every country, and, therefore, we have restricted ourselves to looking briefly at six countries to give the reader a flavour of how the public sector functions across the globe. There is no single model of "the public sector" that is universally adopted, and there are wide differences in remit, size, structure, and complexity.

For similar reasons, the chapter cannot explore every different version of public sector organisations – such a chapter would be many hundreds of pages long. Instead, we present an illustrative example: UK local government. We do not suggest that this is how the whole of the public sector operates, even in the UK; rather we use it as an example to demonstrate that even in a single category, there is considerable complexity and variety.

1.2 Defining "the public sector"

The OED defines the public sector as "the part of a country's economy which is controlled by the State" (OED, 2021). This is fine as far as it goes, but what does this actually mean? As we will see throughout this book, the public sector is responsible for undertaking tasks that are essential for society. Moreover, the nature and diversity of these tasks reflects differences in culture and expectations of the populations of the different countries. For instance, in some countries the large majority of health care providers, teachers, and emergency workers are directly employed by the government. In other countries, these and other types of professionals are employed by the private sector or non-profit organisations (OECD, 2019). These differences are compounded when considering federal and state responsibilities in some countries, and when one takes account of the prevailing political systems which mandate a larger or smaller role for the state. Similarly, the size of the public sector differs considerably from country to country. For instance, in Norway, the public sector represents more than 30% of total employment, whereas in Japan, this figure is fewer than 6%. The average across the OECD is 18% (OECD, 2019).

The public sector is therefore made up of a range of organisations with a wide remit of functions; but despite the diverse nature of these bodies, public sector organisations have a number of common characteristics and operate according to general rules and procedures. This can lead to excessive bureaucracy and "red tape" (Ryan et al., 2008). Some authors feel that this red tape makes the public sector inefficient (Bozeman, 1979). However, this view is by no means universally accepted, with other authors arguing that consistency of rules and obligations is determined by democratic imperatives, which result in legitimacy and accountability (Budd, 2007; Lynn, 2001).

Public organisations have the following characteristics (Weber, 1947):

- Labour is divided by skills and authority, and responsibility is defined by law and administrative regulation.

- Each job and office is independent of its occupant. The job is permanent; the individual temporary.
- Authority is increasingly centralised. At every stage of the organisation, there are superiors and subordinates arranged in a pyramidal hierarchy of powers.
- The organisation operates according to general rules. Individual employees act in accordance with the formal definitions and requirements of their jobs.
- For the sake of organisational continuity, written records are kept.

Although these characteristics were first developed well over half a century ago, they are still relevant (Flynn and Asquer, 2017). Given the nature of the public sector, it is unsurprising that there are significant differences between public and private sector management. For instance:

- The public sector is publicly funded. This means it must ensure both private and public value – i.e. that which is consumed by the public collectively (Moore, 1995).
- Whereas the private sector often focuses significantly, or even exclusively, on shareholders, public sector managers provide their services to a very diverse array of stakeholders (Alford, 2001).
- The public sector faces pressure from politicians to change direction and policies (Joyce, 1999).
- Local government faces quasi-commercial pressures rather than true commercial pressures (Collier et al., 2001).
- Strategy is often instigated and enforced externally (Collier et al., 2001).
- Because if its public funding, it has formalised decision-making processes (Dobuzinskis, 1997).

These differences have led to a view that perhaps public sector management is somehow inferior and that the "proper" managers reside in the private sector. As Appleby and Clark (1997: 34) put it, "When you think management you hardly think public sector". Somehow, management is less "real" and less "important" than within the private sector. However, the differences between the public and private sectors are rather permeable and change according to political influences (Flynn and Asquer, 2017). Indeed, these differences have blurred further in recent decades with the introduction of the new public management (discussed in Section 2); but, nevertheless, differences remain. Moreover, the budgets involved dwarf those of many private sector businesses, and the stakes can be at least as important – these can quite literally be life-and-death decisions. This is compounded by external pressures. For instance, in many countries, the capacity of governments to deliver value is under attack for reasons that relate to factors such as austerity measures, immigration, and dramatic fractures within nations (see, for example, Brexit, les gilets jaunes, and the Catalan separatist movement). Also, in emerging economies, there are growing expectations from the public sector that relate to the rise of a middle class and the call for better public services. Thus, it is important that we understand public sector management, and in particular, the strategic decisions that senior managers make.

The following sections briefly outline the nature and structure of the public sector in several countries. These countries have not been chosen for any particular reason other than to show the diversity and difference in approach in the public sector across the globe.

1.3 Public sector around the world

United States

Here's a good quiz question: How many states does the USA have? If you said 50, you are wrong. The correct answer is 46. Massachusetts, Kentucky, Pennsylvania, and Virginia are commonwealths, not states. However, this is a technicality: there is little, if any, real difference. Indeed, the homepage of www.kentucky.gov refers to its area as both a state and a commonwealth, as does the home page of www.virginia.gov. The four commonwealths and the 46 states have an equal footing and have equal recognition in the constitution. For reasons of simplicity, all 50 areas will be referred to as states throughout the rest of this book.

Within the USA, more than 20 million people are employed in the public sector, which represents almost 15% of the working population (Brock, 2019). Member states are governed by the Federal Government including the President in the Executive Branch supported by a host of Government Departments, Congress and Senate representatives in the Legislation Branch, and the Court structure within the Judicial Branch (Kemp, 2002).

In ultimate control is the US President, although this control is not absolute, and it can be tempered by the Senate or Congress. There are currently 100 Senators (two per state) and 435 Representatives in congress (apportioned between states based on their populations) (Bennett and Jenkins, 2020). However, the most important distinction is between federal and state responsibility McKay, 2001; Conrad, 2020). The National (or Federal) government assumes responsibility for matters such as health, education, welfare, transportation, housing, and urban development (Frymier, 2003), whereas the delivery of local policy and politics within an individual state are delivered locally (Bowman, 2003; Dresang, 2003). There has been an increasing drive towards decentralisation in recent years, with the responsibility for funding moving more towards taxation at a local level (Glaeser, 2013). Within the states, cities and counties own and manage local highways, and the state owns and manages arterial routes that are funded by the Federal Department of Transport through the Federal Highway Administration (U.S. Department of Transportation, 2020). City governments are critically important in the overall pattern of life in America (Cullop, 1999). They provide everything from police and fire protection to sanitary codes, health regulations, education, public transportation, and housing (Ehrenhalt, 2002).

United Kingdom

More than 5 million people are employed in the UK public sector, which represents almost 17% of the working population (ONS, 2019). However, the UK public sector is not easy to define. It is made up of a range of organisations with a wide remit of functions. Some of these organisations may, perhaps, be "obviously public", such as the NHS, local government and the emergency services (Collier et al., 2001; Ferlie et al., 1996; Speller, 2001); whilst others may not be nearly so "obviously public", such as the BBC and the Post Office (Collier et al., 2001). The Freedom of Information Act lists the public sector organisations to which it applies and adds considerably to the above list by including organisations such as the armed forces, some 25 advisory committees, the Bank of

England, the British Library, the Environment Agency, the Tate Gallery, and Remploy Ltd (FOI, 2000: Schedule 1).

The introduction of the Freedom of Information Act in 2000 has had major implications for public sector managers because every decision taken by a public official can now be fully scrutinised (FOI, 2000), and as a result, errors can be front-page news. Consequently, procedures are often established that are designed more to prevent mistakes than achieve success (Brynard, 1995; Dunn, 2008).

Greece

Greece has a similar percentage of public sector employees as the UK – approximately 15% of the workforce (OECD, 2019). Given its relatively small population, Greece has a large number of municipalities – roughly 900 (Cohen, 2008) – and these provide a range of services such as refuse collection, transportation, education, and health services (Doumpos and Cohen, 2014). Unlike countries such as the USA, where local taxation provides much of the funding, Greek municipalities rely heavily on obtaining funding from central government (Doumpos and Cohen, 2014).

The Greek national health service is a universal health care system provided through national health insurance and private health care. It consists of primary care (GP practices), which aims to prevent and treat illnesses, and secondary care (hospitals) which gives aid via hospitalisation. The situation has deteriorated since 2011 due to austerity, and hospitals are now experiencing severe problems (Daley, 2011). According to a major study by POEDIN (ΠΟΕΔΗΝ – the Panhellenic Federation of Employees at Public Hospitals), the Greek health system is in a state of dissolution. The study highlights a lack of beds and medical equipment, the closure of intensive care units and operating theatres, and a national shortage of doctors and staff; in some places, 40% of medical positions are vacant (Giannakos and Papanastasis, 2016). Moreover, government health spending has fallen significantly, and Greece owes $1.2 billion to pharmaceutical companies (Kottasova, 2015).

Denmark

Denmark, together with Norway, has one of the highest ratios of public sector workers in the world – consistently more than 700,000 employees in general government alone (Statistics Denmark, 2020) and approximately 33% of the workforce as a whole (OECD, 2019).

Unlike some parts of the world, Denmark has chosen to embrace technology in a very proactive way throughout the country. Indeed, it has been recognised for the past few years as the most digitalised country in the world (European Commission, 2020; United Nations, 2018). This is reflected in its public sector, to the extent that with a single digital key, citizens can access over 100 different public services together with a range of private services (Denmark.dk, 2021). However, although the mode of access might be different from many nations, the nature of the Danish public sector is similar to most countries and includes health, social care, defence, law and order, environment, and education.

Health care is largely devolved to the local governments in five regions, which are themselves subdivided into 98 municipalities. The national government has less of a role than in the UK, for example, and has more of a strategic role in terms of policy, regulation, and co-ordination (Britnell, 2015). Higher Education (HE) is delivered through a mixture of universities, university colleges, business academies, and HE education institutions and, unlike many parts of the world, education at all levels attracts no tuition fees, with all costs being met by the state (Danish HES Ministry, 2020).

India

The population of India is enormous – roughly 1.3 billion people at the time of writing. Indeed, India is the world's largest democracy in terms of population (BBC, 2019). It has 36 regions, comprising 28 autonomous states, such as Bangalore, Bihar, Punjab, and Karnataka, and eight union territories, such as Delhi, Chandigarh, and Ladakh. These are themselves divided into 729 districts, ranging from 1 to 52 per area (Chandigarh and Madhya Pradesh, respectively).

Prior to India gaining independence in 1947, the public sector in the country hardly existed – certainly in comparison to other countries we are examining in this book. There were perhaps 15–20 public sector enterprises at this point. However, since then, there has been an ever-increasing growth in the public sector and, at the time of writing, the Indian public sector is now among the largest in the world. Central government has driven a massive expansion of the national economy via schemes such as five-year plans for electrification of villages, increased road building, and so forth. There are now roughly 350 public sector enterprises at the national level, and between 700–800 at the state level (Indian Government, 2019). The public sector is, therefore, very diverse and includes hospitals, banks, universities, energy companies, and airlines.

Japan

Japan offers an interesting comparison to other countries due to its relatively small public sector. Out of a total population of more than 125 million (Statistics Bureau Japan, 2021), only 7.7% of the workforce is employed in the public sector (ILO, 2019). The term "public sector" in a Japanese context has been defined as "national and local government organizations involved in both non-industrial and industrial activities" (Koshiro, 2001: 155). This term is revealing because it is underpinned by a difference in governance, with non-industrial public employees being subject to different labour laws than those working in industrial activities (Koshiro, 2001).

Japan's public sector has historically been seen as underperforming, and many reasons for this have been suggested, including differing employment laws, dealing with the demands of an aging population, the need for fiscal decentralisation, and the need to reform the tax system (Doi and Ihori, 2009). As a result, in recent times there has been a move towards privatisation of many aspects of public service. As at 2021, the Japanese economy is now largely based on private enterprise, although there is a significant number of public corporations that are still owned by the government (Statistics Bureau Japan, 2021), including Nippon Telegraph and Telephone Corporation, Tokyo Metro, and Japan Tobacco. Readers may find it odd that a tobacco producer is a publicly owned organisation. One outcome of this drive for privatisation is that fewer than 1% of IT experts work in Japan's public sector, compared to over 10% in the USA, with 70% working in the private sector IT industry, compared to roughly 40% in the USA and Germany (Japan Times, 2020). As a result, there is now a shortage of IT professionals in key fields, and the impacts of this have been felt at a national level, with major delays being experienced in the distribution of COVID-19 financial relief packages to the population.

1.4 Illustrative example: UK local government

Task

- What do you think local government is for?
- What do you think are the responsibilities of local government?

Introduction

As we have seen, the public sector is complex and diverse, thus it is not possible to adequately explore every possible combination and nuance. Therefore, to act as an introduction to the rest of the book, we have chosen to focus on a single illustrative example (local government) in a single country (the UK). As we will see, even this narrow focus contains areas of great complexity, and it, therefore, sets the scene for the rest of the book.

The nature of local government

Local government takes a range of forms depending upon which country is being considered, and the impact of strategic decisions in this context can literally mean life-or-death. This section identifies some of the different approaches taken around the world and draws out both commonalities and areas of difference. By its very nature, where local government is concerned, there are no national employers: each local authority is an autonomous employer. Local government staff are employees only of their own employing authorities, not of some national service. Conformity to national conditions is voluntary (Fowler, 2001).

This means that there can be tensions and areas of confusion around local government management. For instance:

- Central government and local authorities may be governed by different political parties, with different agendas and conflicting concerns (Atkinson and Wilks-Heeg, 2001).
- Local government is subject to extensive public scrutiny and regulation. This has been enhanced by the Freedom of Information Act 2000, which only applies to the public sector.
- Local government has a number of unique features that distinguish it from other parts of the public sector (Appleby and Clark, 1997).
- Local government is based on local election. While local authorities exercise substantive powers they are subject to public accountability for those powers.
- They are multipurpose organisations; this creates challenges of balancing difficult choices both across and within service areas.
- They are multi-contact organisations within the area for which they are responsible,

- They gain their identity from the area for which they are responsible. In that locality, and normally only in that locality, they discharge their functions. They are often the largest employer and biggest property owner in the area, and there are few residents who will not make use of local authority services every year.

In the UK, there is no written constitutional guarantee protecting local government (Barlow and Röber, 1996). It exists by virtue of Acts of Parliament, and hence the structures, functions, funding, and many of the processes of local authorities are determined by law (Barlow and Röber, 1996). The arrangement of local government across the UK is complex and confusing (Chandler, 2001). There are 404 local authorities in the UK, 343 of which are in England (Institute for Government, 2021). Of these, there are 26 county councils, which provide social care and aspects of education and transportation, and these are subdivided into 192 district councils, which manage neighbourhood services such as waste management. Then there are 32 London boroughs, 36 metropolitan districts, and 55 unitary authorities (all figures from Institute for Government, 2021). It should also be noted that there are also approximately a further 9,000–10,000 Parish or Town Councils (Chandler, 2001).

In the USA, the figures are enormous. There are 89,004 local authorities in the US, which include 3,031 counties, 19,522 municipalities, 16,364 townships, 37,203 special districts, and 12,884 independent school districts (all figures from U.S. Census, 2020).

It is beyond the scope of this textbook to explore the structure of local government in more detail – indeed, whole books have been written about this (a search on Amazon conducted by this writer brought up more than 30,000 results!). However, this complexity is reflected in the wide range of theories that have been used to try to study it. These include urban regime theory (Mossberger and Stoker, 2001), public choice theory (Atreya and Armstrong, 2002), stakeholder theory (Laplume et al., 2008), rational choice theory (Donaldson, 1995), and localism theory (Stoker, 1991).

Exercise

Here are a list of services that the public sector normally provides. Which ones do you think are normally delivered by national government, and which are normally delivered by local government?

- defence
- taxation
- road maintenance
- waste disposal
- school-level education

In truth, these are not easy questions to answer definitively. Defence is clearly a matter for central government, but the other services in the list are not so straightforward to address. Taxation is national (e.g income tax rates and collection are the responsibility of national government) and local (e.g. council tax rates and collection fall under local authorities). Within many parts of the world, including the UK, local authorities have statutory responsibilities for a range of services including roads, social services, education, planning, and waste management (Turley, 2008). In some cases, local authorities are effectively monopoly providers (Barlow and Röber, 1996); however, outsourcing of services to the private sector has taken place consistently over recent years (Cooke, 2006). Examples include roads and waste disposal – both questions in the earlier exercise that can commonly be answered as "the service is managed by the local authority but delivered by the private sector". There are many reasons for this including scarcity of resources, strategic fit between the partner and authority, the partner's knowledge of the specific service, and regulatory imperatives (Butler and Gill, 2001). However, local authorities still have the statutory responsibility for delivery of these services and, therefore, bear the ultimate risk while the partner makes the profit (Speller, 2001). Primary and secondary education is usually delivered at a local level but within a national curriculum that is set by the national government.

The structure of local government

Appleby and Clark (1997) suggest that the key processes of decision-making in local government are political ones in which the dominant factor is the political priorities of the majority party on the council. This is, however, a generalisation, and there are also several other significant factors, including the wishes of the electorate, the influence of pressure groups and relationships between officers and councillors (Worthington and Britton, 2000). Woodrow Wilson, in his essay "The Study of Administration" (Wilson, 1887) emphasised the need to separate political decisions and their implementation, and these ideas still have resonance in the modern age (Dobuzinskis, 1997), where distinctions between politicians and officers are built into the organisational structures and decision-making processes (Barlow and Röber, 1996). Hence, decision-making in local government takes place within a framework where elected members and officers have defined roles and levels of authority. This is illustrated in Figure 1.1.

It should be noticed that Figure 1.1 is a generalisation: each council differs slightly in form and structure, and some large cities have chosen to adopt a Mayoral model, with a single elected official in ultimate authority supported by elected councillors.

Although the ultimate responsibility for all that is done by a local authority rests with the full council, in practice the full council is only responsible for taking a small number of major decisions, such as the implementation of the corporate policy framework and formal approval of the annual budget (Appleby and Clark, 1997). In local authorities the key divisions are typically the departments, which are usually headed by a chief officer normally drawn from the dominant profession in that department (e.g. social worker, teacher, or housing officer), and below the chief officers there is normally a multitiered hierarchy. There are also normally several central departments (e.g. finance, legal, or chief executive), sometimes known as the corporate core, which are not directly involved in service provision (Appleby and Clark, 1997). This is illustrated in Figure 1.2.

As before, Figure 1.2 represents a generic local authority, and again, each particular council differs in form and structure.

Within the generalised frameworks outlined above, each local authority's constitution includes a scheme of delegation to its officers. This empowers the chief executive,

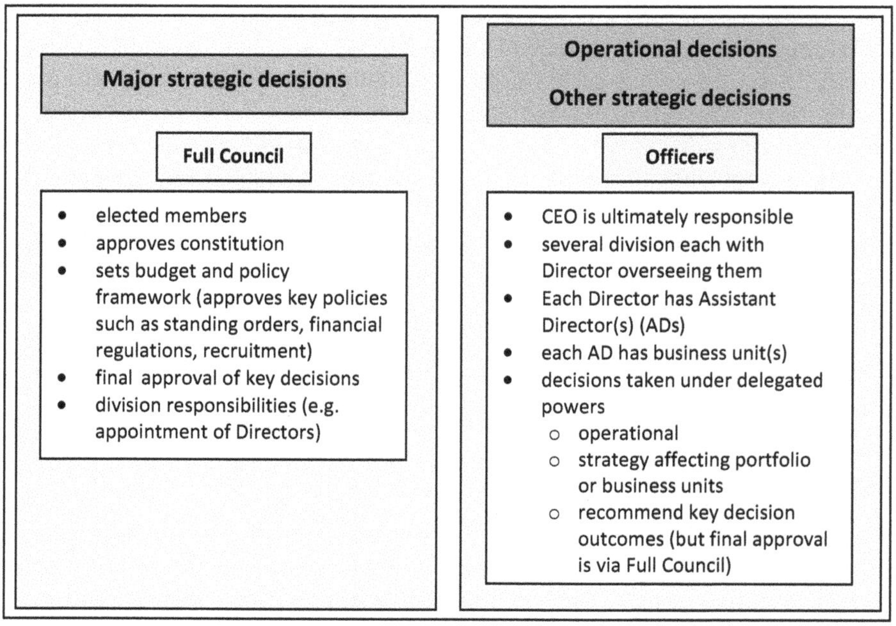

Figure 1.1 Typical local authority management responsibilities in the UK

directors, and other senior managers to make decisions on behalf of the council, although, as noted above, "key decisions" need cabinet approval before they can be implemented. It is impossible to outline every potential decision that officers are able to take; for instance, the scheme of delegation for a typical division is normally many pages long. However, typical examples include the recruitment of staff, emergency decisions, financial decisions (such as the write-off of debts and the virement of budgets between budget lines), procurement decisions (such as acceptance of tenders), and operational decisions (such as those pertaining to individual business units).

The following short exercises will help to set the scene. They all relate to local government.

Exercise 1a Who makes the decision?

Q1. There is a requirement to build a major new retail park. Who makes the decision?

Q2. There is a need to recruit a new secretary for the Chief Executive. Who makes the decision?

Q3. A city council has a highways contract that is due to expire in two years' time, and there is a need to procure a new one. Technical and financial estimates have been provided, and the new contract is expected to run for 15 years and cost a total of £200 million. Who makes the decision?

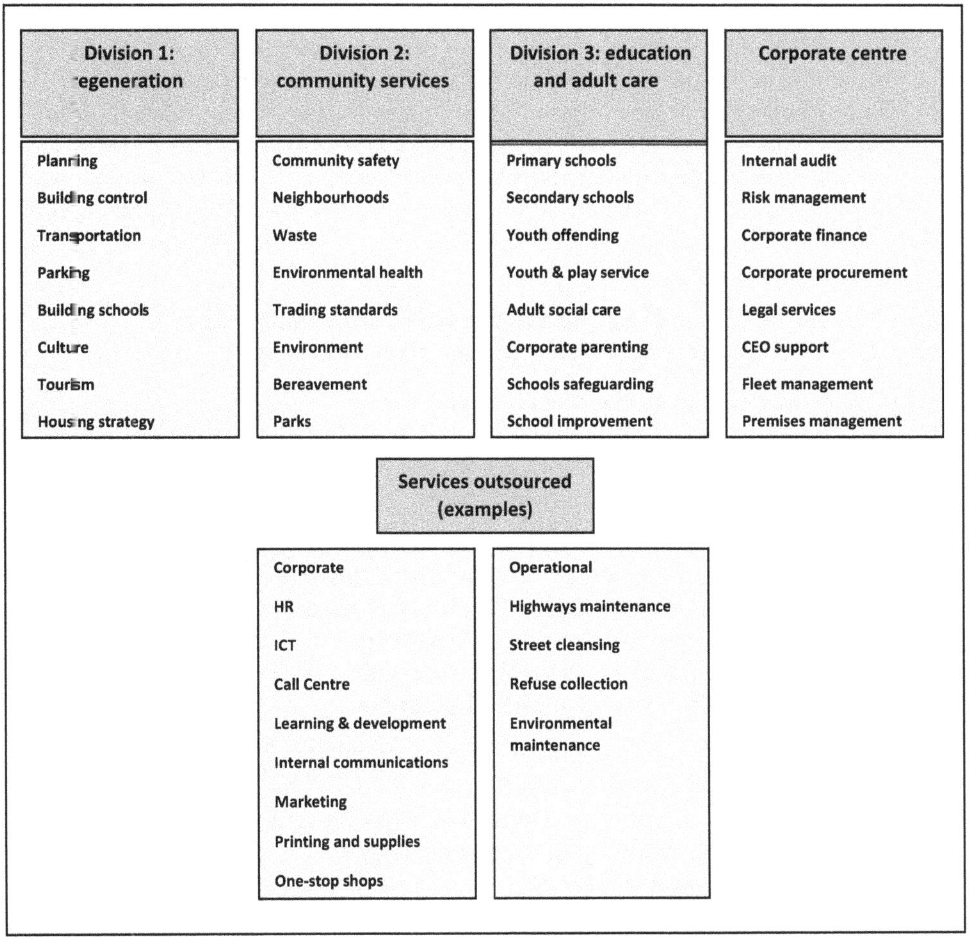

Figure 1.2 Typical local authority structure in the UK

Exercise 1a Who makes the decision? Answers and discussion

Q1 There is a requirement to build a major new retail park. Who makes the decision?

- This will require the disruption of traffic, with consequential impacts on local business for the duration of the work.
- The project will need a major injection of capital funding and will almost certainly be a collaboration of some sort with the private sector.
- There will be a need for major infrastructure work around highways, drainage, power, and so on.

- The new retail park is likely to draw shoppers away from city centre business. This will lead to an economic impact in the city centre, but there may also be benefits in terms of reduced traffic and reduced environmental impact.
- This is a major strategic decision. Typically, the decision will be made by councillors, who will take the views of officers into account. Once the decision has been made, operational decisions will be delegated to officers. Councillors will be kept informed of progress at key stages and intervene at a strategic level if necessary.

Q2 There is a need to recruit a new secretary for the Chief Executive. Who makes the decision?

- This is a decision that only affects one department.
- It is an operational decision. Typically, the decision will be made by an interview panel which includes the Chief Executive.

Q3 A city council has a highways contract that is due to expire in two years' time, and there is a need to procure a new one. Technical and financial estimates have been provided, and the new contract is expected to run for 15 years and cost a total of £200 million. Who makes the decision?

- £200 million is a very significant amount of money. Almost certainly, delegated powers will not cover this and councillors will have the final say.
- The contract lasts for 15 years. This would fall under strategic decisions because the council will be committing itself to expenditure for the foreseeable future, not just for the next few months.
- The project will need a major injection of capital funding and will almost certainly be a collaboration of some sort with the private sector.
- The new highways contract is likely to apply to the whole city at once rather than a small part of it. Although this time there are unlikely to be any major infrastructure changes and massive redevelopment impacts, this is still a major decision.
- This is a major strategic decision. Typically, officers from around the local authority will be involved in the procurement (lawyers, accountants, highways engineers, etc.). Councillors are likely to be involved periodically to make sure any bidders meet the strategic priorities of the council. Officers will make a recommendation but the council will have the final decision.

1.5 Chapter summary

In this chapter, we began by considering the nature of the public sector. We then explored the public sector around the world by means of six exemplar discussions. This led into a more in-depth examination of the public sector using a single illustrative example – UK local government.

Even from this initial chapter, we can see that there is no single model of "the public sector" that covers every possible combination of services, organisations, and countries. We have seen that the public sector is far more complex than a single definition suggests. It covers a range of services, not all of which are obvious, and each of these operates according to distinctive procedures. These vary from function to function and from country to country. Even in this first chapter, we have seen that the public sector and the private sector differ in many important ways.

Since the public sector operates differently from the private sector, its strategy needs to be understood on its own terms, and this is the focus of the remainder of the book. The next chapter begins the process of understanding by exploring how management operates in this context

Self-assessment questions

- What is "the public sector"?
- How is the public sector different from the private sector?
- Does "public sector" mean the same thing in different cultures or countries?
- Given the range of organisations within the public sector, to what extent do you think it is possible to prescribe a single "best" approach to their management?

References

Alford, J. (2001). The implications of 'publicness' for strategic management theory. In G. Johnson & K. Scholes (Eds.), *Exploring Public Sector Strategy*. Harlow: Financial Times Prentice Hall.

Appleby, A. & Clark, A. (1997). Quality management in local government, the same as in the private sector but different. *Leadership & Organization Development Journal*, 18(1), 29–36.

Atkinson, H. & Wilks-Heeg, S. (2001). *Local Government from Thatcher to Blair*. Cambridge: Polity Press.

Atreya, B. & Armstrong, A. (2002). *A Review of the Criticisms and the Future of New Public Management*. Victoria University Working Paper Series. Working Paper 7/2002.

Barlow, J. & Röber, M. (1996). Steering not rowing: Co-ordination and control in the management of public services in Britain and Germany. *International Journal of Public Sector Management*, 9(5/6), 73–89.

BBC. (2019). *India Country Profile* [online]. Retrieved July 28, 2020, from the BBC Website: www.bbc.co.uk/news/world-south-asia-12557384.

Bennett, A. J. & Jenkins, S. (2020). *US Politics Annual Update 2020*. Abingdon: Hodder Education.

Bowman, A. O. (2003). *State and Local Government: The Essentials* (2nd edn). Boston: Houghton Mifflin.

Bozeman, B. (1979). *Public Management and Policy*. New York: St Martin's Press.

Britnell, M. (2015). *In Search of the Perfect Health System*. London: Palgrave Macmillan.

Brock, J. (2019). Public sector employment. In C. Dell'Aringa, G. Della Rocca, & B. Keller (Eds.), *Strategic Choices in Reforming Public Service Employment*. London: Palgrave Macmillan, pp. 97–126.

Budd, L. (2007). Post-bureaucracy and reanimating public governance: A discourse and practice of continuity? *International Journal of Public Sector Management*, 20(6), 531–547.

Brynard, D. J. (1995). Combating red tape in the public sector. *International Journal of Public Sector Management*, 8(4), 38–47.

Butler, R. & Gill, J. (2001). Formulation and control of public-private partnerships: A stakeholder approach. In G Johnson & K. Scholes (Eds.), *Exploring Public Sector Strategy*. Harlow: Financial Times Prentice Hall.

Chandler, J. A. (2001). *Local Government Today* (3rd edn). Manchester: Manchester University Press.

Cohen S. (2008). Identifying the moderator factors of financial performance in Greek municipalities. *Financial Accountability and Management*, 24(3), 265–294.

Collier, N., Fishwick, F. & Johnson, G. (2001). The process of strategy development in the public sector. In G. Johnson & K. Scholes (Eds.), *Exploring Public Sector Strategy*. Harlow: Financial Times Prentice Hall.

Conrad, J. (2020). *What You Should Know about Politics . . . But Don't, Fourth Edition: A Nonpartisan Guide to the Issues That Matter* (4th edn). New York: Arcade Publishing.

Cooke, F. L. (2006). Outsourcing of public services and implications for managerial knowledge and careers. *Journal of Management Development*, 25(3), 269–284.

Cullop, F. G. (1999). *The Constitution of the United States an Introduction*. London: Penguin.

Daley, S. (2011). Fiscal crisis takes toll on health of Greeks. *The New York Times*, December 27. Retrieved July 19, 2020, from www.nytimes.com/2011/12/27/world/europe/greeks-reeling-from-health-care-cutbacks.html.

Danish HES Ministry. (2020). *The Danish Higher Education System*. Retrieved February 11, 2021, from https://ufm.dk/en/education/higher-education/the-danish-higher-education-system.

Denmark.dk. (2021). *The Key to Denmark's Digital Success*. Retrieved February 11, 2021, from https://denmark.dk/innovation-and-design/denmarks-digital-success.

Dobuzinskis, L. (1997). Historical and epistemological trends in public administration. *Journal of Management History*, 3(4), 298–316.

Doi, T. & Ihori, T. (2009). *The Public Sector in Japan: Past Developments and Future Prospects*. London: Edward Elgar.

Donaldson, L. (1995). *American Anti-Management Theories of Organization: A Critique of Paradigm Proliferation*. Cambridge: Cambridge University Press.

Doumpos, M. & Cohen, S. (2014). Applying data envelopment analysis on accounting data to assess and optimize the efficiency of Greek local governments. *Omega*, 46 (July issue), 74–85.

Dresang, D. L. (2003). *Politics and Policy in American States and Communities* (4th edn). New York: Longman.

Dunn, M. D. (2008). Open for business? An evaluation of the current and future impact of New Public Management (NPM) on the UK Ministry of Defence (MOD). Conference Paper: BAM2008, Majestic Hotel, Harrogate, 9–11 September.

Ehrenhalt, A. (Ed.) (2002). *Governing: Issues and Applications from the Front Lines of Government*. Washington, DC: CQ Press.

European Commission. (2020). *The Digital Economy and Society Index 2020*. Retrieved February 11, 2021, from https://ec.europa.eu/digital-single-market/en/digital-economy-and-society-index-desi.

Ferlie, E., Ashburner, L., Fitzgerald, L. & Pettigrew, A. (1996). *The New Public Management in Action*. Oxford: Oxford University Press.

Flynn, N. & Asquer, A. (2017). *Public Sector Management* (7th edn). Thousand Oaks, CA: Sage.

FOI. (2000). *Freedom of Information Act 2000*. London: HMSO.

Fowler, A. (2001). *Human Resource Management in Local Government*. Harlow: Longman Group.

Frymier, J. R. (2003). *Cultures of the States: A Handbook on the Effectiveness of State Governments*. Lanham, MD: Scarecrow Press.

Giannakos, M. & Papanastasis, X. (2016). *Νέα αξονική του ΕΣΥ – ΔΙΑΓΝΩΣΗ: Πλήρη κατάρρευση*. Retrieved July 19, 2020, from www.poedhn.gr/deltia-typoy/item/1803-nea-aksoniki-tou-esy–diagnosi-pliri-katarrefsi.

Glaeser, E. L. (2013). Urban public finance. In A. J. Auerbach, R. Chetty, M. Feldstein, & E. Saez (Eds.), *Handbook of Public Economics* (Vol. 5). London: ScienceDirect, pp. 195–256.

ILO. (2019). *Country Profiles*. Retrieved February 11, 2021, from https://ilostat.ilo.org/?subject=EMP&indicator=PSE_TPSE_GOV_NB&datasetCode=A&collectionCode=YI&_afrLoop=1093627555138474&_afrWindowMode=0&_afrWindowId=null#!%40%40%3Findicator%3DPSE_TPSE_GOV_NB%26_afrWindowId%3Dnull%26subject%3DEMP%26_afrLoop%3D1093627555138474%26datasetCode%3DA%26collectionCode%3DYI%26_afrWindowMode%3D0%26_adf.ctrl-state%3D17m2i1zor1_142.

Indian Government. (2019). *Public Enterprises Survey 2018–19*. Retrieved July 31, 2020, from Department of Public Enterprises Website: https://dpe.gov.in.

Institute For Government. (2021). *Local Government*. Retrieved June 15, 2021, from www.instituteforgovernment.org.uk/explainers/local-government.

Japan Times. (2020). *Less Than 1% of IT Experts Work in Japan's Public Sector*. Retrieved February 11, 2021, from www.japantimes.co.jp/news/2020/11/07/business/tech/it-workers-public-sector/.

Joyce, P. (1999). *Strategic Management for the Public Services*. Buckingham: Open University Press.

Kemp, R. L. (Ed.) (2002). *How American Governments Work: A Handbook of City, County, Regional, State, and Federal Operations*. Jefferson, NC: McFarland.

Koshiro, K. (2001). Japanese public sector employment. In C. Dell'Aringa, G. Della Rocca, & B. Keller (Eds.), *Strategic Choices in Reforming Public Service Employment*. London: Palgrave Macmillan, pp. 155–184. https://doi.org/10.1057/9781403920171_7.

Kottasova, I. (2015). *Inside Greece's Health Care Crisis*. Retrieved July 19, 2020, from http://money.cnn.com/2015/07/10/news/economy/greece-health-care-crisis/.

Laplume, A., Sonpar, K. & Litz, R. (2008). Stakeholder theory: Reviewing a theory that moves us. *Journal of Management*, 34(6), 1152–1189.

Lynn, L. E. (2001). The myth of the bureaucratic paradigm: What traditional public administration really stood for. *Public Administration Review*, 61(2), 144–160.

McKay, D. (2001). *American Politics & Society* (5th edn). Oxford: Blackwell Publishers Ltd.

Moore, M. (1995). *Creating Public Value: Strategic Management in Government*. London: Harvard University Press.

Mossberger, K. & Stoker, G. (2001). The evolution of urban regime theory: The challenge of conceptualization. *Urban Affairs Review*, 36(6), 810–835.

OECD. (2019). *Government at a Glance 2019*. Paris: OECD Publishing.

OED. (2021). *Public Sector*. Retrieved March 7, 2021, from www.oed.com/view/Entry/154052?redirectedFrom=public+sector#eid27763314.

ONS. (2019). *Public Sector Employment, UK: March 2019*. Retrieved July 19, 2019, from the ONS Web Site: www.ons.gov.uk/employmentandlabourmarket/peopleinwork/publicsectorpersonnel/bulletins/publicsectoremployment/march2019.

Ryan, N., Williams, T., Charles, M. & Waterhouse, J. (2008). Top-down organizational change in an Australian Government agency. *International Journal of Public Sector Management*, 21(1), 26–44.

Speller, S. (2001). The best value initiative. In G. Johnson & K. Scholes (Eds.), *Exploring Public Sector Strategy*. Harlow: Financial Times Prentice Hall.

Statistics Bureau Japan. (2021). *Population Estimates Monthly Report December 2020*. Retrieved February 11, 2021, from www.stat.go.jp.

Statistics Denmark. (2020). *Public Sector Employment*. Retrieved February 11, 2021, from www.dst.dk/en/Statistik/emner/arbejde-indkomst-og-formue/beskaeftigelse/offentlig-beskaeftigelse.

Stoker, G. (1991). *The Politics of Local Government* (2nd edn). London: Macmillan.

Turley, A. (2008). *What Is Local Government For?* Presentation at the LGC Fundamentals of Local Government conference. London. December 3, 2008.

United Nations. (2018). *E-Government Survey 2018*. Retrieved February 11, 2021, from https://publicadministration.un.org/egovkb/en-us/Reports/UN-E-Government-Survey-2018.

U.S. Census. (2020). *Census Bureau Reports There Are 89,004 Local Governments in the United States*. Retrieved June 15, 2021, from www.census.gov/newsroom/releases/archives/governments/cb12-161.html#:~:text=Census%20Bureau%20Reports%20There%20Are%2089%2C004%20Local%20Governments%20in%20the%20United%20States,-The%20U.S.%20Census.

U.S. Department of Transportation. (2020). *About DOT*. Retrieved July 12, 2020, from www.dot.gov/about_dot.html.

Weber, M. (1947). *The Theory of Social and Economic Organization*. New York: Oxford University Press.

Wilson, W. (1887). The study of administration. *Political Science Quarterly*, 2(2), 197–222.

Worthington, I. & Britton, C. (2000). *The Business Environment* (3rd edn). Harlow: Financial Times Prentice Hall.

Section 2

Theoretical underpinnings of strategy

Chapter 2

Approaches to developing strategy in the public sector

Learning outcomes

After reading this chapter you should be able to:

- understand the different approaches to management in the public sector
- understand how these different approaches can influence development of strategy
- definee and distinguish between traditional public administration, new public management, and network governance

Pre-chapter questions

- How do you think that public sector organisations are managed?
- What role do you think private sector management techniques can play in the public sector?
- Given what you have learned so far about the diverse nature of the public sector, do you think that there is a single correct way to manage strategy in this context?

Key terms

- Traditional Public Administration (TPA) – the way in which public organisations are "traditionally" structured: functional silos, hierarchies, standardised procedures
- New Public Management (NPM) – private sector management techniques applied to the public sector: performance management, targets, cost control, etc.
- Network governance – collaborative working between public organisations, such as between local authorities and health services: working together to solve common problems

DOI: 10.4324/9780429344305-5

2.1 Introduction

This is a short chapter which discusses how public sector strategy has developed over many decades and demonstrates that there has been a drive towards introducing private sector management techniques into the public sector, despite the fundamental differences between the two sectors. For instance, some concepts that play a central role in business and corporate strategy – such as competition and value appropriation – may bear little relevance in part of the public sector context, where strategy may be more related to collaboration and value (re)distribution. Indeed, it is not always easy to define what "success" looks like in a public sector context. It could be argued that, rather than seeking to make a profit (as in much of the traditional strategy literature), public sector strategy should ultimately deliver public services, and that therefore issues arise concerning criteria for the formulation of "sound" strategies and for the appraisal of the results of strategy implementation

2.2 Traditional Public Administration (TPA)

Traditional Public Administration is, perhaps, the overriding "lay" perception of the public sector – "red tape" (Brynard, 1995). Its key features are long hierarchical structures (Fayol, 1963), complex rules and procedures (Ryan et al., 2008), "disciplinary silos" (Pedersen and Hartley, 2008: 335), and bureaucratic and centralised management (Budd, 2007). Hagen and Liddle (2007) liken this model to Scientific Management, which assumes that organisations are rational entities and seeks to define tasks and management in a very ordered way (Hartley, 2006).

Juran (1967) argues that this "red tape" leads to inefficiency, whereas Brynard (1995) argues that it is essential in a public organisation in the interests of fiscal regularity and operational consistency. The problem comes when "officials realise that . . . errors in the public sector are front-page news and, therefore, they establish procedures that are designed more to prevent mistakes than achieve success" (Brynard, 1995: 42). This has been exacerbated by the UK's Freedom of Information Act, which means that every decision taken by a public official can be scrutinised (FOI, 2000), and therefore there is a rigid adherence to procedure in order to counter outside criticism (Brynard, 1995). Rules can also be beneficial, as case study 2a illustrates.

Case Study 2a Traditional Public Administration in action

Certain parts of the health service are bound by rules and procedures. As one senior manager stated:

> The health service is dealing with people. Everyone has different needs, so one size doesn't fit all. We need to adapt our treatment and look at patients as individuals. But . . . and it's a big but . . . there are times when rules must be invoked. During an operation, if a surgeon doesn't wash their hands properly,

> they'd be thrown out. The surgical team have to count the tools in and count them out again after the operation – imagine if someone left a scalpel blade inside a patient. Rules are there for a reason.
>
> Another health manager explained that:
>
> Rules and procedures mean that the hospital runs smoothly. We know when doctors and nurses are free. We know which bed a particular patient is in. We know what their medical needs are. We know that at such and such a time a particular operation will be taking place, and so all the equipment and materials are there in the right place at the right time. We couldn't function without rules.

Although short, case study 2a reveals the importance of rules in certain contexts. Hence, the idea of traditional public administration being bureaucratic and stifled by red tape is by no means universally accepted. For instance, Lynn (2001: 144) feels that this "is, at best, a caricature and, at worst, a . . . distortion of traditional thought that exhibited . . . respect for law politics [and] citizens". Indeed, this traditional approach had "an emphasis on due process, equity of treatment, probity and accountability" (Ferlie et al., 1996: 1). This view is supported by Budd (2007: 540) who noted that consistency of rules and obligations is determined by "democratic imperatives," which results in legitimacy and accountability. Indeed, Brynard (1995) implies that public accountability requires red tape for reasons of transparency and public scrutiny.

Nonetheless, traditional public administration can be seen as static and inflexible (Ryan et al., 2008), and hence it may not address the current problems faced by the public sector (Hagen and Liddle, 2007). Public management reform can be defined as "deliberate changes to the structures and processes of public sector organisations with the objective of getting them (in some sense) to run better" (Pollitt and Bouckaert, 2011: 2). As the authors themselves admit, this is rather a loose definition, but it aligns neatly with the purposes of this discussion.

2.3 New Public Management (NPM)

Management theory has largely been developed based on private sector research, and it therefore makes the assumption that private sector management principles and practices are equally applicable to public agencies (Atreya and Armstrong, 2002; Cong and Pandya, 2003). However, despite the numerous differences between public and private sector management (e.g. Eskildsen et al., 2004; Parker and Bradley, 2000), the problems faced by the public sector led some authors (for instance Ferlie et al., 1996; Hood, 1991) to seek to find a 'new way" of working that addresses these issues. Thus, New Public Management (NPM) was born.

NPM brought to the public sector many of the principles prevailing in the private sector and the commercial sphere (Emery and Giauque, 2005; Newman, 2001). NPM built upon the work of authors such as Charles Handy, Tom Peters, and Rosabeth Moss Kanter and began as a conceptual framework for the scholarly discussion of contemporary changes in the organisation and management of government. Early versions of NPM chiefly concentrated on efficiency and how private sector management techniques might be applied in the public sector (e.g. Hood, 1991). This approach later expanded to encompass objectives such as quality management, transparency, and a client focus (Rondeaux, 2006), and this in turn led to a shift away from the maintenance of structures, rules, and procedures to the cost-effective achievement of market-oriented outcomes (Ryan et al., 2008).

This has impacted on the individuals within organisations, often leading to feelings of stress and micro-management (see for instance Antoniadou and Crowder, 2021, for a discussion of the effect of initiatives such as NPM on academics in higher education around the world). Nevertheless, it has proved to be very enduring and has influenced virtually every aspect of the public sector to a greater or lesser extent. There are several different approaches to NPM:

- "the efficiency drive" – this was an "attempt to make the public sector more business-like and was led by crude notions of efficiency" (Ferlie et al., 1996: 10)
- "downsizing and decentralization" – this version is characterised by "a shift for flexibility, downsizing and contracting out of functions" (Ferlie et al., 1996: 12)
- "in search of excellence" – this model represents the application to the public sector of the human relations school of management theory (Meek, 1988). It has a "strong emphasis on the importance of organisational culture" (Ferlie et al., 1996: 13)
- "public service orientation" – this model seeks to re-energise public sector managers by outlining a distinct public service mission (Osborne and Gaebler, 1992) but "one compatible with high quality management associated with the private sector" (Ferlie et al., 1996: 13).

In spite of these differences, it is possible to identify common themes. These include improved financial management, performance targets, increased contracting out, and greater competition (Gruening, 2001; Osborne and McLaughlin, 2002; Stoker, 2006). Moreover, NPM sought to achieve a greater orientation towards change, efficiency, and productivity (Orchard, 1998). Hence, although there are many different and overlapping interpretations of what NPM tries to achieve (Martin, 2002), there is a variation in usage which means that can be viewed more as a loose term than a fully established concept (Barzelay, 2002; Hood, 1991, 1995). Nonetheless, factors such as increased competition and a focus on strong financial management are fundamental to all versions (Virtanen, 2000).

Case study 2b offers a view from a local authority.

Case Study 2b New public management in action

> We have targets for everything nowadays. It won't be long before they're asking us for our shoe size and then they'll start comparing that to how many potholes we fill.

This comment was made, not entirely in jest, by a senior manager in a local authority. Targets are an inevitable outcome of NPM. As a different manager in the same organisation put it:

> What gets measured is what gets done. If it's not measured and it's not a legal requirement, then we don't do it. It's as simple as that.

This manager explained that the targets, not the manager, sometimes set the priorities for his department. Targets can be imposed from elsewhere, and therefore politicians or people who do not understand the intricacies of a department are effectively deciding what is important, not the manager. However, she recognised that this can be helpful in a local authority:

> The politicians are elected. They are answerable to the public, so it's only fair that they should be involved. They give us targets, we report back to them, and they report back to the public. It's democracy in action.

A difficulty can arise if the wrong targets are set. A manager in Parks and Gardens made the following statement:

> Councillors were interested in grass cutting, and they gave us a series of meaningless targets. We were required to cut the grass every so many weeks, and the time of year made no difference. Grass hardly grows in the winter, but still we were expected to cut it just as often as we did in the summer. If the grass was covered by snow, we still had to cut it. Eventually, the councillors realised how ludicrous it was, and then asked us to work with them to set targets. Finally, we were able to make sensible targets. We factored seasonality into it, so we cut the grass more often in the summer and less often in the winter. We broke the targets up into frequency measures and performance measures. Frequency – how often should we cut? Performance – what length should we cut? And so on. Now we have meaningful targets, and the councillors have a real idea what is going on. Having the right targets makes all the difference.

Hence, these measures are tools to be used. As with all tools, they need to be used properly and with caution if the desired outcomes are to be achieved.

It has been suggested that NPM is internationalist and the principles of NPM can be applied in any location to produce similar outcomes (Boston et al., 1996; Osborne and Gaebler, 1992). Perhaps this is unsurprising – for instance, the UK and US political parties have broadly similar policies: those of the UK Labour Party are roughly the same as the US Democratic Party, those of the UK Conservative Party are generally compatible with the US Republican Party, and those of the UK Liberal Democrat Party most closely resemble the US Reform Party (McSweeney, 2002). Indeed, it is possible that the implementation of NPM is resulting in different countries' public sectors becoming more similar to one another in terms of structures, processes, role conceptions, and performance (Maor and Jones, 1999). However, in other areas such as performance-related pay, the degree of privatisation, and the level of central government control, significant differences remain (Maor and Jones, 1999). Cheung (1997) also questions the globalist interpretation on the ground that there is no one best approach to public sector reform, and thus there is no ready-made solution applicable to all countries. Barlow and Röber (1996) support this argument and highlight a number of differences between the British and German approaches to the implementation of NPM, resulting in different impacts in the respective countries. Common (1998) takes a more neutral position, indicating that claims of internationalism are largely unsubstantiated, and states that globalisation of NPM is a misnomer for the scattering of management techniques around the world.

The issue of new public management remains a hot topic in many academic discussions, and we return to this in the next chapter when we discuss the balanced scorecard.

2.4 Network governance

In some parts of the world, such as the US and the UK, there has been a gradual move to a post-NPM environment (Addicott, 2008). This introduced a different emphasis to the modernisation agenda (Morphet, 2008). It became apparent that knowledge and resources can sometimes be difficult to locate in a single organisation, and that instead, the necessary capabilities are more likely to be found across a network of different businesses and contractors. This approach became known as network governance, and it sought to ensure that public sector decision-making processes were efficient, transparent, and accountable, and that local communities were actively involved and engaged in decision-making (Addicott, 2008; Morphet, 2008).

As with NPM, more than one model of network governance has been identified. The "principal-agent" model has one dominant party (the principal), which then contracts out to other parties (Broadbent et al., 1996), whereas the "inter-organisational" form involves organisations negotiating joint projects in which by blending their capacities they are better able to meet their own objectives (Stoker, 1998). The latter may take the form of a "dominated" network, with one organisation taking the lead, or of a "equal partner" network, consisting of several similarly sized organisations (Buchanan and Huczynski, 2019).

Despite these differences, again there are similarities, such as the development of public/private partnerships and formal agreements, and thus collaboration, innovation, and flexibility are vital (Addicott, 2008; Budd, 2007). This means that public sector management must rely on discretion, trust and negotiation (Budd, 2007; Hagen and Liddle, 2007; Klijn and Koppenjan, 2000). This results in collaborative, co-operative, and competitive arrangements between and within networks (Klijn and Koppenjan, 2000). As Addicott (2008: 150) states, "collective culture, rather than strong line management, is . . . the glue that holds an organisation together".

As NPM began to be superseded across the world, networks, partnerships, and agreements began to replace internal markets, managerialism, and contracts (Addicott, 2008), and a collaborative approach was taken to regional problems, with partnerships being formed between different local authorities and between local authorities and, for example, the National Health Service in the UK (Addicott, 2008). Such approaches open up opportunities for information sharing and learning from each other (Stoker, 2006), and partners therefore work together on the basis of trust rather than on the basis of a formalised, contractual relationship (Hagen and Liddle, 2007). Case study 2c illustrates how this can work in a health care setting.

Case Study 2c Network governance in action

In a large UK city, there was a major local authority and an important health care trust that operated a series of hospitals. Previously, there had been little interconnectivity. Each organisation had focused on its own priorities. As one health care manager stated:

> People were falling through the cracks. Some people were in our hospitals who would have been better placed in social care . . . in their own communities. This was bad for them because they weren't getting the care they needed, but it was bad for the hospital because they were taking up beds that could have been used by people who we could help more.

A key local government manager agreed:

> There was a boundary between us and the hospital. Everyone recognised that this boundary was there – it was real – but nobody was quite sure where it was. It was blurred. That meant responsibility was blurred. Sometimes, we ended up doing the same job as the hospital. Patients got frustrated because they were being asked the same questions over and over, and often they got contradictory advice because neither of us knew what the other was doing. Sometimes, we assumed the hospital was dealing with a patient, but they assumed we were doing it. In the end, nobody was looking after the patient.

Both parties agreed that something had to be done.

Space constraints do not permit a detailed account of the discussions that took place between the organisations, or the detailed legal and financial negotiations that went on, or the complex discussions between the different trades unions and the organisations concerned (etc). In brief, it was decided to set up a series of informal meetings and workshops. These developed into regular sessions – first monthly, then weekly. Eventually, it was agreed that the working arrangements should be formalised and a formal partnership was established. Ultimately, this involved sharing resources. Both organisations set aside part of their budgets to effectively create a dedicated budget for the partnership. Certain key staff were jointly employed by both organisations. Staff from both organisations worked together in the same office. Information was shared wherever legally possible. Disagreements were resolved through discussion and negotiation.

Both organisations were happy with the outcome. The local government manager put it this way:

> It took ages to get sorted, but even during the initial stages things started to get better. Just by our two organisations speaking to each other, things improved. It was obvious to everyone that we weren't in competition. We didn't need to be fighting. By working together, things could be better for everyone.

These views were echoed by health service manager:

> You have to remember that we aren't dealing with nuts and bolts here. We aren't dealing with commodities. We are dealing with people . . . vulnerable people. They have needs. They aren't statistics or numbers. Our patients need to come front and centre. It was difficult to get everything nailed down and agreed. We had to agree on where certain responsibilities were shared, where other responsibilities were split, and so on. It took forever, but now that things are in place, patients are happier and nobody is being missed by the system.

Network governance, therefore, has a significant focus on human relations and the importance of organisational culture in managing change and innovation (Addicott, 2008). It is a form of collective decision-making (Stoker, 2006), although accountability can be unclear if partners are dissatisfied or when things go wrong (Stoker, 1998).

2.5 Chapter summary

This chapter outlines some of the key developments in public sector strategy, and it shows how thinking has developed over time. There has been a drive towards introducing private sector management techniques into the public sector, and this has continued internationally despite the fundamental differences between the two sectors and the different national contexts. There is no single approach that describes the public sector. Traditional Public Administration (TPA) is concerned with standardisation of procedures, bureaucracy, and gaining efficiency through silo management, where specialists can focus on their own areas of expertise. New Public Management (NPM) introduced many private-sector management techniques into the public sector, such as performance management, target setting, and an increased focus on cost control; and this led, it is argued, to an increase in managerial accountability. Finally, network governance seeks to encourage organisations to collaborate beyond traditional boundaries and work together to tackle common issues, such as where social work and health care overlap. Many public bodies adopt a combination of TPA. NPM and network governance in their approaches in different parts of their organisation. We build upon these issues again in the next chapter, which explores some seminal academic approaches to strategy and introduces some key authors.

Self-assessment questions

- Compare and contrast the different approaches identified in this chapter – traditional public administration, new public management, network governance.
- To what extent do you think that new public management improved the public sector?

- What performance measures might be appropriate for health services and for academia? Why do you think these measures might be different for each group?
- Given the diverse range of services offered by local government, which performance measures might be appropriate for the organisation as a whole?
- Following the financial crisis of 2008 and the subsequent implementation of austerity measures, do you think the measures outlined in this chapter were effective in managing the public sector? Why (or why not)?

References

Addicott, R. (2008). Models of governance and the changing role of the board in the 'modernised' UK health sector. *Journal of Health Organization and Management*, 22(2), 147–163.

Antoniadou, M. & Crowder, M. (2021). *Emotion Management in Higher Education*. Bingley: Emerald.

Atreya, B. & Armstrong, A. (2002). *A Review of the Criticisms and the Future of New Public Management*. Victoria University Working Paper Series. Working Paper 7/2002.

Barlow, J. & Röber, M. (1996). Steering not rowing: Co-ordination and control in the management of public services in Britain and Germany. *International Journal of Public Sector Management*, 9(5/6), 73–89.

Barzelay M. (2002). Origins of the new public management: An international view from public administration/political science. In K. McLaughlin, S. P. Osborne, & E. Ferlie (Eds.), *New Public Management: Current Trends and Future Prospects*. Abingdon: Routledge.

Boston, J., Martin, J., Pallot, J. & Walsh, P. (1996). *Public Management: The New Zealand Model*. Aukland: Oxford University Press.

Broadbent, J., Dietrich, M. & Laughlin, R. (1996). The development of principal-agent, contracting and accountability relationships in the public sector: Conceptual and cultural problem. *Critical Perspectives on Accounting*, 17, 259–284.

Brynard D. J. (1995). Combating red tape in the public sector. *International Journal of Public Sector Management*, 8(4), 38–47.

Buchanan, D. A. & Huczynski, A. (2019). *Organizational Behaviour: An Introductory Text* (10th edn). Harlow: Pearson Education.

Budd, L. (2007). Post-bureaucracy and reanimating public governance: A discourse and practice of continuity? *International Journal of Public Sector Management*, 20(6), 531–547.

Cheung, A. B. L. (1997). Understanding public-sector reforms: Global trends and diverse agenda. *International Review of Administrative Science*, 63, 435–457.

Common, R. (1998). Convergence and transfer: A review of globalisation of new public management. *International Journal of Public Sector Management*, 11(6), 440–450.

Cong, X. & Pandya, K. V. (2003). Issues of knowledge management in the public sector. *Electronic Journal of Knowledge Management*, 3(2). Retrieved January 4, 2020, from www.ejkm.com/volume-1/volume1-issue-2/issue2-art3.htm.

Emery, Y. & Giauque, D. (2005). Employment in the public and private sectors: Toward a confusing hybridisation process. *International Review of Administrative Sciences*, 71(4), 639–657.

Eskildsen, J. K., Kristensen, K. & Juhl, H. J. (2004). Private versus public sector excellence. *The TQM Magazine*, 16(1), 50–56.

Fayol, H. (1963). *General and Industrial Management* (C. Storrs, Trans). London: Pitman & Sons (Original work published in 1917).

Ferlie, E., Ashburner, L., Fitzgerald, L. & Pettigrew, A. (1996). *The New Public Management in Action*. Oxford: Oxford University Press.

FOI. (2000). *Freedom of Information Act 2000*. London: HMSO.

Gruening, G. (2001). Origin and theoretical basis of New Public Management. *International Public Management Journal*, 4(1), 1–25.

Hagen, R. & Liddle, J. (2007). Changing strategic direction for executive development in the public sector. *International Journal of Public Sector Management*, 20(4), 325–340.

Hartley, N. T. (2006). Management history: An umbrella model. *Journal of Management History*, 12(3), 278–292.

Hood, C. (1991). A public management for all seasons? *Public Administration*, 69(1), 3–19.

Hood, C. (1995). The 'new public management' in the 1980s: Variation on a theme. *Accounting Organizations and Society*, 20(2/3), 93–109.

Juran, J. M. (1967). The diseases can be cured. In D. C. Rowat (Ed.), *Basic Issues in Public Administration*. New York: Macmillan.

Klijn, E-H. & Koppenjan, J. F. M. (2000). Public management and policy networks: Foundations of a network approach to governance. *Public Management*, 2(2), 135–158.

Lynn, L. E. (2001). The myth of the bureaucratic paradigm: What traditional public administration really stood for. *Public Administration Review*, 61(2), 144–160.

Maor, M. & Jones, G. W. (1999). Varieties of administrative convergence. *International Journal of Public Sector Management*, 12(1), 49–62.

Martin, S. (2002). Best value: New public management or new direction? In K. McLaughlin, S. P. Osborne, & E. Ferlie (Eds.), *New Public Management: Current Trends and Future Prospects*. Abingdon: Routledge.

McSweeney, D. (2002). Political parties. In G. Peele, C. J. Bailey, B. Cain, & B. Guy (Eds.), *Developments in American Politics 4*. Basingstoke: Palgrave MacMillan.

Meek, V. L. (1988). Organisation culture: Origins and weaknesses. *Organization Studies*, 9(4), 453–473.

Morphet, J. (2008). *Modern Local Government*. London: Sage.

Newman, J. (2001). *Modernising Governance: New Labour, Policy and Society*. London: Sage.

Orchard, L. (1998). Managerialism, economic rationalism and public sector reform in Australia: Connections, divergences, alternatives. *Australian Journal of Public Administration*, 57(1), 19–32.

Osborne, D. & Gaebler, T. (1992). *Reinventing Government: How the Entrepreneurial Spirit Is Transforming the Public Sector*. Reading, MA: Addison-Wesley.

Osborne, S. P. & McLaughlin, K. (2002). The New Public Management in context. In K. McLaughlin, S. P. Osborne, & E. Ferlie (Eds.), *New Public Management: Current Trends and Future Prospects*. Abingdon: Routledge.

Parker, R. & Bradley, L. (2000). Organisational culture in the public sector: Evidence from six organisations. *International Journal of Public Sector Management*, 13(2), 125–141.

Pedersen, D. & Hartley, J. (2008). The changing context of public leadership and management: Implications for roles and dynamics. *International Journal of Public Sector Management*, 21(4), 327–339.

Pollitt, C. & Bouckaert, G. (2011). *Continuity and Change in Public Policy and Management*. Cheltenham: Edward Elgar.

Rondeaux, G. (2006). Modernizing public administration: The impact on organisational identities. *International Journal of Public Sector Management*, 19(6), 569–584.

Ryan, N., Williams, T., Charles, M. & Waterhouse, J. (2008). Top-down organizational change in an Australian government agency. *International Journal of Public Sector Management*, 21(1), 26–44.

Stoker, G. (1998). Governance as theory: Five propositions. *International Social Science Journal*, 50(155), 17–28.

Stoker, G. (2006). Public value management: A new narrative for networked governance? *The American Review of Public Administration*, 36(1), 41–57.

Virtanen, T. (2000). Changing competences of public managers: Tensions in commitment. *International Journal of Public Sector Management*, 13(4), 333–341.

Chapter 3

Traditional approaches to strategy and value creation

Learning outcomes

After reading this chapter you should be able to understand:

- how organisations impact on their environments and vice versa
- the importance of both external analysis and internal analysis in developing and refining strategy
- the fundamental differences between public sector and private sector strategy

Pre-chapter questions

- Do you think there are any fundamental differences in the strategies of public sector and private sector organisations? Why? Give examples
- How would you define the industry that Walmart operates in? E.g. is it an airline? Is it a supermarket?
- How would you define the industry that Tata operates in? E.g. is it a consultancy company? Is it a company that makes tea?
- Is profitability the main driver of public sector strategy?

Key terms

- Resources – What organisations have that allows them to do what they do. These are assets, organisational processes, firm attributes, information, knowledge, etc. controlled by an organisation that enable the organisation to conceive of and implement strategies that improve its efficiency and effectiveness (Barney, 1991)
- Value chain – How organisations do what they do. This is the "how", and it contrasts with resources (the "what"). It is the set of activities that a firm operating in a specific industry performs in order to deliver a valuable product or service to its market (Porter, 1985)

DOI: 10.4324/9780429344305-6

3.1 Introduction

Value creation is at the heart of strategy. This chapter outlines some of the main theoretical models and frameworks within the area of strategic management focusing on how value is created. Over the past few decades, several theories and frameworks have been developed to answer the "holy grail" of strategic management: why organisations in the same competitive domain outperform one another. In this chapter we review some of the influential frameworks that underpin how value is perceived and captured before focusing on some of the more contemporary approaches about value creation. The objective of this chapter is to draw on key theories within the field of strategy and how they inform value creation within public sector.

3.2 Competitive advantage and the rise of strategy frameworks

In this section, we review and discuss some of the traditional frameworks that underpin the value creation argument within strategic management. We track the historical development of these frameworks within strategy to provide a better context to understanding of public sector strategy.

The competitive advantage conception is one of the most complex and yet fundamental areas of strategic management studies. There is little known about the origin of competitive advantage notion. The majority of traditional and contemporary literature on competitive advantage point to organisational strategy as being the key factor behind competitive advantage. Competitive advantage stems from the idea that long-term prosperity of an organisation is closely tied into developing an edge over your rivals. Pitts and Lei (1996: 6) state that "each firm's strategy needs it to develop a competitive advantage that enables it to compete effectively [as organisation] strategy refers to the ideas, plans, and support that firms employ to compete successfully against their rivals. [Organisation] strategy is designed to help firms achieve competitive advantage".

Similar to the above, some strategy researchers have proposed that the competitive advantage view gathered momentum in the 1980s amid the fierce competition between pharmaceutical companies. For instance, Cockburn et al. (2000) believe that rivalry among pharmaceutical firms to employ "science-driven drug discovery techniques" in order to outperform other firms was the major driver behind the emergence of competitive advantage view. Other strategists (see Ghemawat, 2017) primarily trace research on competitive advantage to the earlier work of Selznick (1957), Andrews (1971: 5) and particularly the work of Alfred Chandler (1962). Cockburn et al. (2000) suggest that "early studies of competitive advantage were rooted firmly in historical analyses and careful qualitative research. This work could be interpreted that as suggesting that competitive advantage was a complex phenomenon that depended crucially on the active presence of superior leadership". It is believed that based on competitive advantage some organisations have a superior performance compared to their industry rivals. To make the matters more complex, as of yet there is no universally accepted theory of competitive advantage. What it is widely accepted is that competitive advantage in its simplest form is a position of advantage that an organisation assumes against its rivals. There are, however, some useful frameworks, which have been developed to unravel the complexities of competitive advantage and provide basic groundwork for future research on this topic, including mapping organisation advantages within the public sector.

To date, the majority of existing theoretical and frameworks have focused on competitive advantage within for-profit or private industries. Nevertheless, modelling of how competitive advantage can be achieved and maintained are increasingly employed within public sector.

Definition and frameworks

Reviewing the literature on competitive advantage, it is evident that there is no single universal definition of competitive advantage. The general consensus tends to indicate that when a company attains profits that surpass the average for its industry, the company has a competitive advantage over its competitors. According to Barney (1991: 101) "a firm experiences competitive advantages when its actions in an industry or market create economic value and when few competing firms are engaging in similar actions". This school of thought relates competitive advantage to organisational performance relying on the internal characteristics of the firm. Peteraf (1993: 179–191) employs a similar perspective on competitive advantage but also highlights the importance of "imperfectly mobile resources" and rent generation as "competitive advantage is sustained above normal returns . . . [and imperfectly mobile] resources can be a source of competitive advantage . . . as any Ricardian or monopoly rents generated by the asset will not be offset entirely by accounting for the asset's opportunity costs".

Exercise 3.1 What do we mean by "the environment in which a business operates"?

- What industry would you say Walmart operates in?
- What industry would you say Manchester United operates in?

Exercise 3.1 Discussion

What industries do Walmart and Manchester United operate in? These questions sound simple. Obviously, Walmart is a supermarket, right? Obviously, Manchester United is a football club, right?

Are these statements true?

Yes, Walmart is a supermarket. However, it is also a bank. It is also a mobile phone provider. It is also an insurance provider.

Yes, Manchester United is a football club. Does this mean men's football, women's football, or both? It also sells clothing. It also works with the local community to help disadvantaged young people in Manchester.

So what? Why does this matter?

If Walmart is a supermarket, then perhaps its competitors would be Kroger or Publix. If Walmart is a bank, its main competitors might me JPMorgan Chase, Bank of America, or Wells Fargo. If Manchester United is a football club, its competitors might be Liverpool, Bayern Munich, or Barcelona. If Manchester United is an organisation that helps disadvantaged children in Manchester, maybe there is no competition at all – organisations might work together and co-operate for the good of those they are trying to serve.

In other words, how we define an organisation and how we specify the industry in which it operates are crucial. These decisions tell us who our competitors are, who our customers are, who our suppliers are, and so on. It is, therefore, of the greatest importance that we take time over this analysis because our assessment of strategy flows directly from this.

Five forces

Another clarification on competitive advantage which is comparable with the above but is from a dissimilar point of view is offered by Porter (1998). According to Porter competitive advantage is fundamental to an organisation's performance in "competitive markets". Compatible with Porter's view competitive advantage implies lower costs, differentiation advantage, or a successful focus strategy. Porter argues that competitive advantage is generated essentially out of value a company is capable to create for its customers that surpasses the company's cost of generating it. This latest take on competitive advantage by Porter has arguably become the most dominant framework on competitive advantage.

As stated earlier, the origin and evolution of competitive advantage could be traced back to as early as the 1960s. Nevertheless, it was Michael Porter who revolutionised competitive advantage and turned this idea to a strategic management paradigm. In transforming the study of imperfect competition into the analysis of competitive advantage, Porter shifted the focus of strategy research outward, towards the analysis of the firm's microeconomic environment. Porter's approach provided effective tools for understanding exactly why some firms (and industries) were likely to be more profitable than others. Porter developed what he referred to and subsequently became widely known as five forces (Figure 3.1) analysis that determines industry attractiveness. A five forces analysis is essentially a structural map of the underlying economics of an industry; a map of the degree to which competitors, entrants, substitutes, and vertical power exert pressure on the margins of a firm in a particular industry (Cockburn, 2000; Levy et al., 2003; Narayanan, 2005; Grundy, 2006).

According to Porter (1998), a firm operating in an industry in which there are substantial returns to scale coupled with opportunities to differentiate, that buys from and sells to perfectly competitive markets and that produces a product for which substitutes are very unsatisfactory, is likely to be much more profitable than one operating in an industry with few barriers to entry, and a large number of similarly sized companies who are reliant on a few large suppliers and are selling commodity products to a few large buyers (Cockburn, 2000).

> The collective strength of these five competitive forces determines the ability of a firm in an industry to earn, on average, rates of return on investment in excess of the cost of capital . . . The five forces determine industry profitability because they influence the prices, costs, and required investment of firms in an industry (the elements

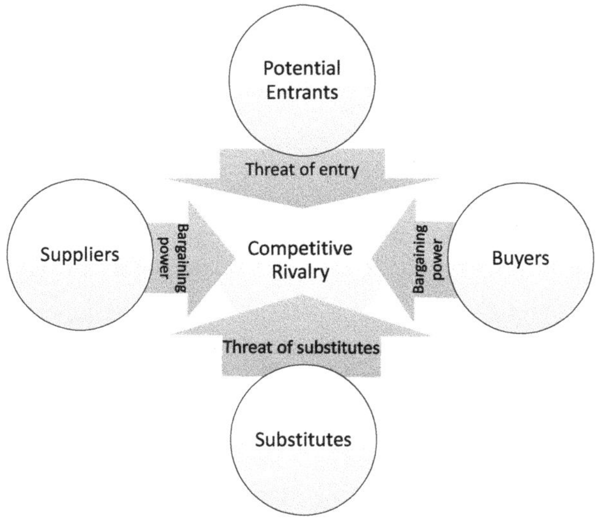

Figure 3.1 Porter's five forces analysis

Source: adapted from Porter (1998: 5)

> of return on investment). Buyer power influences the prices that firms can charge, for example, as does the threat of substitution. The power of buyers can also influence cost and investment because powerful buyers demand costly service. The bargaining power of suppliers determines the costs of raw materials and other inputs. The intensity of rivalry influences prices as well as the costs of competing in areas such as plant, product development, advertising, and sales force. The threat of entry places a limit on prices, and shapes the investment required to deter entrants.
>
> (Porter, 1998: 4–5)

Case study 3a illustrates how the five forces model might be applied in the public sector. It uses as its example the context of building control, which often competes with the private sector on the open market.

Case study 3a Five forces analysis

In the UK, there are two types of building control bodies: a local authority building control service and a private sector–approved inspector building control service. As long as the legal regulations are complied with, customers are free to choose which type they wish to use on their project. There are a small number of exceptions, but for the purposes of this case study, we can assume full competition in the industry. Therefore, the five forces model is applicable.

The following analysis has been extracted from a detailed assessment that was undertaken by a local authority building control service.

Threat of new entrants

Low. There are many barriers to entry, such as the cost of becoming certified and the cost of maintaining this certification. It is practically mandatory to be ISO9001 certified also, and this brings additional costs. There are additional difficulties about training staff, specialising in certain types of structure, and staying up to date with legislation.

Bargaining power of customers

Moderate. There is a need to understand customers. Many are single households. Although they have a wide choice and low switching costs, and can therefore choose from many suppliers taken individually, they have little impact on the industry. However, there are some corporate customers, and these have much more power.

Threat of substitutes

Low. Building regulations are a legal requirement. There is a substitute of ignoring the regulations, but this is rare. Other substitutes include building temporary structures and other similar constructions that are subject to less regulation. Again, numbers and impact are small.

Bargaining power of suppliers

Moderate. There are large numbers of small firms who supply the industry, and therefore the industry has almost all of the power. However, employees are an important supplier in this industry. The service that they provide is essentially the service that the organisation provides. Therefore, employee power is high.

Competitive rivalry

Fierce. There are many national (and even international) firms who have large client bases and strong reputations. At a regional and local level there are also many players who are competing for work. Competition includes aggressive marketing, heavy discounting, loyalty rewards, headhunting of employees, etc.

Having developed this analysis, management were keen to assess the implications for their own organisation. The quotes below all come from members of the senior management team and have been anonymised at their request.

> The analysis applies to the industry as a whole. So, it's not a five forces analysis of [our own organisation]. So, we needed to see what it meant for our industry – the building control industry.

Threat of new entrants

This was low. Basically, we don't need to spend long worrying about it. If there is no threat, or only a low threat, then all we need to do is keep an eye on it every now and then. It would be a waste of money trying to erect barriers or build a fence around the industry. The threat is low – move on.

Bargaining power of customers

This is more difficult. The assessment showed that individual customers don't have a lot of power in our industry. Perhaps we can ignore them, like we're doing for new entrants, but we can't really do that. We are a local authority. We serve our citizens. We can't be seen to ignore them. So, we have to put some effort into promoting our service. We have to do a good job. We have to listen to feedback. I think we're a bit different to the private sector here.

Yes, but we need to really look after our corporate customers . . . our big customers. The analysis shows that they have lots of power because of the size of the project. Something high profile like a hospital or a football stadium – they really matter. They could move to another supplier. We need to be seen to be doing a good job. We want the big customers to come back. So we really have to be nice to them and involve them in everything.

Threat of substitutes

Again, this was low. This is not something to worry about at the moment. If anything, it's an opportunity to take enforcement action if anyone is breaking the law, but that's not our responsibility – it's [another part of the council]'s responsibility.

Bargaining power of suppliers

The analysis showed that our staff are our most important supplier. If we lost our staff, we would be in trouble. This is true across our whole industry. So, we need to pay our staff well. We need to look after their workloads. We need to support them if there are any claims against them. We work closely with the unions, and we bend over backwards to address staff complaints.

Competitive rivalry

It's dog-eat-dog out there. Our competition is going after us, so we need to go after them too, otherwise we will go under. We've had to persuade the politicians to leave us alone when budget cuts are being mooted. We bring in far more money than we cost, so if we were getting our budgets hammered, there would be a massive impact on our service. That would mean that council revenues fell. So, yes we are expensive, but look how much money we bring in.

It was important that management noticed the interplay between different parts of the five forces model.

> That's right. You can't disconnect competitive rivalry from the rest of it. It ties in with customers – if we can attract big customers and then build our relationship, that helps with staying competitive. If we can attract and then retain the best staff, then that helps with our competitiveness. You can't decouple everything. It's all part of the same thing.

Generic strategies and the value chain

Building upon his work on analysing the competitive forces in an industry (five forces model), Porter developed four non-specific business strategies that would enable an organisation to gain competitive advantage (Figure 3.2) and determine an organisation's position within its industry.

These four strategies relate to the extent to which the scope of an organisation's activities are narrow versus broad, and the extent to which a business seeks to differentiate its products. According to this model, the differentiation and cost leadership strategies seek competitive advantage in a broad range of market or industry segments. By contrast, the differentiation focus and cost focus strategies are adopted in a narrow market or industry.

> Each of the generic strategies involves a fundamentally different route to competitive advantage, combining a choice about the type of competitive advantage sought with the scope of the strategic target in which competitive advantage is to be achieved.

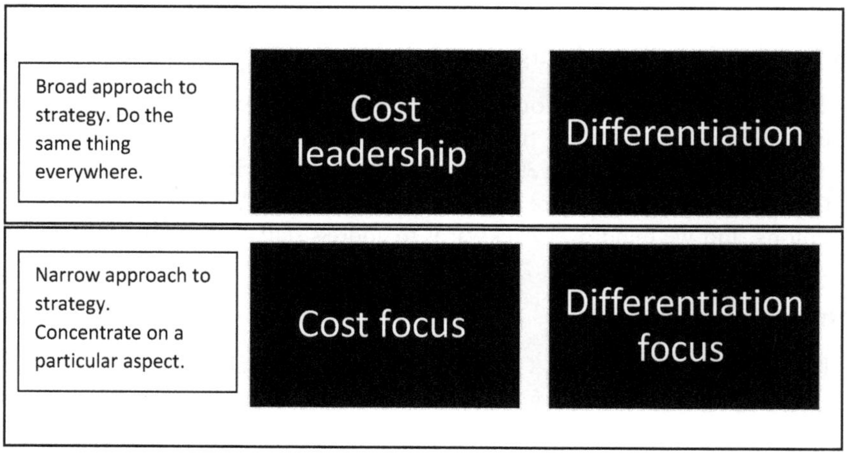

Figure 3.2 Business strategies for competitive advantage

Source: adapted from Porter (1998: 12)

> The cost leadership and differentiation strategies seek competitive advantage in a broad range of industry segments, while focus strategies aim at cost advantage (cost focus) or differentiation (differentiation focus) in a narrow segment. The specific actions required to implement each generic strategy vary widely from industry to industry, as do feasible generic strategies in a particular industry. While selecting and implementing a generic strategy is far from simple, however, they are logical routes to competitive advantage that must be probed in any industry.
>
> (Porter, 1998: 11)

The "specific actions" necessary to implement any of the generic strategies relates to one of the enduring arguments around value creation and competitive advantage, namely *the value chain* described by Porter (1998: 33) as a "systematic way of examining all the activities a firm performs and how they interact". The value chain separates an organisation to a set of value adding strategic activities which underpins the potential sources of differentiation or cost advantages. Every organisation is a collection of activities designed to source, produce, offer, deliver, and support their products and services. The value chain divides the organisation to a set of value adding primary activities and a set of secondary activities designed to support the primary activities. Support activities on their own do not add or create value unless linked to primary activities, whereas primary activities could create value on their own. Figure 3.3 below shows an organisation's value chain and how these activities are performed taking into account the organisation's history, strategy, and how it is implemented (Porter, 1998).

According to Porter (1998), differences between individual organisation value chain is the source of competitive advantage where the value is what buyers/clients/customer are willing to pay for what an organisation offers. The value argument is why linking generic

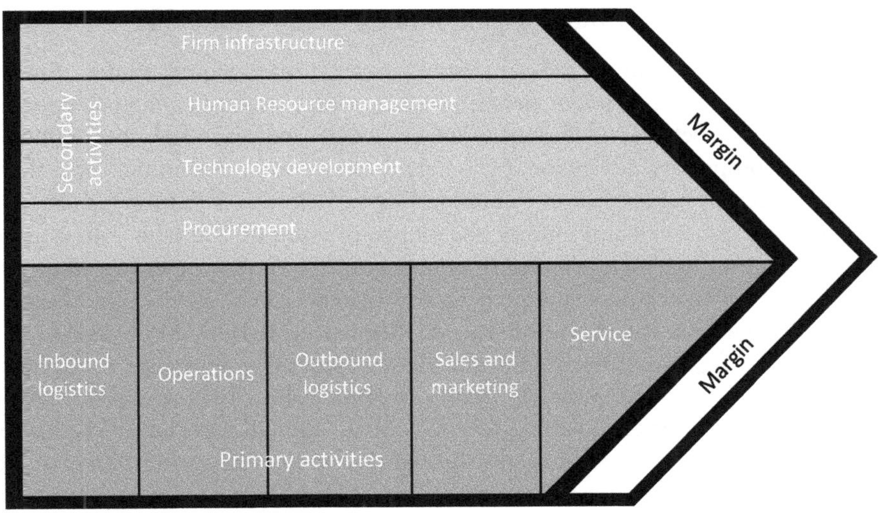

Figure 3.3 Value chain

Source: Adapted from Porter (1985)

strategies and positioning to the value chain is paramount. Porter (1998: 38): clearly highlights this when he asserts:

> Value is measured by total revenue, a reflection of the price a firm's product commands and the units it can sell. A firm is profitable if the value it commands exceeds the cost involved in creating the product. Creating value for buyers that exceeds the cost of doing so is the goal of any generic strategy. Value instead of cost, must be used in analysing competitive position since firms often deliberately raise their cost in order to command a premium price via differentiation.

One key factor to consider is that value adding activities are not entirely mutually exclusive, and it is the collection of these interdependent activities which provides pathways to value creation and competitive advantage. This is achieved either through optimisation of activities or through their coordination, and there are myriad ways of how these processes work within the value chain and support the overall positioning of the organisation using the generic strategies. For example, an organisation with a cost leadership position would optimise their value chain to achieve economies of scale and reduce cost across activity system, whereas one with a differentiation may coordinate its activities to ensure quality of service or product is maintained through the whole of the value chain.

Essentially, competitive advantage frameworks such as the five forces, generic strategies, and the value chain put emphasis on how an organisation positions itself in its external environment. Therefore, Porter strongly relates competitive advantage to organisational strategy with less emphasis on firm resources. In other words, Porter assumes an outside-in view of competitive advantage. In contrast to Porter's view, the RBT takes a different approach to accounting for competitive advantage, which is discussed in the following section.

The Resource-Based Theory (RBT) approach to competitive advantage

RBT is one of the most influential concepts of strategic management studies. Essentially the RBT accounts for a different perspective on competitive advantage as opposed to Porter's perspective. Peteraf and Barney (2003; cited in Barney and Clark, 2007: 24) believe a firm "has a competitive advantage if it is able to create more economic value than the marginal (breakeven) competitor in its product market". In this definition (which is based on the RBT logic), as well as resources, the emphasis is also on the value-based approach or "economic value" which is "created by an enterprise in the course of providing a good or service is the difference between the perceived benefits gained by the purchasers of the good and the economic cost to the enterprise" (Peteraf and Barney, 2003; cited in Barney and Clark, 2007: 25). Consistent with this view, competitive advantage is expressed in terms of the ability to create relatively more economic value. To create more value than its rivals, a company must produce greater net benefits through superior differentiation or lower costs. Creating higher net benefits through lower costs or greater differentiation is where the RBT perspective on competitive advantage and Porter's competitive strategies view are most comparable.

Nonetheless the RBT perspective on competitive advantage is not concluded with the above argument. As important as it is to explain the existence of competitive advantages among firms, the sustainability of these advantages is also important as some competitive advantages are fleeting while others are long-lasting (Black and Boal, 1994). This is where competitive advantage and sustainable competitive advantage fundamentally differ.

According to the RBT, an organisation possesses sustainable competitive advantage "when it is creating more economic value than the marginal firm in its industry and when other firms are unable to duplicate the benefits of this strategy" (Barney and Clark, 2007: 52). It is obvious that the definition of competitive advantage and sustainable competitive advantage based on RBT are relatively analogous. However, there are a couple of remarks that highlight the dissimilarity between competitive and sustained competitive advantage.

> First, unlike the concept of competitive advantage, sustained competitive advantage does not focus exclusively on a firm's competitive position vis-a-vis firms that are already operating in its industry. Rather a firm's competition is assumed to include not only all of its current competitors, but also potential competitors poised to enter an industry at some future date. Second, the definition of sustained competitive advantage . . . does not necessarily depend on the period of calendar time during which a firm enjoys a competitive advantage. One indicator that a firm may have sustained competitive advantage is that it has a competitive advantage that lasts a long time. . . . However, in some industry settings, a sustained competitive advantage may not last a long period of calendar time. In such settings, it may be possible for a firm to have a competitive advantage that lasts for a relatively short period. But if that advantage is not competed away through other firms duplicating strategy of the firm with a competitive advantage, then that advantage may still have been sustained.
>
> (Barney and Clark, 2007: 52–53)

The above argument reflects the fact that the sustainability of a competitive advantage ultimately depends on what might be referred to as the "condition of duplication" (Wright et al., 1994). If other organisations competing in the same industry do not duplicate the competitive edge of a successful organisation, that organisation will manage to sustain its competitive advantage.

Sustainable competitive advantage based on RBT logic further draws on the attributes of the resources that a firm possesses (Conner, 1991; Conner and Prahalad, 1996; Acedo et al., 2006). In order for resources to be considered as important for sustainable competitive advantage, the resources must have four different characteristics. Firstly the resource must be valuable, meaning that it exploits opportunities and/or neutralises threats in a firm's environment; secondly, it must be rare among a firm's current and potential competition; thirdly, it must be imperfectly imitable; and, finally, it must be of a position to be exploited by organisational processes (Wright et al., 1994; Grant, 1996; Wiklund and Shepherd, 2005; Beard and Sumner, 2004; Barney and Clark, 2007). This is what has become widely known as the VRIO framework in the strategic management literature. In the following sections, we look at each aspect in detail.

For organisational resources to be a source of competitive advantage or sustained competitive advantage, they must be valuable. Resources are valuable when they would enable an organisation to envisage and employ strategies that would lead to greater efficiency and effectiveness (Barney and Clark, 2007). Valuable resources assist a firm to provide a lower cost than competitors or offer differentiated products and services (Collis and Montgomery, 2008). The fact that resources need to be valuable to be considered a source of competitive advantage also highlights an important linkage between environmental models of competitive advantage and the competitive advantage based on the RBT.

Resources, in spite of how valuable they are, could not be the source of competitive advantage or sustained competitive advantage if they are possessed by a large number of rivals or potential competitors (Smith et al., 1996). If a valuable organisation resource is owned by large number of rival companies, then any of the competitors could exploit the resources in a similar way that would threaten competitive advantage of the firm. The rarity of a resource implies that a company that acquires a particular resource may produce either superior returns or better sales volumes from a similar value base to rivals (Bowman and Ambrosini, 2003).

It is not straightforward to identify how rare a valuable organisation resource must be to generate a competitive advantage. According to Barney and Clark (2007: 59),

> it is not difficult to see that if a firm's valuable resources are absolutely unique among a set of competing and potentially competing firms, those resources generate at least a competitive advantage and may have the potential of generating a sustained competitive advantage. However, it may be possible for a small number of firms in an industry to possess a particular valuable resource and still generate a competitive advantage.

Consistent with this, as long as the number of firms that possess a particular valuable resource is less than the number of firms needed to generate perfect competition dynamics in an industry, that resource has the potential of generating a competitive advantage.

Valuable and rare firm resources could generate a competitive advantage or be the sources of sustained competitive advantage if firms that do not own these resources are unable to attain them by direct replication or substitution (Barney et al., 2011). There are three conditions under which organisation resources can be imperfectly imitable or too expensive to imitate. While not all conditions are necessary for firm resources to be imperfectly imitable, one or a combination of three is essential. Barney and Clark (2007: 60) identify these three conditions as "(a) the ability of a firm to obtain a resource is dependent on unique historical conditions, (b) the link between the resources possessed by a firm, and a firm's sustained competitive advantage is causally ambiguous, or (c) the resource generating a firm's advantage is socially complex". These conditions protect the firm's resources from imitation and preserve the value created through them. Assessing limitability stipulates insight into the nature of the resource and how it was fashioned. A comprehensive awareness of the organisation history may be required considering the path dependency nature of many resources (Black and Boal, 1994).

Based on the RBT, the above conditions are highly significant in determining if organisation resources are seen as imperfectly imitable. For instance, to be a source of sustained competitive advantage, both the organisations which possess resources that generate a competitive advantage and the organisations that do not possess these resources but seek to imitate them must be faced with the same level of causal ambiguity (Boxall and Steeneveld, 1999). If a company with a competitive advantage understands the relationship between the resources it possesses and its advantage, the other companies can also learn about the linkage, obtain the essential resources (supposing that they are not imperfectly imitable because of the other conditions), and employ appropriate strategies (Barney and Clark, 2007). This would lead to duplication of the organisation's competitive advantage and hence, the competitive advantage would not be sustained.

In contrast,

> when a firm with a competitive advantage does not understand the source of its competitive advantage and better than firms without this advantage, that competitive advantage may be sustained because it is not subject to imitation. Ironically, in order for causal ambiguity to be the source of sustained competitive advantage, all competing firms must have an imperfect understanding of the link between the resources controlled by a firm and a firm's competitive advantages.
>
> (Barney and Clark, 2007: 63)

This is where the argument of competitive advantage based on the RBT exhibits a certain degree of ambiguity as the latter statement by Barney and Clark means successful organisations should not attempt to identify and understand why they are successful as doing so would result in that particular competitive advantage to be fleeting. This is where critics of the RBT rightly suggest this concept has deficiency in accounting for competitive advantage (Priem and Butler, 2001b; Arend, 2006) Nevertheless, unique historical conditions, causal ambiguity, and social complexity can all raise the cost of another company duplicating the resources of a certain company. However, if substitutes for these resources exist, and these substitutes are not expensive to duplicate, then organisations without these resources can imitate their effects by substituting resources they can duplicate at low cost. This is where the question of resource non-substitutability is brought into attention.

The last attribute which imperfectly imitable resources should have to generate a competitive advantage and be a source of sustained competitive advantage is non-substitutability. A resource is deemed to be non-substitutable if it cannot easily be replaced or duplicated by a similar or different resource (Bowman and Ambrosini, 2003). Substitutability of resources are in two forms according to Barney and Clark (2007: 66), "first, though it may not be possible for a firm to imitate another firm's resources exactly, it may be able to substitute a similar resource that enables it to conceive and implement the same strategies . . . second, very different firm resources can also be strategic substitutes". This claim of the non-substitutability is again problematic as this logic implies that no firm can ever have sustained competitive advantage without artificial protection.

Therefore, consistent with the VRIO framework, non-substitutability is an important attribute of resources to be imperfectly imitable in the similar way attributes of historical conditions and causal ambiguity are. This is an interesting assumption as reviewing the literature reveals a common mistake by the scholars regarding the VRIO framework. In fact many have used the term VRIN (which is essentially incorrect) instead of VRIO. They have assumed that non-substitutability is a condition of resources parallel to valuable, rare, and imperfectly imitable conditions. However it is argued here this assumption is fundamentally inaccurate as non-substitutability is an attribute necessary for resources to be imperfectly imitable. Evidently, there is no VRIN framework as some authors refer to. The viable framework based on the RBT, which discusses resource characteristics that supposedly generate a competitive advantage or can be a source of sustained competitive advantage, is VRIO.

Valuable, rare, and imperfectly imitable resources can only create competitive advantage or be a source of sustained competitive advantage if the organisation is structured to exploit the potential offered by these resources. There are various factors of an organisation's structure which influences its capacity to exploit the full competitive prospective of its resources and capabilities. These elements are referred to as "complimentary resources and capabilities" as they have inadequate capacity to create competitive advantage in isolation (Barney and Clark, 2007). It is the combination with other resources and capabilities that enables an organisation to achieve its potential for competitive advantage (Mahoney, 2001).

Organisational processes are the fourth and final condition necessary for firm resources to create competitive advantage or be a source of sustained competitive advantage. Interestingly, this is where one of the major assumptions of dynamic capabilities emerges as the reconfiguration of resources and capabilities to achieve competitive advantage. This raises the question of added value of dynamic capabilities as discussed in earlier sections.

Value, rarity, imitability, and organisational processes together form the VRIO framework which expresses the major parameters in resource-based analysis for creating and sustaining competitive advantage. This according to Barney and Clark (2007: 69–70) poses a series of question about a company's activities:

- The question of Value: Do a firm's resources and capabilities enable the firm to respond to environmental threats or opportunities?
- The question of Rarity: Is a resource currently controlled by only a small number of competing firms?
- The question of Imitability: Do firms without a resource face a cost disadvantage in obtaining or developing it?
- The question of Organisation: Are a firm's other policies and procedures organised to support the exploitation of its valuable, rare, and costly to imitate resources?

The above questions provide a single framework to understand the return potential associated with exploiting organisational resources or capabilities. Table 3.1 provides a comprehensive outlook to this framework.

If a resource or capability possessed by a company is not valuable, then that resource would not allow a company to pick or employ strategies that exploit environmental opportunities or counteract threats. Organising to exploit these types of resources will increase an organisation's costs or decrease its profits. If an organisation opts to exploit these types of resources, they are likely to be in a position of competitive disadvantage compared to its rivals which do not control these non-valuable resources. Consequently, these types of resources are the firm's weaknesses.

Table 3.1 Competitive advantage based on the VRIO framework

Is a resource or a capability . . .				
Valuable?	*Rare?*	*Costly to Imitate?*	*Exploited by organisation?*	*Implications*
No	No	No	No	Competitive disadvantage
Yes	No	No	No	Competitive parity
Yes	Yes	No	No	Temporary competitive advantage
Yes	Yes	Yes	No	Unused competitive advantage
Yes	Yes	Yes	Yes	Sustained competitive advantage

Source: Adapted from Barney and Clark (2007)

If a resource or capability is valuable but not rare and the firm chooses to utilise this resource or capability, this could result in competitive advantage parity. Therefore, no competitive advantage could be gained from exploiting this type of resources, but failure to utilise them could position the firm at a competitive disadvantage (Barney and Clark, 2007). Thus, these types of resources or capabilities are the firm's strength.

A temporary competitive advantage could be obtained when the exploited resource or capability is valuable and rare but not expensive to imitate. However, rivals firms could also achieve this temporary competitive advantage through duplication or substitution since it is not too costly to imitate the relative resources or capabilities. Subsequently, this sort of resource or capability could be referred to as the firm's strength and distinctive competences (Barney and Clark, 2007).

It should be noted that unused (unrealized or unexploited) competitive advantage does not appear in Barney's original formulation, or in Barney and Clark's subsequent work. Nevertheless, it is found a lot in practitioner documentation. There is support for it in academic literature, and this has been gaining more recognition in recent years (see for instance Anastasya and Widjaja, 2019; Berisha Qehaja and Kutllovci, 2015; Lopes et al., 2020; Min et al., 2016). Essentially, if a resource or capability is valuable, rare, difficult to imitate but is not properly exploited within the organisation, there is a potentially significant advantage that is being neglected. The organisation needs to make full use of its resources if it is to maximise its competitive advantage.

Ultimately, if a resource or capability is valuable, rare, and too costly to imitate, it will be a source of sustained competitive advantage. Rival companies encounter a considerable cost disadvantage if they attempt to directly duplicate a successful company's resources and capabilities. Even if competing firms were successful in acquiring or developing the associated resources or capabilities, the significant cost of achieving this would position them at a competitive disadvantage compared to the firm that already controls the valuable, rare, and imperfectly imitable resources or capabilities. As a result, these kinds of resources and capabilities are organisational strengths and "sustainable distinctive competences" (Barney and Clark, 2007).

Nonetheless, while the VRIO framework has developed as an influential view in strategic management, as stated earlier there are some general ambiguities and questions regarding the competitive advantage based on the RBT (see Priem and Butler, 2001a). The limitations of the RBT and the subsequent VRIO framework has given rise to an alternative view on how competitive advantage is achieved and maintained by looking at how resources and competences can be reconfigured as a response to the ever-changing external environment. These viewpoints attempt to link the internal characteristics of the organisation to the external environment and the industry. We will review some of these suppositions in chapter 3.3.

Case study 3b provides a worked example of a VRIO analysis.

Case study 3b A VRIO analysis

Jillian was the head of a local authority department in Denver, Colorado. Her department was involved in a range of activities and had developed several processes

	V	*R*	*I*	*O*
IT department	Yes	No	No	No
HR department	No	No	No	No
Red process	Yes	Yes	Yes	No
Blue process	Yes	Yes	No	No
Green process	Yes	Yes	Yes	Yes

Figure 3.4 Extract from consultant's VRIO analysis

that were very attractive to the marketplace. She was unsure how she should proceed, so she invited a team of management consultants into her department to undertake an analysis of what they did, how they did it, and what might be the best way to build on the current situation.

The consultants spent two months looking at every aspect of the business and undertook a range of strategic analyses. One of these was a VRIO analysis. Below is an extract of their report (Figure 3.4).

Question:

1 Based on this analysis, how would you advise Jillian? What should she focus on?

Case study 3b (continued): A VRIO analysis – Discussion

Jillian needs to understand what the implication of the consultant's analysis is for her department. Therefore, the first stage would be to interpret the VRIO analysis by adding in an extra column – "implications". Essentially, we are asking "so what"? and we do this by referring back to the theoretical discussion presented earlier in this chapter. One possible interpretation is shown below in Figure 3.5

In other words:

- The IT department is keeping Jillian's department level with the others in the field – they have parity.
- The HR department is a drain. It doesn't even add value to Jillian's operation.
- The red process has potential. It is not being fully exploited, and Jillian's department is therefore missing out on something it could gain a significant advantage from.
- The blue process is giving the department a temporary competitive advantage.
- The green process is giving the department a sustained competitive advantage. This is the single source of long-term difference over the competition.

	V	*R*	*I*	*O*	*Implications*
IT department	Yes	No	No	No	Competitive parity
HR department	No	No	No	No	Competitive disadvantage
Red process	Yes	Yes	Yes	No	Unused competitive advantage
Blue process	Yes	Yes	No	No	Temporary competitive advantage
Green process	Yes	Yes	Yes	Yes	Sustained competitive advantage

Figure 3.5 Extract from consultant's VRIO analysis – implications for Jillian's department

Now that we understand the implications of what the consultants are saying, we can advise Jillian. Obviously, because the green process is giving her a significant advantage, this is where she should focus her energy and budget . . . or is it? Perhaps the advice could be different.

We move into the realm of speculation. The exact advice might depend on the specifics of the situation. However, there are other possibilities besides the obvious.

Firstly, based on the consultant's analysis, the HR department is a drain on resources. Jillian is spending money and getting nothing back. In fact, the money she is spending on HR is money that could be more profitably spent elsewhere. Therefore, there is a good argument that Jillian should address this issue first. Perhaps she could restructure the HR function? Perhaps she could outsource it? Once she has dealt with this issue, then she can move onto other things. Therefore, one reasonable recommendation might be:

- **Jillian's first priority should be to deal with the HR department**

An alternative approach might be to focus on the red process. Based on the consultant's analysis, this is delivering an unused competitive advantage. The process is valuable, rare, hard to imitate, but is not being utilised by the organisation. Thus, perhaps the organisation needs to find a way to exploit what it already does, and this might be the most important priority. The green process is already delivering a sustained competitive advantage, so if Jillian can keep that going while exploiting the red process, then she would have two sources of sustained competitive advantage. Thus, a reasonable recommendation might be:

- **Jillian's first priority should be to find a way to fully utilise the red process**

As we said, since the green process is already delivering a sustained competitive advantage, the recommendation might be to focus everything on this and try to build on its success. However, the blue process is already delivering a competitive advantage – albeit a temporary one. It might, therefore, be a mistake to focus exclusively on the green process, because then Jillian might lose the short-term advantage offered by the blue process. Because advantages are already being realised, perhaps she needs to continue as she is, and the recommendation might be:

- **Jillian should continue with her current model of delivery**

In reality, consultants are unlikely to offer a single solution. Instead, they may outline a list of alternatives and leave management to choose between them. None of these three options above can be said to be "best". Because strategy is ultimately trying to predict the future, there are rarely any objectively "correct" answers.

What this example clearly shows is that the completion of a VRIO analysis is only the first stage. The organisation needs to understand the implications of the analysis. Then, the analysis needs to be used to shape strategy and should not be left on a shelf gathering dust. VRIO is a key tool in the strategist's armoury but it does need to be **used**, not merely described.

3.3 Contemporary approaches and redefining value creation

More recently, the contemporary approaches to competitiveness and value creation has focused on the ideas that incorporate the dynamic interplay of the internal and external environment as well as the increasing importance of stakeholders in strategy-making. Concepts such as the dynamic capability view (DCV) are progressively becoming one of the most debated issues of strategic management studies. The origin of this relationship is traced back to the RBT and its linkage to competitive advantage. Essentially, the DCV supposedly enables explanation for creating and sustaining competitive advantage where the RBT becomes inadequate. Firstly, the RBT does not explain how certain companies can sustain competitive advantage in rapidly changing and turbulent external environments. The RBT becomes rather obsolete in fast changing environments where sustaining competitive advantage is an exigent issue since "the duration of [sustaining competitive] advantage is inherently unpredictable, where time is an essential aspect of strategy, and the DCs that drive competitive advantage are themselves unstable processes that are challenging to sustain" (Eisenhardt and Martin, 2000: 1106). Secondly, the RBT offers little clarification of how companies could extend their competences and create new capabilities. Whereas the RBT perceives resources and capabilities as idiosyncratic, the DCV argues that these may have some common features among companies with idiosyncratic details. According to dynamic capabilities, creating competitive advantage is not exclusively from organisational resources but how they are configured by the managers (Cavusgil et al., 2007).

Previous studies on the dynamic capabilities-competitive advantage relationship have built on three seminal papers on dynamic capabilities by Teece et al. (1997), Eisenhardt and Martin (2000) and Winter (2003) discussed in the earlier part of this review. Perhaps one of the studies that offer useful insights into the dynamic capabilities–competitive advantage relationship is carried out by Helfat et al. (2007). They allege that to understand dynamic capabilities–competitive advantage relationship, one must assess how much value a dynamic capability creates.

> Dynamic capabilities create value by conferring upon an organisation the ability to perform a particular function . . . The value of a dynamic capability depends on whether or not its function creates value and to what degree. The value of a function is always context dependent. It depends in part on the environmental need (in terms of derived demand and, therefore, willingness to pay) for the function to be performed and on any environmental constraints.
>
> (Helfat et al., 2007: 13)

According to this model, changes in the environment could increase or decrease the value created by a particular dynamic capability. This value creation of dynamic capabilities could lead to competitive advantage over rivals. An organisation could gain advantage if its dynamic capabilities create higher value than competing firms (Helfat et al., 2007). This, however, by no means confirms that dynamic capabilities necessarily lead to competitive advantage. Similar to competitive advantage based on the RBT, there are several conditions to be met in order for dynamic capabilities to be considered the source of competitive advantage. The first condition is that the same dynamic capabilities must exhibit heterogeneity in the technical fitness (Helfat et al., 2007). Secondly, the application of dynamic capabilities must be in demand since they only have value when in use, and competitive advantage could only be generated when dynamic capabilities are applied. Finally, similar to VRIO resources, dynamic capabilities must be rare simply because no competitive advantage could be generated if firms possess similar dynamic capabilities.

One of the other contributions of Helfat et al. (2007: 14–15) to understanding the dynamic capabilities–competitive advantage relationship is addressing the issue of sustainability. In order to realise whether competitive advantage derived from dynamic capabilities is sustained, one requires considering competitive, environmental, and internal factors. In terms of competitive forces, "sustainability derives from barriers to imitation and/or substitution that prevent rivals from matching the value created by a capability". The question of sustainability concerns environmental factors as well. When the environments are reasonably stable, "a competitive advantage can persist, abstracting from the imitative efforts of the competitors. In more turbulent environments, the need for some previously valuable functions can diminish, detracting from the value gained from deploying the capability. In a high-velocity environment, the fact that imitation barriers prevent duplication of a capability's functionality may be immaterial if the capability no longer serves a need".

The internal factors that influence sustainability mainly emerge from the argument of how dynamic capabilities are managed. How a capability is managed and maintained could affect both the level and the sustainability of its value.

At the heart of the value creation argument based on the DCV is the idea of resource-based reconfigurations by managers. This is perhaps why more recent theoretical and empirical work on the DCV have focused on the idea of sensing, seizing opportunities, and reconfiguring as dynamic managerial capabilities (Teece, 2009; Teece, 2012; Helfat and Martin, 2015). Sensing opportunities and threats, particularly in periods of rapid external change necessitates scanning, searching, and exploration while seizing opportunities is to do with making the right decisions and executing them (Harreld et al., 2007; O'Reilly and Tushman, 2008; Teece, 2009). Reconfiguring which may require managers to reallocate resources is the final element of the tripartite taxonomy of dynamic capabilities (Teece, 2009). When opportunities are identified, the role of managers is to figure out how to interpret new events and developments, which technologies to pursue, and which market segments to target (Helfat et al., 2007).

The key distinction between these contemporary approaches to value creation and the traditional frameworks are the increasing importance of different stakeholder groups and the role they play in strategy-making. More recent analytical models of value creation take into account the influence of different stakeholders as well as how value is perceived by and created for these groups beyond the monetary and financial indicators. Frameworks such as "shared value" put stakeholder groups at the heart of value creation (Porter and Kramer, 2006). The principles of the shared value centre around the fact that value creation needs to be of benefit to the society and the organisation. As a result, the importance of stakeholders are paramount in assessment of any organisation value creation irrespective of the type of sector and industry. In the next section, we will discuss some of the analytical tools geared towards evaluating value creation within the public sector.

3.4 Towards a value framework for the public sector

Strategic management is a field that has mainly focused on developing tools and frameworks for the private sector. One of the key ensuing debates has always been if these tools and frameworks developed in the private sector are relevant and applicable in the public sector (Alford and Greve, 2017). This stems from the fact that there are many strategic management tools and frameworks and undoubtedly, given the diversity and idiosyncrasy of public sector organisations and the environment they operate in, not all these frameworks would be applicable or appropriate.

Before we discuss the applicability of the value frameworks for public sector organisations, it is worth noting that the meaning of value creation both in the private and public sector is subject to a fierce debate (Porter, 2011), some of which we have alluded to in the previous section. This debate is of particular interest in the public sector domain as the social value creation becomes more meaningful, and this is why many scholars have argued that public sector organisations should focus on creating public value (Moore, 1995; Chun and Rainey, 2005; Bryer, 2007; Thompson and Rizova, 2015). Several authors have argued for different meanings and interpretation of public value (see Moore, 2000; Andersen et al., 2012) but it is argued that public organisations should aim to increase social efficiency and social value while the implications of both often create dilemma for these organisations (Vining, 2016). This is why, as discussed in the previous section, stakeholder analysis is an important part of any value creation analysis within the public sector.

Nevertheless, several important frameworks designed to map the value creation of an organisation can either be used directly or adopted to the context of public sector organisations. This is because even though most of public and third sector organisations have a not-for-profit status, many compete for funds from donors or governments while others have to compete on the basis of sector quality and service metrics (e.g. schools, hospitals). Therefore, while there might be no clear profit objectives, competitive strategy is still very much relevant. We have discussed some of these frameworks such as the VRIO and the DCV in the previous section. Other frameworks such as PESTEL or Porter's five forces could easily be adopted to reflect the unique characteristics of an external environment of a public sector organisation. There are also other frameworks that are more applicable to the public sector organization; some of these in fact would be less relevant to the private sector context even though the inherent nature of many of these frameworks is rooted in the Business Policy Model (Christensen et al., 1982) and the resulting frameworks discussed earlier.

Perhaps one of the most popular of these frameworks is the new public management (Hood, 1991) where the focus is how value is created through the dynamic interplay of the environment and organisational capabilities. Emerging as yet another framework with close relationship to business policy model (BPM), at the heart of New Public Management (NPM) is the notion of strategic intent encouraging many aspects of BPM such as leadership and accountability, corporate planning, performance management, positioning, and how products and services align to specific markets (Alford and Greve, 2017). The NPM model emerged as the most dominant framework throughout the 1970s and 1980s and was employed by the public sector with the ultimate aim of increasing efficiency that was allegedly apparent in the private sector (Boston et al., 1996; Greve, 2015). Nevertheless and despite some of the advantages offered by employing NPM in the public sector, the viewpoint has faced significant criticism over the past two decades for several reasons. One argument is that public service managers and leaders are public servants and, therefore, the public trust could be undermined if public executives are to manage public agencies as a business, while others have questioned the effectiveness of the model in the public sector (Hood and Dixon, 2015). Consequently, the interest in the use of value creation models in the public sector has shifted towards alternative approaches where the emphasis on value creation is on the challenges that public and third sector organisations face (Alford and Greve, 2017). The reader will remember that we discussed NPM in more detail in the previous chapter.

The public value framework (PVF) has emerged as a popular tool in the public sector context and is widely employed and adopted by scholars and practitioners over the past few years (Moore, 1995; O'Flynn, 2007; Poister, 2010; Weinberg and Leeman, 2013; Bryson et al., 2015; Crosby et al., 2017; Neuroni et al., 2019; Torfing et al., 2021). The importance and relevance is due to the fact that it clearly distinguishes between public and private sector organisations across the three organisational strategic domains. This allows both scholars and practitioners to utilise and adopt the framework where necessary. Figure 3.6 depicts an assumption of PVF and the relevant strategic factors.

There is another useful feature of the PVF model as opposed to BPM and NPM, which makes for a compelling case why this framework has gained much attention over the last few years. The PVF has the flexibility to allow for integrating other analytical models in any of the three strategic factor domains. For example, dependent on the public sector organisation and the external context, one could use any external analysis framework that would be applicable and appropriate to the said organisation and its external stakeholders. This suits the idiosyncratic characteristics of public sector organisations and is of significance especially in application of value creation mapping tools where the primary focus is the external environment of a public sector organisation.

The majority of frameworks that analyse external environment of the public sector organisations are derived from Porter' s five forces framework but given that public sector external environment often has far less focus on competition and a greater emphasis on other factors (Vining, 2016), the competitive element of the five forces is replaced by a more important context-specific force. Therefore, despite the benefit of employing the five forces model in the public sector, it usually requires considerable alternations as the value creation objectives of public sector organisations often significantly vary compared

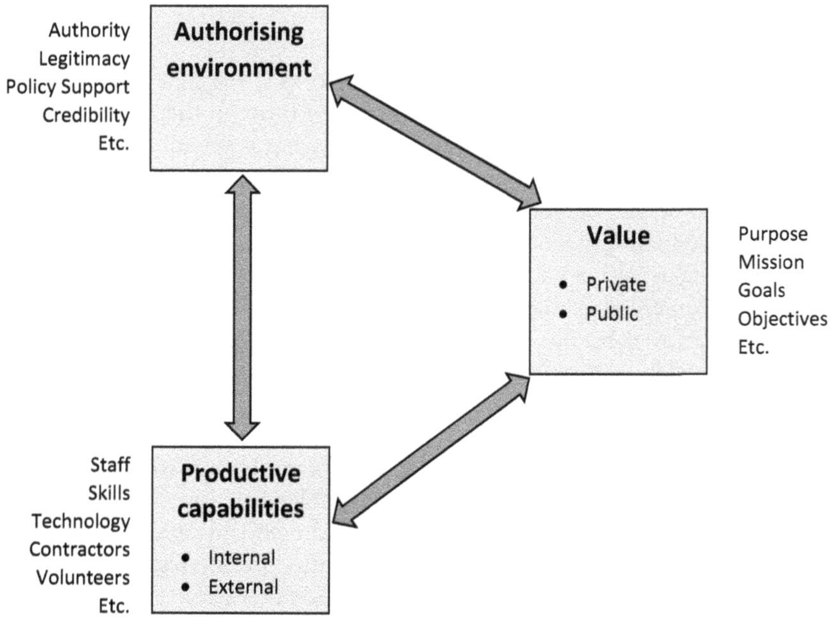

Figure 3.6 PVF and strategic factors
Source: Adapted from Moore (1995)

to the private sector. In addition to this, there are often other external forces affecting the public sector environment stemming from the high power of some external stakeholders such as the government, and as such, political force is one of the most crucial factors in any public sector outside-in analysis. There is in fact a strong argument to consider the political factor as a separate force in the five forces (Grundy, 2006), and this perhaps is even more applicable for public sector organisations. Figure 3.7 illustrates an adoption of five forces to the public sector organisations external environment.

From the model above it is apparent why there is a need for significant modification of external analytical frameworks as public sector organisations would significantly vary in the nature of stakeholders/participants. While some of the forces such as bargaining power of suppliers and threat of substitutes are directly applicable to public sector organisations, other forces such as bargaining power of customers would require significant amendment prior to any analysis. This is because the term customer could have several meanings in the public sector context such as citizens, tax payers, clients, users, students, patients, residents, and community, and eventually it is dependent on the public sector environment of specific organisation how the bargaining power of this force unfolds.

Similarly, other scholars have used the aforementioned approach to propose models of public sector external analysis based on the five forces framework. For instance, McKevitt's model of external analysis for public sector organisations (2000) (Figure 3.7) takes into account the importance of regulation while adopting the competitive force elements of five forces to what he refers to as street-level public organisation (SLPO). The model also highlights the role of central government as a clear and distinctive force influencing the

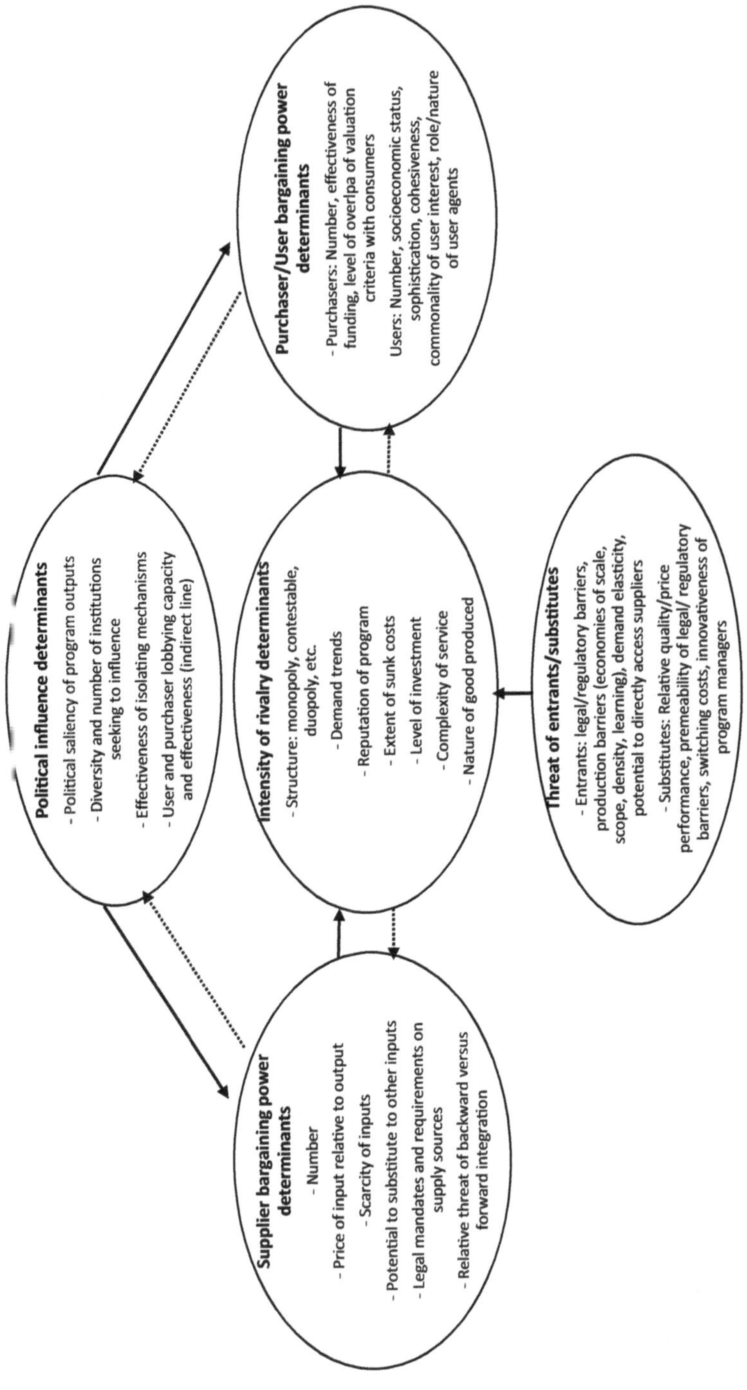

Figure 3.7 Public sector external forces analysis

Source: Adapted from Vining (2016: 10)

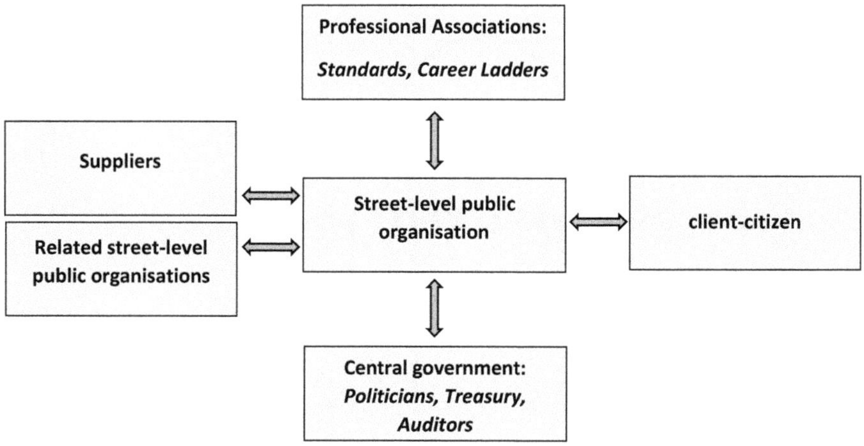

Figure 3.8 the external analysis of SLPOs

Source: Adapted from McKevitt (1998)

external environment dynamics. For the majority of public sector organisations, the government also acts as the funding/donor. Figure 3.8 shows SLPO and its related external environment.

The second differing force identified in this model is other street-level public organisations, which may act as either substitutes or collaborators to the SLPOs. The third important force in McKevitt's model is Professional Association Standards as often there are governing or legislative organisations that provide training, education, career paths as well as industry level guidelines for professionals/workers in the public service sector. As an example, the National Governor's Association is an independent organisation representing School Governor in the UK, or the General Medical Council is the organisation that oversees and regulates doctors in the UK.

Ultimately and as discussed in earlier section, whether it is the private or public sector, value creation analysis is highly dependent on the interplay of the external environment as well as what transpires at an organisational level. Equally important is taking into account the idiosyncratic differences of public sector organisations as well as their related external environment. Therefore, formulating an effective value framework for public sector organisations requires an integrative approach to both internal and external strategic management analytical models with a careful consideration of how and where these models require adoption and modification to reflect the context of any given public sector organisation.

3.5 The balanced scorecard

Original formulation of the scorecard

The balanced scorecard was developed by Robert Kaplan and David Norton in 1992 (Kaplan and Norton, 1992), and in subsequent decades its popularity has grown to the extent that it is now regarded as one of the key tools in the strategist's armoury. It is used by senior management to aid the formulation of strategy, improving operational alignment, and enhancing communication with internal and external stakeholders (Gumbus and Lyons, 2002).

At its heart is a simple idea. When company performance is being assessed, it is common to talk in financial terms such as profitability and market share. However, the balanced scorecard demonstrates that there a range of non-financial measures that need to be taken into account when devising strategy. This means that senior management have the potential to deliver even greater performance because decisions are made on a more complete and rounded set of information (Kaplan and Norton, 1992). Importantly, it pulls together external and internal factors into a holistic model that considers all aspects of strategy. Many versions of the model have been developed over the years, but they are essentially variations on a theme. In this book, we present the following version (Figure 3.9), which is based on the original.

Figure 3.9 shows that finance is important. It may, indeed, be the single most important factor when making strategic decisions, since at its most basic level, a company that is not financially sound is potentially in trouble regardless of any other attributes it may have. Hence this area is shaded in the diagram to emphasise its importance to the organisation. Nevertheless, many other factors should be considered, but the precise nature of these varies from industry to industry. In certain industries, innovation is key, and it is vital that new products are developed rapidly and regularly – how often do Microsoft, Apple, and Google bring out new technology that is substantially different from what has gone before? In other industries, the need for such frame-breaking innovation is different; the trousers that George Washington wore are still recognisably trousers, and the shoes King Henry VIII wore are still recognisably shoes.

Within each of the four categories, for each subcomponent, the scorecard asks management to identify objectives, measures, targets, and outline the initiatives they plan to undertake to deliver these. Effectively, therefore, the balanced scorecard is a graphical

Financial	*Internal Processes*
How do shareholders see us?	What must we excel at?
• operating efficiency • financial health • revenue streams	• innovation • new products • understand customers • response
Learning and growth	*Customer*
How do we grow and prosper?	How do customers see us?
• recruitment • training • productivity • information	• service excellence • trusted • complaint resolution

Figure 3.9 Example of traditional (private sector) balanced scorecard

Source: Based on Kaplan and Norton (1992)

representation of an organisation's strategy (Nørreklit, 2003), or a strategy map (Kaplan and Norton, 2001). It shows the internal processes that an organisation adopts in order to achieve its results (Kaplan and Norton, 2004), and it can show how the different interactions within the organisation (such as those between communication, control systems, and management) can influence the overall outcome (Atkinson, 2006). The idea of causality is fundamental – what actions cause the observed results (Kober and Northcott, 2021)? Indeed, some forms of the model include arrows to show the interconnectivity between the components: a financially sound company is likely to recruit more effectively; a company with excellent customer service is likely to reap financial benefits from repeat customers; and so on. Kaplan and Norton (2004) argue that this causality means that performance measures should be derived from the identified cause-and-effect relationships. Organisations can, therefore, identify all of the important aspects of their strategy to drive improvement.

There have been criticisms levelled at the balanced scorecard. For instance, it takes a somewhat static view of the situation (Othman, 2008), assumes that organisations are somewhat mechanistic (Bessire and Baker, 2005), and uses somewhat subjective measures (Chiang and Lin, 2009) that underplay the role of employees in organisational success (Nielsen et al., 2017). Nevertheless, it remains widely used (Soderberg et al., 2011), although the model has been updated over the years, for instance with an explicit consideration of environmental, social, or ethical issues; this has become known as the sustainability balanced scorecard (Gurd and Ifandoudas, 2014; Bento et al., 2017). This version can be used to explore relationships between CSR and business performance, and it stresses the significant influence that each of these aspects has on the other (Hansen and Schaltegger, 2016; Kang et al., 2015).

Public sector scorecard

As we have seen throughout this book, despite some similarities with the private sector in terms of strategy, there are also a number of significant differences. Thus, there has been a demand for an adaptation of the balanced scorecard so that it reflected the unique characteristics of the public sector. The performance of public sector organisations is not easily measured by financial indicators; instead they are judged by how effectively they meet the needs of their stakeholders. This was recognised by Kaplan and Norton, who modified their model for non-profit organisations by adding in a new element called "mission" (Kaplan and Norton, 2001), and this is so fundamental to success that it underpins the entire model (Urrutia and Eriksen, 2005). This version of model is sometimes known as the public sector scorecard, and it often varies from sector to sector, and even from organisation to organisation, to address the specimoullofic culture and values of the particular organisation (Moullin, 2017).

As with the private sector model, the public sector variant has been widely adopted (Grigoroudis et al., 2012). For instance, it can be found in health care (Grigoroudis et al., 2012; Gurd and Gao, 2007), education, (Barndt et al., 2011; Dreveton, 2013) and local and national government (Nisson, 2010; Northcott and Taulapapa, 2012), and its use is evident in many countries including Taiwan (Chang et al., 2008), Ethiopia (Geru, 2020), Vietnam (Pham et al., 2020), New Zealand (Northcott and Taulapapa, 2012), and extensively across Europe (e.g. Ax and Bjornenak, 2005; Dreveton, 2013; Malmi, 2001; Speckbacher et al., 2003). Interestingly, its prevalence and focus on performance measures has led some to present the public sector balanced scorecard as a symbol of New Public Management (Dreveton, 2013), which has been explored in the previous chapter, and it is therefore a useful tool when public sector organisations wish to report publicly (Griffiths, 2003).

One version of the public sector balanced scorecard is presented below (Figure 3.10), and this is the version that is explored in more detail in the case study that follows:

Mission	
Stakeholders	*Internal Processes*
How do stakeholders see us?	What must we excel at?
• citizen • environment • society	• understand customers • complaint resolution • response • deliver more with less • financial management
Learning and Growth	*Regulatory framework*
How do we grow and prosper?	What must we do?
• recruitment • training • partnerships • information	• statutory functions we must deliver • statutory functions we must manage • best value (and similar)

Figure 3.10. Example of public sector balanced scorecard

Source: Adapted from a UK local authority

Figure 3.10 has been sourced from a UK local authority. In this organisation, the authority is divided into different portfolios, as shown earlier in this book, and each portfolio has its own particular balanced scorecard. This example comes from the regeneration portfolio. The importance of satisfying stakeholder needs is pre-eminent in the public sector, and in this organisation, and thus, this section has been shaded in the diagram to reflect its importance.

It is interesting that in this example, finance occupies a completely different place in the model. Here, rather than it being a separate aspect in its own right (as in the private sector version), it forms part of internal processes. This reinforces the fact that it is merely one of many factors that need to be considered and is not the fundamental driving force that it is for many in the private sector.

The application of this model is shown in case study 3c.

Case Study 3c Balanced scorecard in the public sector

Local authority A is comprised of five portfolios. Each portfolio has its own balanced scorecard. This case explores the version in Figure 3.6, which is drawn from the regeneration portfolio. The portfolio in question is responsible for services including parks, bereavement, highways and lighting, waste disposal, grounds maintenance, libraries, neighbourhood services, and public realm infrastructure.

A key part of the portfolio is the Business Management department. This is responsible for providing advice and guidance across the whole range of services and offers oversight and a sense of cohesion that allows the disparate parts of the portfolio to work together towards a common cause. The department gives direction and, as one employee puts it, "it is the glue that holds everything together".

As part of its role, the department was tasked with developing a strategy for the portfolio, and the balanced scorecard was a key element of this. The manager explains the process:

> Our first job was to establish definitively exactly what the portfolio was for. What is its purpose? Why does it exist? What is it trying to achieve? From that, we could identify a mission statement, and this allowed us to focus our thinking. Basically, if something didn't fit with our mission statement, then we needed to stop doing it, unless it was a legal requirement.

The Business Management department met with the heads of each of the other departments, and collectively, the following wording was agreed as the portfolio's mission:

> To grow the local economy while safeguarding local jobs and industry

The manager continued:

> OK, so once we had our overall mission, we began to plug various things into the balanced scorecard. One problem we had was that the different directors all started banging their pet projects into the plan without any overall objective. Everyone thought their own work was more important than everyone else's work.

The Business Management department held a series of workshops where they facilitated discussions, and gradually things began to take shape. The deputy manager explained how it began.

> Money was important – of course it was – but there were many other important things too. How could we grow the economy? What did that even mean? How do we measure this growth? Also, we were safeguarding jobs, but we can only directly employ so many people. That means we have to influence, take away barriers, make the employment situation more favourable. How do we do that? We had to get these basic ideas down on paper and agreed before we could look at the detail.

This was not always an easy process. During the discussions, managers sometimes found it difficult to decide on the appropriate dimensions to include in the balanced scorecard. It was not always easy to define who 'the customer' was, and it was often difficult to identify a manageable number of appropriate KPIs because of the range and complexity of organisational activities. This was overcome through a further series of meetings between directors and other senior managers, again facilitated by the Business Management department. Further details are not provided here, but the interested reader might look at Northcott and Taulapapa (2012), who found similar issues in their own research.

The resulting balanced scorecard is shown in Figure 3.11.

The final version of the scorecard illustrates the key points raised earlier. Underneath each of the main sections – stakeholders, internal processes, learning and growth, regulatory framework – are a series of key objectives, or main headings. These show what the organisation ultimately wants to address. For each of these headings are measures, targets, and initiatives.

Measures were not always easy to develop. Essentially, this section identifies the document, system, statistic, etc. In many places, the organisation has been precise, and it is clear what is intended: number of one-stop shops can be counted; international standards will be achieved or they won't; customer satisfaction surveys will contain important results, and so on. However, looking at the measures for this book, our view is that some are still rather nebulous: It is not particularly clear how "provide leadership of complex cross-organisational strategic themes" can be measured or how effectiveness can be judged.

Targets explain what the organisation intends to do to address the measures. In Figure 3.11 the targets are precise. Exact timescales and/or specific percentages are provided, and thus it will be possible for management to monitor progress. In this particular organisation, targets were cascaded down through the portfolio so that individual departments could work on their own discrete areas whilst contributing to the whole.

Initiatives outline what the organisation will do in order to meet the targets that have been set. In the example provided, these are largely statements of intent, and they help to give context to the figures provided in the document. This helps staff to understand the reasoning behind why they are doing what they are.

Managers in the organisation felt that the balanced scorecard was an important tool for many reasons. The following quotes were made by senior managers in preparation for this book, and they have been anonymised at their request:

> The scorecard shows finance in its proper place. It is important, but there are other factors too, and they are often just as important.
>
> It gave us a way to communicate to councillors. Councillors often tend to focus on their own wards and on their own particular constituents. Now they could see the big picture. There are bigger things going on. It was important for our relationship with them, but it was important for them too. They had to explain things to their constituents, and that gave the public a better understanding and allowed them to understand how the competing priorities played out on the ground.

Mission: To grow the local economy while safeguarding local jobs and industry

Stakeholders				*Internal processes*			
Objectives	*Measures*	*Targets*	*Initiatives*	*Objectives*	*Measures*	*Targets*	*Initiatives*
Citizen	Provide leadership of complex cross-organisational strategic themes	Establish cross-institution working groups and terms of reference in year 1	Facilitate shared working between health care providers and social services	Understand customers	Customer satisfaction surveys	95% customer satisfaction rating	Introduce customer satisfaction surveys in all parts of portfolio
			Facilitate shared working between local authorities in the region				Extend customer surveys to include internal customers
Environment	Certification against environmental standards	Obtain ISO14001 in parks and bereavement in year 2. Extend to events by year 3	Establish quality management team within portfolio to oversee accreditation against ISO and EFQM standards	Complaint resolution	Customer satisfaction surveys, number of complaints, pattern of complaints, nature of complaints	Resolve 95% of complaints within five working days, 95% customer satisfaction rating	Expand the use of the xxx system into one-stop shops. Provide training for front-facing staff
Society	Number of one-stop shops	Establish three One Stop Shops in year 1, and four more each year for five years	Create synergy by bringing common customer issues into one place	Response	Response rates	90% of call-outs to be responded to within 48 hours	Expand the use of the xxx system into one-stop shops. Provide training for end-point staff

			Create seamless customer experience at point of contact	Deliver more with less	Value of contracts awarded	Successfully let contracts for highways in year 1; waste management in year 2; grounds maintenance in year 3. For each, 5% net saving on current contracts	Create economies of scale through shared cross-portfolio procurement
	Preserve historic sites and monuments	Maintain current level of repair and maintenance costs	Undertake pro-active assessment of sites and monuments. Target remedial measures based on risk	Financial management	Inventory turnover	Reduce by 3% in year 1 and by 5% annually thereafter for five years	Improve asset utilisation
	Number of journeys by public transport	Reduce car journeys by 5% and increase use of public transport by 5% within five years	Improve bus and train infrastructure over five years		Budget	Reduce by 5% in year 1 and by 3% annually thereafter for five years	Generate cost savings through shared use of back-office staff, systems, and processes

(*Continued*)

Figure 3.11 Public sector scorecard for regeneration portfolio in a UK local authority

Figure 3.11 (Continued)

Learning and Growth				*Regulatory framework*			
Objectives	*Measures*	*Targets*	*Initiatives*	*Objectives*	*Measures*	*Targets*	*Initiatives*
Recruitment	Staff satisfaction surveys	95% staff satisfaction	Increase number and relevance of staff surveys	Statutory functions we must deliver	Specific to each contract	100% legal compliance	Specific to each contract
	Diversity surveys	Equality statistics	Achieve representation of BAME, LGBT+ and other disadvantaged sectors of society		Specific to each contract	Early awareness of changes to regulation and legislation	Work with professional bodies (specific to each contract). Benchmark with local authorities to identify and plan for likely changes to legal and regulatory regimes
Training	Gap analysis	Address major issues (not possible to be more specific until skills audit completed)	Perform skills audit of staff comparing competency to business need	Statutory functions we must manage	Vehicle exhausts emissions measured in parts per million	Reduce carbon footprint by 5% over three years	Upgrade fleet, prioritising heavy vehicles within first three years. Explore the potential of electric vehicles

	Course enrolment and completion figures	20% increase in number of staff completing management training courses within five years	Work with local university to develop MBA for senior management, PGDip for middle management, PGCert for junior or aspiring managers. These to be arranged so that progression to the next course is possible, and thus aid career progression		Number of complaints. Number of emergency call outs	Successfully let contracts for highways in year 1; waste management in year 2; grounds maintenance in year 3. For each, 15% reduction in customer complaints and emergency call outs within two years of contract commencement	Successfully implement programme of city-wide infrastructure contracts by year 3
Partnerships	Number of community partnerships	Establish one new community partnership each year for five years	Work with local "friends" groups to develop relationships and identify need	Best Value (and similar)	Compare	At least parity with benchmark authorities' results	Benchmark performance against key local authorities
	Number of successful bids	Successfully bid to host one international event within five years	Work with other local authorities in the region to submit a series of joint bids on behalf of the region		Challenge	At least parity with benchmark organisations' results	Benchmark performance against key private sector organisations in comparable areas

(*Continued*)

Figure 3.11 (Continued)

Learning and Growth				*Regulatory framework*			
Objectives	*Measures*	*Targets*	*Initiatives*	*Objectives*	*Measures*	*Targets*	*Initiatives*
Information	Timeliness of reports	98% of reports delivered on time. Remaining 2% delivered within two working days	Expand the use of the xxx system into one-stop shops. Provide training for front-facing staff		Consult	95% stakeholder satisfaction rating	Introduce customer satisfaction surveys in all parts of portfolio. Increase number and relevance of staff surveys. Identify other stakeholders and develop ways to engage with them
			Develop new decision-support system		Compete	Introduce three new work streams within five years	Explore areas where private sector might be challenged

There was a consensus that it was very important that the portfolio-level scorecard was cascaded down to individual departments so that they could develop their own strategies whilst supporting the overall position. These departments did not use formal scorecards, but their own strategic documents had to include a section showing how their work supported the wider aims of the scorecard. As one departmental manager put it:

> It allows everyone to see how they fit in. It's hard to explain to a grave digger how their work helps the council achieve its strategy. Now staff in individual departments could see themselves represented in the document. They could see that they actually impacted many different parts of the strategy, from Environment to Customers, and from Society to Best Value.

One important aspect that might be overlooked is the need for the scorecard to be a live document. This was borne out repeatedly in discussions with managers. It is a key tool in the armoury of the public sector strategist, but like any tool, if it is to be effective, it needs to be *used* and maintained.

3.6 Chapter summary

This chapter has outlined the traditional approaches to developing strategy. The following key points were identified:

- Strategy needs to be understood in relation to the environment in which an organisation operates.
- Once the organisations strategy with relation to its industry is assessed, it is necessary to examine the internal workings of the organisation to determine the extent to which its own processes and resources are contributing to strategic objectives.
- Some approaches to strategy can be applicable to both the public sector and private sector. However, these sectors also have fundamental differences in strategic purpose. Generally speaking, the private sector is interested in concepts such as profitability or market share, whereas the public sector is more fundamentally concerned with value creation and value maximization.
- There may be some linkages that can be made between models that were originally formulated for the private sector, such as the value chain, the rise of new public management, and the public sector drive for value creation.
- However, although some commonly taught models of strategic analysis may be equally applicable regardless of sector, in many cases it is necessary to view public sector strategy as something different and distinct from the private sector, and therefore, different concepts, models, and theories should be used in this context.

References

Acedo, F. J., Barroso, C. & Galan, J. L. (2006). The resource-based theory: Dissemination and main trends. *Strategic Management Journal*, 27(7), 621–636.

Alford, J. & Greve, C. (2017). Strategy in the public and private sectors: Similarities, differences and changes. *Administrative Sciences*, 7(4), 35.

Anastasya, A. & Widjaja, A. W. (2019). The addition of channel distribution and media campaign in SME Abelarosa collection. In *12th International Conference on Business and Management Research (ICBMR 2018)*. Atlantis Press, pp. 236–241.

Andersen, L. B., Jørgensen, T. B., Kjeldsen, A. M., Pedersen, L. H. & Vrangbæk, K. (2012). Public value dimensions: Developing and testing a multi-dimensional classification. *International Journal of Public Administration*, 35(11), 715–728.

Andrews, K. J. (1971). *The Concept of Corporate Strategy*. Irwin (Ch. 1–5).

Arend, R. J. (2006). Tests of the resource-based view: Do the empirics have any clothes? *Strategic Organization*, 4(4), 409–421.

Atkinson, H. (2006). Strategy implementation: A role for the balanced scorecard? *Management Decision*, 44(10), 1441–1460.

Ax, C. & Bjornenak, T. (2005). Bundling and diffusion of management accounting innovations – the case of the balanced scorecard in Sweden. *Management Accounting Research*, 16, 1–20.

Barndt, R., Mcgee, C. & Cataldo, A. (2011). Failure to benchmark: An out-of-balance scorecard at an academic institution. *Management Accounting Quarterly*, 12(2), 49–56.

Barney, J. B. (1991). Firm resources and sustained competitive advantage. *Journal of Management*, 17(1), 99–120.

Barney, J. B. & Clark, D. N. (2007). *Resource-Based Theory: Creating and Sustaining Competitive Advantage*. Oxford: Oxford University Press.

Barney, J. B., Ketchen, D. J. & Wright, M. (2011). The future of resource-based theory revitalization or decline? *Journal of Management*, 37(5), 1299–1315.

Beard, J. W. & Sumner, M. (2004). Seeking strategic advantage in the post-net era: Viewing ERP systems from the resource-based perspective. *The Journal of Strategic Information Systems*, 13(2), 129–150.

Bento, R. F., Mertins, L. & White, L. F. (2017). Ideology and the balanced scorecard: An empirical exploration of the tension between shareholder value maximization and corporate social responsibility. *Journal of Business Ethics*, 142(4), 769–789.

Berisha Qehaja, A. & Kutllovci, E. (2015). The role of human resources in gaining competitive advantage. *Journal of Human Resource Management*, 18(2), 47–61.

Bessire, D. & Baker, C. R. (2005). The French Tableau de bord and the American balanced scorecard: A critical analysis. *Critical Perspectives on Accounting*, 16(6), 645–664.

Black, J. A. & Boal, K. B. (1994). Strategic resources: Traits, configurations and paths to sustainable competitive advantage. *Strategic Management Journal*, 15(S2), 131–148.

Boston, J., Martin, J., Pallot, J. & Walsh, P. (1996). *Public Management: The New Zealand Model*. Oxford: Oxford University Press. ISBN-13:978–0195583250.

Bowman, C. & Ambrosini, V. (2003). How the resource-based and the dynamic capability views of the firm inform corporate-level strategy. *British Journal of Management*, 14(4), 289–303.

Boxall, P. & Steeneveld, M. (1999). Human resource strategy and competitive advantage: A longitudinal study of engineering consultancies. *Journal of Management Studies*, 36(4), 443–463.

Bryer, T. A. (2007). Toward a relevant agenda for a responsive public administration. *Journal of Public Administration Research and Theory*, 17(3), 479–500.

Bryson, J. M., Crosby, B. C. & Stone, M. M. (2015). Designing and implementing cross-sector collaborations: Needed and challenging. *Public Administration Review*, 75(5), 647–663.

Cavusgil, E., Seggie, S. H. & Talay, M. B. (2007). Dynamic capabilities view: Foundations and research agenda. *The Journal of Marketing Theory and Practice*, 15(2), 159–166.

Chandler, A. D. (1962). *Strategy and Structure: Chapters in the History of American Enterprise*. Boston: MIT Press.

Chang, W. C., Tung, Y. C., Huang, C. H. & Yang, M. C. (2008). Performance improvement after implementing the balanced scorecard: A large hospital's experience in Taiwan. *Total Quality Management*, 19(11), 1143–1154.

Chiang, C. Y. & Lin, B. (2009). An integration of balanced scorecards and data envelopment analysis for firm's benchmarking management. *Total Quality Management*, 20(11), 1153–1172.

Cockburn, I., Henderson, R. & Stern, S. (2000). Untangling the origins of competitive advantage. *Strategic Management Journal*, 21(11), 1123–1145.

Collis, D. J. & Montgomery, C. A. (2008). Competing on resources. *Harvard Business Review*, 86(7/8), 140.

Conner, K. R. (1991). A historical comparison of resource-based theory and five schools of thought within industrial organization economics: Do we have a new theory of the firm? *Journal of Management*, 17(1), 121–154.

Conner, K. R. & Prahalad, C. K. (1996). A resource-based theory of the firm: Knowledge versus opportunism. *Organization Science*, 7(5), 477–501.

Christensen, C. R., Andrews, K. R., Bower, J. L., Hamermesh, R. G. & Porter, M. E. (1982). *Business Policy Text and Cases* (5th edn). Homewood: Richard D. Irwin. ISBN 0256014515.

Chun, Y. H. & Rainey, H. G. (2005). Goal ambiguity and organizational performance in US federal agencies. *Journal of Public Administration Research and Theory*, 15(4), 529–557.

Crosby, B. C., 't Hart, P. & Torfing, J. (2017). Public value creation through collaborative innovation. *Public Management Review*, 19(5), 655–669.

Dreveton, B. (2013). The advantages of the balanced scorecard in the public sector: Beyond performance measurement. *Public Money & Management*, 33(2), 131–136.

Eisenhardt, K. M. & Martin, J. A. (2000). Dynamic capabilities: What are they? *Strategic Management Journal*, 21(10/11), 1105–1121.

Geru, A. A. (2020). Examining the achievements of the balanced scorecard as public sector reform tool: The case of some selected Oromia regional government bureaus. *Public Policy and Administration Research*, 10(3), 15–25.

Grant, R. M. (1996). Toward a knowledge-based theory of the firm. *Strategic Management Journal*, 17(S2), 109–122.

Greve, C. (2015). Ideas in public management reform for the 2010s. Digitalization, value creation and involvement. *Public Organization Review*, 15, 15–49.

Griffiths, J. (2003). Balanced scorecard use in New Zealand government departments and crown entities. *Australian Journal of Public Administration*, 62(4), 70–79.

Grigoroudis, E., Orfanoudaki, E. & Zopounidis, C. (2012). Strategic performance measurement in a health care organization. *Omega*, 40, 104–119.

Grundy T. (2006). Rethinking and reinventing Michael Porter's five forces model. *Strategic Change*, 15(5), 213–229.

Gumbus, A. & Lyons, B. (2002). The balanced scorecard at Philips electronics. *Strategic Finance-Montvale*, 84, 45–49. Retrieved May 26, 2021, from https://pdfs.semanticscholar.org/78d1/83e58794f5a5f7de3768a1353a8cdca539a1.pdf.

Gurd, B. & Gao, T. (2007). Lives in the balance: An analysis of the balanced scorecard (BSC) in healthcare organizations. *International Journal of Productivity and Performance Management*, 57(1), 6–21.

Gurd, B. & Ifandoudas, P. (2014). Moving towards agility: The contribution of a modified balanced scorecard system. *Measuring Business Excellence*, 18(2), 1–13.

Hansen E. G. & Schaltegger, S. (2016). The sustainability balanced scorecard: A systematic review of architectures. *Journal of Business Ethics*, 133(2), 193–221.

Harreld J. B., O'Reilly III, C. A. & Tushman, M. L. (2007). Dynamic capabilities at IBM: Driving strategy into action. *California Management Review*, 49(4), 21–43.

Helfat, C. E., Finkelstein, S., Mitchell, W., Peteraf, M., Singh, H., Teece, D. & Winter, S. G. (2007). *Dynamic Capabilities: Understanding Strategic Change in Organizations*. John Wiley & Sons.

Helfat, C. E. & Martin, J. A. (2015). Dynamic managerial capabilities: Review and assessment of managerial impact on strategic change. *Journal of Management*, 41(5), 1281–1312.

Hood, C. (1991). A public management for all seasons? *Public Administration*, 69, 3–19.

Hood, C., & Dixon, R. (2015). What we have to show for 30 years of new public management: *Higher costs, more complaints*. *Governance*, 28(3), 265–267.

Kang, J. S., Chiang, C. F., Huangthanapan, K. & Downing, S. (2015). Corporate social responsibility and sustainability balanced scorecard: The case study of family-owned hotels. *International Journal of Hospitality Management*, 48, 124–134.
Kaplan, R. S. & Norton, D. P. (1992). The balanced scorecard: Measures that drive performance. *Harvard Business Review*, 70(1), 71–79.
Kaplan, R. S. & Norton, D. P. (2001). *The Strategy Focused Organization*. Boston: Harvard Business School Press.
Kaplan, R. S. & Norton, D. P. (2004). The strategy map: Guide to aligning intangible assets. *Strategy and Leadership*, 32(5), 10–17.
Kober, R. & Northcott, D. (2021). Testing cause-and-effect relationships within a balanced scorecard. *Accounting & Finance*, 61, 1815–1849.
Levy, D. L., Alvesson, M. & Willmott, H. (2003). Critical approaches to strategic management. *Studying Management Critically*, 14, 92–110.
Lopes, J., Oliveira, J. & Silveira, P. (2020). Applying regional VRIO model to Island regions: An evaluation of RIS3. In L. Farinha, D. Santos, J. Ferreira, & M. Ranga (Eds.), *Regional Helix Ecosystems and Sustainable Growth. Studies on Entrepreneurship, Structural Change and Industrial Dynamics*. Cham: Springer, pp. 67–84.
Mahoney, J. T. (2001). A resource-based theory of sustainable rents. *Journal of Management*, 27(6), 651–660.
Malmi, T. (2001). Balanced scorecards in Finnish companies. *Management Accounting Research*, 12, 207–220.
McKevitt, D. (1998). *Managing Core Public Services*. Oxford: Blackwell.
McKevitt, D., Millar, M. & Keogan, J. F. (2000). The role of the citizen-client in performance measurement: The case of the street level public organization (SLPO). *International Review of Administrative Sciences*, 66(4), 619–636.
Min, B. S., Min, J. H., Jang, W., Han, S. H. & Kang, S. Y. (2016). VRIO model based enterprise capability assessment framework for plant project. *Korean Journal of Construction Engineering and Management*, 17(3), 61–70.
Moore, M. H. (1995). *Creating Public Value: Strategic Management in Government*. Cambridge: Harvard University. ISBN 9780674175587.
Moore, M. H. (2000). Managing for value: Organizational strategy in for-profit, nonprofit, and governmental organizations. *Nonprofit and Voluntary Sector Quarterly*, 29(1_suppl), 183–204.
Moullin, M. (2017). Improving and evaluating performance with the public sector scorecard. *International Journal of Productivity and Performance Management*, 66(4), 442–458.
Narayanan, V. K. & Fahey, L. (2005). The relevance of the institutional underpinnings of Porter's five forces framework to emerging economies: An epistemological analysis. *Journal of Management Studies*, 42(1), 207–223.
Neuroni, A. C., Haller, S., van Winden, W., Carabias-Hütter, V. & Yildirim, O. (2019). Public value creation in a smart city context: An analysis framework. In *Setting Foundations for the Creation of Public Value in Smart Cities*. Cham: Springer, pp. 49–76.
Nielsen, C., Lund, M. & Thomsen, P. (2017). Killing the balanced scorecard to improve internal disclosure. *Journal of Intellectual Capital*, 18(1), 45–62.
Nisson, K. (2010). Expectations from administrative reforms: An attempt to implement the balanced scorecard in a public sector organization. *International Journal of Public Administration*, 33(14), 822–831.
Nørreklit, H. (2003). The balanced scorecard: What is the score? A rhetorical analysis of the balanced scorecard. *Accounting, Organizations and Society*, 28(6), 591–619.
Northcott, D. & Taulapapa, T. M. (2012). Using the balanced scorecard to manage performance in public sector organizations: Issues and challenges. *International Journal of Public Sector Management*, 25(3), 166–191.
O'Flynn, J. (2007). From new public management to public value: Paradigmatic change and managerial implications. *Australian Journal of Public Administration*, 66, 353–366.

O'Reilly C. A. & Tushman, M. L. (2008). Ambidexterity as a dynamic capability: Resolving the innovator's dilemma. *Research in Organizational Behaviour*, 28, 185–206.

Othman, R. (2008). Enhancing the effectiveness of the balanced scorecard with scenario planning. *International Journal of Productivity and Performance Management*, 57(3), 259–266.

Peteraf, M. A. (1993). The cornerstones of competitive advantage: A resource-based view. *Strategic Management Journal*, 14(3), 179–191.

Peteraf, M. A. & Barney, J. B. (2003). Unraveling the resource-based tangle. *Managerial and Decision Economics*, 24(4), 309–323.

Pham, C. D., Vu, S. T., Pham, Y. T. K. & Vu, N. T. (2020). Evaluating performance of Vietnamese public hospitals based on balanced scorecard. *Journal of Asian Finance, Economics and Business*, 17(6), 339–349.

Pitts, R. A. & Lei, D. (1996). *Strategic management: Building and sustaining competitive advantage*. Minneapolis: West Pub.

Poister, T. H. (2010). The future of strategic planning in the public sector: Linking strategic management and performance. *Public Administration Review*, 70, 246–254.

Porter, M. E. (1985). Creating and sustaining superior performance. *Competitive Advantage*, 167, 167–206.

Porter, M. E. (1998). *Competitive Strategy: Techniques for Analyzing Industries and Competitors: With a New Introduction*. New York: Free Press.

Porter, M. E. (2011). *Competitive advantage of nations: Creating and sustaining superior performance*. Simon and Schuster.

Porter, M. E. & Kramer, M. R. (2006). Strategy and Society: The link between competitive advantage and corporate social responsibility. *Harvard Business Review*, December, 78–92.

Priem, R. L. & Butler, J. E. (2001a). Is the resource-based "view" a useful perspective for strategic management research? *Academy of Management Review*, 22–40.

Priem, R. L. & Butler, J. E. (2001b). Tautology in the resource-based view and the implications of externally determined resource value: Further comments. *Academy of Management Review*, 26(1), 57–66.

Selznick, P. (1957, September). Law and the structures of social action. *Administrative Science Quarterly*, 2(2), 258–261.

Smith, K. A., Vasudevan, S. P. & Tanniru, M. R. (1996). Organizational learning and resource-based theory: An integrative model. *Journal of Organizational Change Management*, 9(6), 41–53.

Soderberg, M., Kalagnanam, S., Sheehan, N. T. & Vaidyanathan, G. (2011). When is a balanced scorecard a balanced scorecard? *International Journal of Productivity and Performance Management*, 60(7), 688–708.

Speckbacher, G., Bischof, J. & Pfeiffer, P. (2003). A descriptive analysis on the implementation of balanced scorecards in German-speaking countries. *Management Accounting Research*, 14, 361–387.

Teece, D. J. (2012). Dynamic capabilities: Routines versus entrepreneurial action. *Journal of Management Studies*, 49(8), 1395–1401.

Teece, D. J. (2009). *Dynamic Capabilities and Strategic Management: Organizing for Innovation and Growth*. Oxford: Oxford University Press.

Teece, D. J., Pisano, G. & Shuen, A. (1997). Dynamic capabilities and strategic management. *Strategic Management Journal*, 18(7), 509–533.

Thompson, F. & Rizova, P. (2015). Understanding and creating public value: Business is the engine, government the flywheel (and also the regulator). *Public Management Review*, 17(4), 565–586.

Torfing, J., Ferlie, E., Jukić, T. & Ongaro, E. (2021). A theoretical framework for studying the co-creation of innovative solutions and public value. *Policy & Politics*, 49(2), 189–209.

Urrutia, I. & Eriksen, S. D. (2005). Application of the balanced scorecard in Spanish private health-care management. *Measuring Business Excellence*, 9(4), 16–26.

Vining, A. R. (2016). What is public agency strategic analysis (PASA) and how does it differ from public policy analysis and firm strategy analysis? *Administrative Sciences*, 6(4), 19.

Weinberg, M. L. & Leeman, K. (2013). Creating strategic value: Thinking, acting and learning. In Carol A. Scott (Ed.), *Museums and Public Value: Creating Sustainable Futures*. London and New York: Routledge, pp. 17–31. ISBN 9781409446439.

Wiklund, J. & Shepherd, D. (2005). Entrepreneurial orientation and small business performance: A configurational approach. *Journal of Business Venturing*, 20(1), 71–91.
Winter, S. G. (2003). Understanding dynamic capabilities. *Strategic Management Journal*, 24(10), 991–995.
Wright, P. M., McMahan, G. C. & McWilliams, A. (1994). Human resources and sustained competitive advantage: A resource-based perspective. *International Journal of Human Resource Management*, 5(2), 301–326.

Section 3

Factors that influence strategic decision-making

Chapter 4

Influences on strategy development

Classical models

Learning outcomes

After reading this chapter you should be able to:

- explain the difference between normative and behavioural decision-making models
- identify philosophical positions
- critique positivistic approaches in the development of strategic analysis
- have a deeper clarity and recognition of any unconscious assumptions

Pre-chapter questions

- Do classical approaches to strategy work in the public sector
- Do I need to think about my preconceptions before I undertake strategic thinking?
- Is what I observe and an accurate interpretation of reality? Is my reality real?

Key terms

- Positivist philosophy – knowledge is only valid if it is verifiable by observation or experiment, reason, or logic
- Ideology – a system of ideas or beliefs
- Strategy tools – concepts, models, frameworks, or methods for the analysis and exploration of strategic thinking
- Social construction – a philosophy wherein the perception of reality is not based on objective facts but on knowledge derived through cultural society and social interaction

DOI: 10.4324/9780429344305-8

4.1 Introduction

Strategic decision-making does not simply just "happen". Rather, strategy is the result of a series of decisions, each of which builds upon the last. However, although senior managers like to think that they are immune from influence and always make decisions dispassionately and objectively, this is not the case in reality. This section explores how managers are influenced and the impact this has on their decisions. This will, therefore, help practitioners and academics alike to become more aware of these factors and to factor them into their thought processes and, as a result, improve the quality of their decision-making.

Within his seminal text "What is strategy and does it matter", Whittington offers four perspectives on strategy: classical, evolutionary, systemic and processual, or emergent (see Figure 4.1).

This chapter explores two of these perspectives in detail. In the first section, we will critique the philosophical underpinnings within the classical framework and challenge its positivistic underpinning through a brief exploration social constructionism. In Chapter 5, we will dive deeper into the Systemic perspective, specifically the neo-institutional drivers that may underpin strategic thinking. The intent is to give the public sector strategist a critical eye when undertaking strategic development and to unmask any unconscious assumptions that may influence or affect strategic thinking.

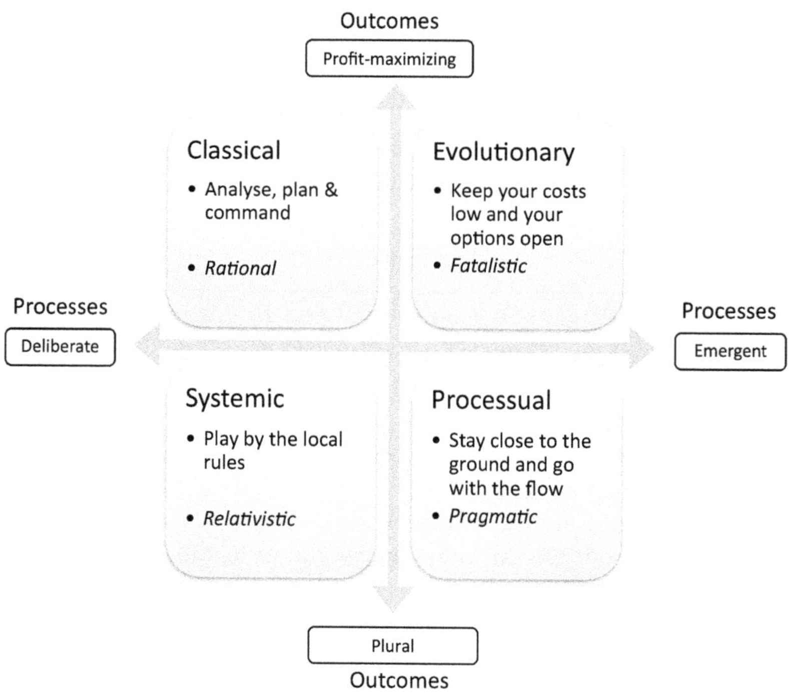

Figure 4.1 Whittington's four perspectives on strategy

4.2 Exploring positivism and social constructionism within strategy

Introduction

The aim of this section is to review the current literature in respect of the nature of management knowledge and the philosophical and contextual underpinnings of management and strategic management. The argument is that the strategic management field is dominated by universal theory applicable to any situation or context. Whittington (2001) describes this as the Classical perspective, based on a rational process, using deliberate and long-term calculation and analysis. This approach is fundamentally underpinned by economics wherein a rational economic man can use perfect rationality to maximize economic advantage (Hollis, 1975). The method tends towards the top down, following an analysis and command a planned, militaristic, and hierarchical approach.

The strategist is viewed as master of the internal and external environments (Ansoff, 1965), and a range of traditional strategy tools are typical of the process: such as SWOT, Porter's five forces, Boston matrix, PESTEL, resources and competencies, and value chain analysis. The fundamental philosophical underpinning this rationality is positivism. The following chapter will be an exploration of the generalisability and underpinning philosophical assumptions of the broader setting of management knowledge and more specifically, strategic management. It will explore the contextual development of strategic management leading to this philosophical position, the inherent paradoxes within strategic management and its leanings towards ideology in order to express and justify the basis of some of these issues. We then give the reader a brief introduction to an alternative philosophical position, social constructionism, and use this to help the reader establish a different perspective on what they perceive as real or observed.

The wider context of management science

In reviewing the wider contextual setting of strategic management within management science, it can be observed that management science is currently undertaken within a diverse range of philosophical viewpoints and research approaches, with a plurality of philosophies and methodologies endemic within the literature. The foundation of management science is, however, broadly based upon, and dominated by, a fundamentally modernist, logical positivist, and empiricist philosophy (Mingers, 2006). This scientific and lawlike approach and underlying management research is based on three assumptions (Whitley, 1984b).

Firstly, there is one true way of generating knowledge applicable to all situations, and management science is not significantly different from the natural sciences (Terry, 1977). Management science is positioned as "the application of scientific methodology, or principles, to management decisions" (Dannenbring and Starr, 1981: 1); it is a specific philosophical approach that was uncritically adopted in the 1950s (Whitley, 1984b). Although receiving much critique (Suppe, 1977: 617–632) it was reinforced in the mid 1990s when a move towards a more pluralist or rural approach to management research was perceived as a deviation and move away from the position of consensus. A consensus was deemed indispensable by some and necessary for the advancement of knowledge, and any move away from this consensus was viewed as limiting scientific progress (Pfeffer, 1993). The result was that scholars in organisation/management made recommendations to centrally control, limit, and restrict diverse research development. Subsequent publications were then controlled by an elite group, restricting views, generating a controlled consensus, and purging areas of low consensus (Pfeffer, 1993; Tranfield and Starkey, 1998).

The second of these three assumptions (Whitley, 1984b) is that this single scientific method is directly valid to, or relevant within, a social setting and that the range of application of theory is applicable in all contexts and contingencies, as seen in the positivistic scientific enquiry model (Koontz and O'Donnell, 1976). Positivism is reliant on the assembly of facts, the claim being that the approach is factually underpinned. The assumption is that the social or human world can be studied in the same way as any natural science, producing comparable knowledge; and it does not account for the context and meaning within human action (Whitley, 1984b). An assumption demonstrated by a significant element of management research is based upon single case studies leading to broad generalisations (Tranfield and Starkey, 1998). However, positivistic approaches alone are unable to accurately validate social theories (Burrell and Morgan, 1985) and is critiqued as being a restrictive approach for the analysis of social issues (Shrivastava, 1986).

These two assumptions align with a number of Tranfield and Starkey's (1998) propositions that management research has been too embedded in the physical sciences, developing universal laws and adhering to predominantly American models (stable/growing economy, market-dominated, individualistic and capitalistic [Whittington, 2001]) and that management is essentially non-reductionist, mode 2 (more real/applied), plural, and cross disciplinary.

A final assumption is that knowledge or theory is relevant and usable by managers and unaffected by use of the operational requirements of those managers. Applied knowledge relies on the notion that there is a current condition, framework, or problem within a management area that can be improved in a measurable way by the manager utilising the research or theory (Whitley, 1984a). However, current beliefs and practices amongst managers are widely variant; there is no one way of viewing, perceiving, organising, and managing organisations, and as such, there are no unified and identical conditions, frameworks, or problems within organisations on which to apply generalisable theory. The quest for generalisability then de-emphasises the importance of context and the usability by managers within that context (Whitley, 1984b).

A fundamental critique of this logical positivist philosophy is explored through the investigation of the impact of research on organisations (Hodgkinson and Starkey, 2011). Here the focus is on whether management research "mattered" (Porter and McKibbin, 1988; Hambrick, 1994) and whether it succeeds in meeting the needs of students, by business schools overemphasising the scientific model (Khurana, 2010). The current consensus endorses the double hurdles of management philosophy, rigour, and relevance (Pettigrew, 2001; Hodgkinson and Starkey, 2011), and asserts that management research is grounded in two issues: its diverse and fragmented nature and its applied nature (Tranfield and Starkey, 1998). The cognitive components of business managemnt (Becher and Trowler, 2001) can be mapped against two substantive dimensions of disciplines: the hard versus soft and the pure versus applied (Tranfield and Starkey, 1998). Hardness being the extent of consistency and consensus within in the field thus defining boundaries, soft implies divergent and rural (the research area being broad and wide ranging as opposed to urban, tightly packed and occupying a small space (Becher and Trowler, 2001)). Social sciences and business areas are found to be soft in that they do not share single a philosophy or paradigm (Biglan, 1973). Whether business and management is pure (knowing what) or applied (knowing how, the application to real-world problems (Tranfield and Starkey, 1998)) was observed to be, for the UK in mid 1970s at least, leaning towards the pure. More recently there is consensus that there is no single philosophical paradigm within which broader management research operates (Whitley, 1984b). Thus the field can be viewed as soft, having attributes of engineering, crafts, or medicine; and the argument that disseminated knowledge should have a sympathy with the "managerial and broader societal context" (Tranfield and Starkey, 1998: 346) aligns with and exhibits a soft, applied paradigm. The conclusion is that management research must be linked to practice. Here praxis, whereby theoretical considerations inform practice and practice is integrated with theoretical truth, (Marcuse, 1964; Habermas and Shapiro, 1972) is arguably an appropriate concept for capturing this view. Being action linked to informed theory for practical change, a movement in this direction was, however, hampered by a positivist dialogue (Shrivastava, 1986).

A tension arises in that management science retains attributes of the natural sciences in its adherence to generalisable models in the majority of texts while at the same time acknowledging that management knowledge is, to a notable extent, fragmented, localised, and contextualised. It could be argued that the underpinning philosophical approach to management science is, therefore, wrong in its key assumptions and should be explored as a post-modern social science (Pettigrew, 2001).

4.3 Strategic management, a positivist ideology? An introduction to paradigms, context, ideology, and normative thinking

Although management science seems underpinned with a positivist paradigm, the need for management knowledge to reflect context is acknowledged. Contemporary strategic management theory, however, appears to assume a modernist universality that can appear to be dominated by rational (Starbuck, 2004), economic/macro (Stander and Pretorius, 2016), law-like, systematic, generalisable models (Freeman and McVea, 2001) and philosophically leans towards a logical positivist epistemology (Evered, 1980; Whitley, 1984a; Daft and Buenger, 1990; Bettis, 1991; Pettigrew, 2001) which aims towards a development of universal criteria driven by dominant logics (Prahalad and Bettis, 1986; Rasche, 2008). Arguably, driven by a view that economic theory is the correct, cleaner (Hirsch et al., 1987), and proper underpinning philosophical approach to theory development for the strategy field, however simplistic and unrealistic the abstract theories become (Jarzabkowski and Whittington, 2008).

This relatively uncritical philosophical position and leaning towards a single scientific approach can be explored further within the dominant paradigms (Rasche, 2008) and the contingent factors prevalent in the field though strategic management's development. Including its focus on universality and lack of attention to how context influences generalisable strategic management theory (Note: here the author is referring to the extent to which context influences generalisable theory rather than the use of contexts within theoretical models.)

The most prominent documented approach to strategy can be broadly referred to as the classical perspective (Whittington, 2001), a traditional, American, or western view of strategy which is formal, top-down, planning-oriented and analytical, a perspective that dominates the classroom (Greiner et al., 2003a; Jarzabkowski and Whittington, 2008). The classical perspective is conceived from a rational approach to the process, being both deliberate in actions and typically focused on profit maximisation. This includes the prescriptive approaches of the Design School, Planning School, and Positioning School (Mintzberg, 1978). These schools and perspectives tie in with traditional definitions of Strategy such as military theory describing "large scale, long term planning and development" (Random House Dictionary), Chandler's definition ". . . determination of the basic long-term goals and objectives of an enterprise, and the adoption of courses of action and the allocation of resources necessary for carrying out these goals" (1962: 13), and Porter's definition (1980) encompassing a broad and frequently generalised formula for how an organisation will compete, detailing goals and policies. Strategy is described as a deductive and deliberate process which has a causal relationship from strategy analysis and development down the chain into operational effectiveness, and should not be over-extended into contingent factors such as "employees and organizational arrangements" (Porter, 1997: 162).

The foundation for strategic management's dominant paradigm was established within a unique set of contingent factors influenced by the organisational challenges of World War 2, which required vast resource allocation across the United States. This was significant in underpinning the context for the development of strategy concepts such as experience curves (Hedley, 1976; Greiner et al., 2003b) and the work of Peter Drucker (1946), developing the rationale that conscious formal planning could exert control over market forces. The context of the post-war period was one of significant growth in the USA (Bracker, 1980), "Growth was easy" (Greiner et al., 2003b: 406). The boom period produced a period of market stability (Hill and Westbrook, 1997), reduced competition through high demand and the reduced number of European multinational competitors affected by the war (Greiner et al., 2003b). A very different environment to the one experienced by organisations in the 1990s (Bettis, 1991) and currently. This background as a setting for the development of strategic management concepts had a narrow, ethnocentric (Bettis, 1991) context, using large North American firms during economic periods of growth (Shrivastava, 1986). Theory was grounded within economic theory and developed through studies of organisations and their environments as they were constituted at that time (Bettis, 1991).

The underlying positivistic position of theory development during this distinct time period did not take into account the unconscious philosophical underpinnings and environmental context within which theory was developed. This setting resulted in a number of enduring common sense tools, for example, SWOT (Weihrich, 1982; Humphrey, 2005), which has been critiqued as being both ineffective as an analysis tool and questioned as to whether it even constitutes as a structured form of analysis (Hill and Westbrook, 1997: 50), or the Positioning School, which is contingent upon and critiqued (Mintzberg et al., 2001) as having a narrow context, focusing, in the main, on large traditional, established, and mature businesses operating in stable conditions.

Standardised, generalisable, and universal approaches

The positivist paradigm was further embraced by strategic management researchers in the early 1970s (Evered, 1980). Groups of consultancy practices also referred to as "strategy boutique(s)" (Ghemawat, 2002: 45), for example the Boston Consulting Group (BCG) and McKinsey & Company, grew during the period in response to demand within a growing stock market (Schoeffler et al., 1974).

These groups formulated and delivered strategic methodologies within organisations, responding to a need for more formal planning by businesses (Brandenburger et al., 1996). Specific strategic management approaches were developed and then championed by these strategy consultancies, achieving a normative status and becoming an "obsession" with businesses in America (Mintzberg et al., 2001: 97). Within a positivistic standpoint and a focus on logic, the strategy boutiques produced a range of standardised, generalisable, and universal approaches (Henderson, 1979). Generic tools emerged, such as BCG Growth–Share Matrix (Henderson, 1979), BCG Experience Curve (Henderson, 1979), Porter's five forces and Porter's generic strategies (Porter, 1980), Porter's value chain analysis (Porter, 1985), McKinsey Nine-Block Matric (Hax and Majluf, 1984), game theory (von Neumann et al., 1944). Within these models, aspects of uniqueness and pluralism where lost as the process of Strategic Management was delivered through clear, steps and models. These universal approaches were perceived to be effective in all contexts regardless of the nature of that context. For example; Sidney Schoeffler founder of the Profit for Impact of Market Strategies (PIMS) model stated "product characteristics don't matter" and "all business situations are essentially alike" (Schoeffler, 1972; cited in Mintzberg et al., 2001: 98).

Early analysis of the underpinning philosophical assumptions of theory used at this time; for example within PIMS (Schoeffler et al., 1974), BCG-BPM (Hedley, 1977), and the experience curve (Hedley, 1976), established that their theoretical approaches exist within or are founded upon the (positivist) empiricist philosophical stance (Mitroff and Mason, 1982a). The assumption that these strategic rules and tools can be applied in a generalised way to all organisations, implies that the rules are "full" of meaning prior to their usage (Rasche, 2008: 8 emphasis in original text). This relies on an idealised perception of the world which believes that it can be represented, articulated and expressed clearly (Leiss, 1975), effectively turning nature into a form of maths (Husserl, 1970). To illustrate this, Porter's industry analysis (1980) establishes a set of rules, which can be applied to any industry for analysis (specifically Porter's Five Forces [1980]). Within the model, a list of effective determinants are gone through in order to establish a useful outcome. These rules have no reference to the context in which the industry exists, for example, an alignment with "American East-Coast Business Ideals" (Harfield, 1997: 8) did not seem relevant or contextually appropriate to smaller businesses in New Zealand (Harfield, 1997). A second example is Porters' generic strategies (1985), which define the scope (broad and narrow) and competitive advantage (low cost or differentiated) of possible strategic positions, resulting in three generic strategies: cost leadership, focus, and differentiation. The rules to fit with and achieve these generic strategies are a given and are to be followed, regardless of context. A further example can be found within SWOT (Humphrey, 2005) which ignores organisational diversity and promotes generic solutions. Although this can be appealing to individuals tasked with making sense of diverse markets and developing strategies (Hill and Westbrook, 1997), the specific and unique insights and actions required by managers to realise and implement a strategic choice are not accounted for. So, although generic rules and tools appear to have meaning, they are effectively empty without undergoing some contextual and unique modification to adapt to a local context.

Strategy consultancy organisations thus influenced strategy development in championing specific generalisable techniques, thereby dictating and consolidating the prevalent form of strategy in the era. The 1960s boom in this type of consultancy dictated the approach to how strategy was done in the following period. With little modification of theory in regards to organisational characteristics or context and reinforcing the positivist, empiricist standpoint (Mitroff and Mason, 1982b).

Ideology within strategy

This drive towards a single philosophical position and control of the subject paradigm (Pfeffer, 1993) can be critiqued as a form of ideology (Mannheim, 1936), whereby control of ideas perpetuated "dominion" (Shrivastava, 1986: 364), enabling control of the field for the dominant groups. An ideology being defined here as idea systems that are part tradition and prejudice constructed within discourse by dominant groups and institutionally though codes of conduct, structures, resources, and power (ibid). Arguably, this has occurred in strategic management and supported the development of the current paradigm (Rasche, 2008). A paradigm being a set of assumptions, view, or a filter that, sometimes unconsciously, legitimate approaches and techniques (Ratcliffe, 1983) in order to make sense of a problem. Paradigms are directly linked to metaphysical assumptions (Mitroff and Mason, 1982a; Mingers, 2003) and underlying philosophical stances. A critique of an adherence to a particular paradigm is that it will restrict research and impact on the inherent methods and approaches utilised for research, thereby reducing the progress of a subject area (Daft and Buenger, 1990).

The approaches championed within the foundations of strategic management are underpinned by assumptions that rationality will garner better understanding (Starbuck, 2004), that internal complexities can be ignored within a rational classical perspective (Whittington, 2001), and that all business contexts are fundamentally alike (Schoeffler, 1972; Tranfield and Starkey, 1998; Boyne, 2002). Strategic management has been critiqued as being dominated by an ideology and normative models that assume a perfectly rational approach with knowledge that is complete, but this status was ". . . not factually validated" (Shrivastava, 1986: 367), the subject viewed as being too closely entangled in the ". . . rituals and paraphernalia of normal science" (Daft and Buenger, 1990: 82) and stuck within the straitjacket of normal science (Bettis, 1991). Strategists have been criticised in their loyalty to the simplification of complexity within social systems and an underpinning use of a positivist philosophy. This simplicity had resulted in generalisable "systematic, definable strategy procedures and structures that can be measured analysed and compared" (Daft and Buenger, 1990: 91), negating any contextual or social influences on a strategy-making process.

An example of applied simplicity within social systems is the assumption that a single approach is relevant to all contexts. An assumption which obscures the paradox inherent within strategic management of viewing the organisation and its environment as two separate entities. The positivistic underpinnings of strategic management would describe an analysis of an environment that is unambiguous and that that environment exists separately to the organisation. In actuality, the organisation invents the reality in the process of observation, as there is more than one perceived reality due to the complexity differential between the organisation and the environment; i.e. the complexity of the external environment is so vast as to require sense-making by the organisational actor. The social actors construct a reality from the perspective of the organisation; each organisation thus creates its own reality as to the nature of its environment and the value of, for example, resources to a customer within that reality. The environment is then a construction which cannot be evaluated with generalisable rules, as it is unique to the organisation and actors within that organisation (Berger and Luckmann, 1966; Rasche, 2008).

A second level of simplicity, formed within a positivistic philosophy, is the linear and separate approaches to the acts of strategy formulation and strategy implementation (Mintzberg, 1994). A formula that is unquestioned within the early forms of strategic management. These are described as two distinct acts assumed to be undertaken in a linear process separated in thought and action. This highlights a second paradox referred to by Rasche (2008: 7) as "double contingency" within strategy. The first element being the organisation reacting to, for example, competitor actions and vice versa; the decision action divide becomes blurred as decisions are co-dependent on competitor actions and vice versa. The decision-making process, in choosing between a number of options, potentialises all options, as all are potentially possible, but at the same time all options are not fully justifiable, as no option can be fully and absolutely justified. Only after a decision is made can a full justification be made, and this is an ongoing process. Applying a fixed model to a constantly varying set of circumstances that are self-reliant on the decision being made cannot be achieved within fixed rules that are valid in all organisations and contexts. Using a positivistic philosophy within strategic management goes against the nature of reality and exposes an inherent paradox (Rasche, 2008).

Mainstream strategy texts

If we accept the argument that management science and, more specifically, strategic management was founded and developed from a positivist paradigm (Evered, 1980; Whitley, 1984a; Daft and Buenger, 1990; Bettis, 1991; Freeman and McVea, 2001; Pettigrew, 2001; Starbuck, 2004; Rasche, 2008; Stander and Pretorius, 2016), the functional "strategy tools" (Jarzabkowski and Kaplan, 2015) that have emerged can be observed to be taught and utilised in a generalisable manner across all contexts and deemed applicable to all organisations (Greiner et al., 2003a; Jarzabkowski and Whittington, 2008). Academic research within strategy may have matured into utilising a range of methodological and epistemological approaches. However, within mainstream strategy texts, utilised within undergraduate, postgraduate, CPD, and executive education in business schools there remains an expression of strategic management processes and theory that articulates a generic approach to any organisation, regardless of context (Greiner et al., 2003a; Jarzabkowski and Whittington, 2008). For example, a seminal text advocates that strategy-making models are "relevant in most organisations" (Johnson, 2013: 19). Within this text, aspects of complexity or context are briefly explored, with no underpinning research, and there remains an adherence to a generic approach of analysis, choice, and implementation

The most recognisable strategy tool, SWOT (Humphrey, 2005) analysis, is an endemic and recognised tool utilised for the development of strategy in an identical manner regardless of any organisations contexts or specifics (Chermack and Kasshanna, 2007). Although receiving much critique for its effectiveness and lack of underpinning research (Hill and Westbrook, 1997; Chermack and Kasshanna, 2007; Helms and Nixon, 2010), SWOT (Humphrey, 2005) retains an "unmerited position in the thinking used in education, management development, consultancy and in the real world of managing businesses" (Hill and Westbrook, 1997: 52).

Strategy education and theory, while suggesting that generic strategy processes, tools, and decision-making might be influenced by context, is applied with minimal acknowledgement of differing contexts or complexity (Whitley, 1984b) and provides limited description of the nature or extent of that influence (Greiner et al., 2003a). There is acknowledgement that there are differences between contexts or organisational dimensions e.g. size, structure, environment, and goals (McKinley, 2010); and a critique of the use of generic generalisable approaches is that they potentially produce generic strategies across all contexts (Freeman and McVea, 2001), raising the need to incorporate varying contingent factors (Ackermann and Eden, 2011). However, there remains an adherence to a set of generalised approaches that is at odds with that acknowledgment, and there is little guidance on exactly what is different in certain organisations and why, with existing studies highlighting the need for more detailed work (Shepherd and Rudd, 2014).

Origins of the design school: a counterpoint

The argument that the classical approach is entirely positivistic does ignore some of the core attributes of the earlier design school. A key aspect of these was that, although utilising a standardised process, the resultant strategies produced are unique and specific to an individual situation and not subject to any generalisations (Christensen et al., 1982). Early Design School Harvard academics during the 1960s remained fixed to the case-by-case and unique strategy development approach (Brandenburger et al., 1996). They did not attempt to develop generalisable strategies across any contingency or context. In this aspect they did not entirely embrace a positivist philosophical standpoint, to some extent leaning towards an idealist or interpretivist stance (Mitroff and Mason, 1982b). Further to this, a key study found a range of strategic management approaches were found to be distinctly placed within an interpretative philosophical stance (Mitroff and Mason, 1982a), for example SWOT (Humphrey, 2005) (herein referred to as WOTS-UP [Channon, 1983]) and Case Method (Andrews, 1971). Recent work found that the use of strategy tools can vary within contexts and the perception of tools should not be separate from their use (Jarzabkowski and Kaplan, 2015). This effectively critiques the standpoint that strategic management is purely positivist in its philosophical leanings. However, the assumption that strategy can be undertaken by a deliberate conscious thought process, derived from the "certain" and absolute knowledge of the Rational Economic Man (Hollis, 1975). Supported by the use of reason, logic, and an accurate all-encompassing analysis of the internal and external environment, using a standard set of analysis tools, has an undoubted positivistic leaning.

Cognition, construction, and practice

We have argued that theory within mainstream strategy is arguably dominated by rational (Starbuck, 2004), economic/macro (Stander and Pretorius, 2016), law-like, systematic, generalisable models (Freeman and McVea, 2001) and philosophically tends towards a logical positivist epistemology (Evered, 1980; Whitley, 1984a; Daft and Buenger, 1990; Bettis, 1991; Pettigrew, 2001) in the development of universally applicable theory.

Although researchers within the strategy field acknowledge that there are differences between contexts (Spender, 1989; Bettis, 1991; Whittington, 2001), there remains an adherence to high-level generalisable theory that does not describe the nature or extent of that influence (Jarzabkowski et al., 2016). The dominating literature within the strategic management field leaning towards a positivistic philosophical standpoint, where strategic management theory is universally applied to any context (Evered, 1980; Whitley, 1984a; Daft and Buenger, 1990; Bettis, 1991; Freeman and McVea, 2001; Pettigrew, 2001; Starbuck, 2004; Rasche, 2008; Stander and Pretorius, 2016).

However, ontologically, organisations are subjectivist social constructions (Downing, 2005) that differ in makeup and form and are driven by the perceived reality of individual agents If we accept that agents function within a Weberian-bounded rationality (Simon, 1957; Dimaggio and Powell, 1983) (i.e. the limited information available to actors upon which to interpret and make decisions), then within this individual practice, we will encounter agentic actors undertaking strategy in ways which are unique to the actors perception of reality and the imperfect information that is available to them.

Cognitive school and social constructionism

Taking the concept further, we can view strategy as a subjective interpretation of the actors' reality. Mintzberg et al.'s (2001) view of strategy is shown in Figure 4.2.

The individuals construction of organisational phenomena or schema (Hogarth, 1987) is not a reproduction of the environment but is created or enacted (Smircich and Stubbart, 1985) in the minds of actors. This social constructionist (Berger and Luckmann, 1966; Burr, 1996) view argues that there is no single truth within an analysis of the environment. The idea of an objective environment which is concrete is replaced by actors forming, understanding, and creating the environment. Strategic analysis and formation is placed within the mind of the actor or manager as a purely cognitive process, which can be formed and understood through cognitive mapping (Axelrod, 1976) and schemas (Mintzberg et al., 2001).

Mintzberg refers to the cognitive school in linking social constructionism to strategy. Exploring not "requisites for thinking" (2001: 150) but the thinking itself. He divides this school into two areas of thinking: the first leans towards positivistic, the second subjective. Within the first, the strategist observes and produces a picture of the world, which

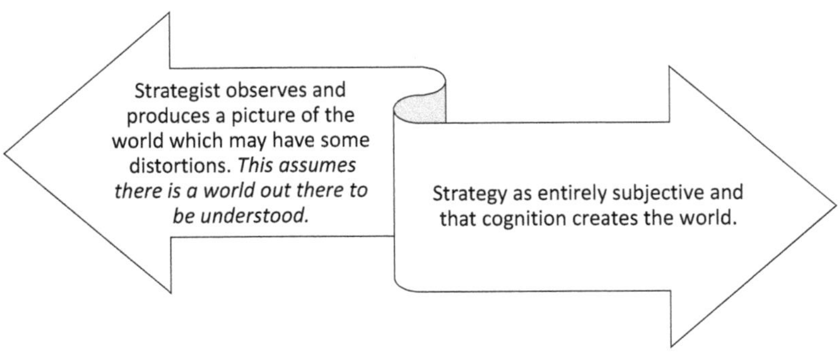

Figure 4.2 Mintzberg's positivism versus the cognitive school

may have some distortions; this assumes there is a world out there to be understood. The second, which aligns more closely with this work is the view that strategy is entirely subjective and that cognition creates the world.

Case study 4a Social construction, strategic decisions for a University satellite centre

This case study considers the operation and subsequent closure of a satellite centre of a large UK university. The university in question had, over the prior 20 years, expanded by subsuming local colleges and higher education establishments into a single post-1992 University. This led the organisation to have multiple faculties and physical locations spread quite widely across the region, one of which was some 30 miles from the central operation. This particular faculty had previously been a college of further and higher education and had resided in the community for 100 years as a teacher training college. The faculty was well established within the local community and a key player in various council, government, industrial, and education partnerships. The region itself was experiencing significant growth, with a number of high-profile national developments underway.

Given this background, staff and stakeholders within the organisation and wider community felt secure and well linked with the local economy. The main organisational actors felt that the faculty was a necessary and required part of the community, one which local stakeholders, businesses, government, and the broader community felt was essential and needed for further growth. If asked does the region need a university faculty, the answer from local stakeholders or organisational actors would be a resounding "yes."

However, the University itself was exploring strategic growth from a different perspective. Rather than considering the regional needs, it considered the organisation's needs and asked a very different question: "does the University require satellite centres"? This question was not asked in particular relation to a specific satellite centre but more broadly about satellite centres and university campuses away from the central business. With a question framed in this manner, and the bulk of business and transactions taking place at the University Centre, the answer to this question was quite straightforward: "no, the University does not require satellite centres". This resulted in the satellite centre being closed down and redeveloped by separate organisations.

In many ways the actors within the satellite centre and stakeholders in the local community had constructed a reality that the university campus was essential and required. The area was in growth; the community needed a University, and there had always been a university in the area. Although always seen as a risk that the faculty may close, the perceived overwhelming need for the faculty outweighed this perception. Taking a social constructionist viewpoint, this overwhelming perception of need was a construction, an enacted reality by both organisational actors and the wider community. This enacted environment clouded any perception of the strategic environment and impacted on the strategic decision-making of the local actors. The central team themselves would arguably also experience a constructed reality – but this was significantly dissimilar and resulted in a different strategic decision.

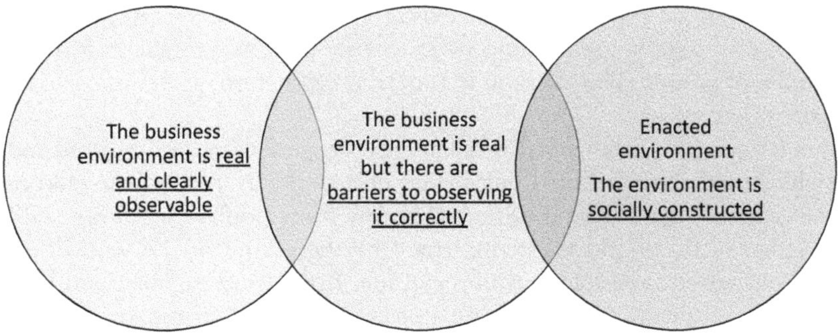

Figure 4.3 The real observable environment to the enacted environment

Smircich and Stubbart (1985) clarify this further, exploring three positions: the objective environment, the perceived environment, and the enacted environment (see Figure 4.3).

Firstly, they referred to strategy as exploring an objective environment. Here an organisation exists within an environment that is independent and external; analysis within this perspective assumes there are information and facts waiting to be found – then actors can create a strategy to meet them. They next explore the distortions and inaccuracies that can be undertaken by actors within a perceived environment. Here the environment remains a real, separate and external object but actors/managers are trapped by bounded rationality (Simon, 1957) and imperfect interpretations. Within this perspective, the aim for the strategist is to recognise the imperfect nature of their analysis and minimise the gap between reality and interpretation. This brings us to their final insight, one which aligns social constructionism with strategy, the enacted environment. The insight being that a separate objective environment does not exist; instead actors and organisations label patterns of activity. What they see as their environment is entirely generated by human action and efforts to make sense of these actions.

Social constructionism describes knowledge aspects of our world as not real in themselves but a construction that only exist through social agreement within society (Burr, 1996). One interpretation of this (weak social constructionism) is that although there is one literal universe, the interpretation and categorisation of that single world creates different realities. A second interpretation (strong social constructionism) is that the realities created by agents produce fundamentally different realities, not just an interpretation of that reality.

Weak social constructionism is based on brute facts, fundamental facts that do not rely on any other facts or information, something that cannot be explained by something else. A brute fact is separate from an institutional fact created by a social convention which do rely on other facts. Strong social constructionism states that the whole of reality and all knowledge is a social construct and that no facts just exist they are dependent on a societal or constructive explanation. Social constructionism does not explain natural phenomena, only phenomena dependent on human social practices.

Four aspects are necessary within social constructionism:

1 It is critical of the idea that observations of phenomena can reveal their true nature and that it is possible to have an unbiased and objective study. This is counter to

positivism within more traditional science arenas and takes a view that what exists is based on our perception of what exists. This also includes categorisation such as music genres, there being nothing within music itself that results in it being divided into different genres. This division is a social construction, and music can be divided in many other ways.

2 How we understand the world is reliant and dependent on our culture and history. Knowledge elements within a culture are effectively artefacts of the culture and are no closer to any truth than another worldview from a different culture and history.
3 Knowledge of the world is not informed by the nature of the world but through interaction between people within social life. Knowledge is fabricated through this interaction and practices, truth being a product of social process of engagement and interaction.
4 Social action and socially constructive knowledge are interdependent. A social construction of the world support enables different kinds of actions from the actors within that world. The example given within Burr (1996) is that of alcoholism being seen as a crime moving to it being seen as addiction and illness. (Burr, 1996)

Strategic management arguably retains a hidden ideology and value assumptions, constantly underpinning theory development. It is one that continues to be restrained by the positivistic stance and research norms of economic analysis (Rasche, 2008). If strategic management research needs to matter (Porter and McKibbin, 1988; Hambrick, 1994) and aspire to practical use in the field, this position limits the range and types of research undertaken (Daft and Buenger, 1990).

OK. Now what?

If we accept that a positivistic approach to strategic management is limiting, then what do we do when making strategy? Figure 4.4 offers one possible approach.

Firstly we can recognise that strategy formation is a cognitive process and that there is no single truth or objective social reality – it is interpreted by the managers or actors within the organisation. If environments are constructed, assessment of internal or external environments is merely a product of actors' beliefs. Analysis then starts by exploring the beliefs of organisational actors, exploring not "requisites for thinking" (Mintzberg et al., 2001: 150) but the thinking itself. Strategies then can be seen as perspectives or

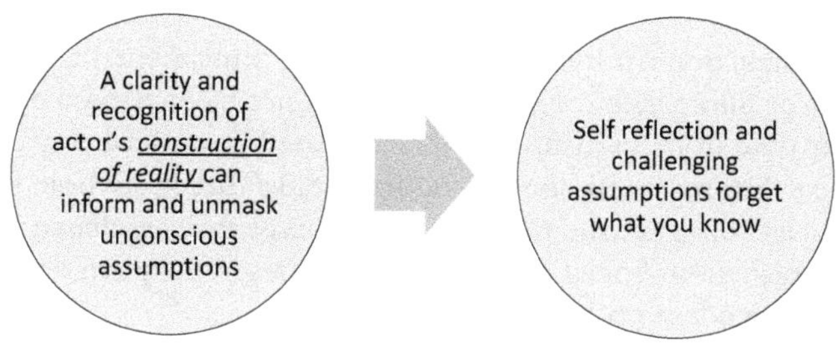

Figure 4.4 Unmasking unconscious assumptions

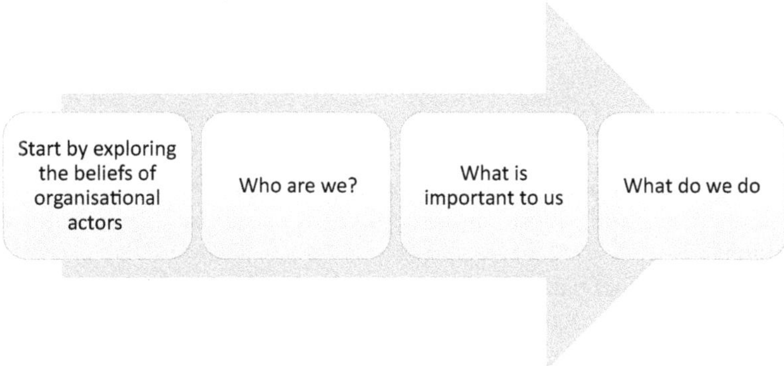

Figure 4.5 Exploring beliefs

interpretations, and if it is interpreted, we need to understand this to "make strategy" in an informed manner.

By exploring, clarifying, and recognising our colleagues' construction of reality we can inform and unmask unconscious assumptions. Smircich and Stubbart (1985) argue in Figure 4.5 that this can be achieved by self-reflection and challenging these assumptions, exploring the context.

The answers to these questions can help initiate strategy formulation and offer strategists a framework to guide their thinking.

4.4 Chapter summary

At this point it is important to not let the ideological or philosophical pendulums swing too far in any particular direction. The insights and methodological approach of more classical methods alongside emergent and intuitive thinking can yield a more thorough/broader level of analysis. The author's aim in this chapter is not to dismiss classical theory but to critically accept its limitations and utilise its benefits. As we will see in the strategy workshop guide, after the participants have explored issues at the forefront of their thinking, we then recommend the use of classical models to ensure participants have mentally explored a wider range of potential strategic issues: internal, external, macro, industry, and competitive.

An analogy might be to go grocery shopping with a list of required items (i.e. the strategic issues at the forefront of our thinking), but by going down every isle in the supermarket (Classical models – thereby exploring multiple areas of strategic interest), we jog memories and use the process to explore other needed items.

We also accept that this cannot be undertaken in a truly scientific or positivistic manner, as the institutional and constructed realities of the participants and organisational field will affect what and how actors think and perceive reality. Overall then there are philosophical limitations to how actors and groups think, and it would be a mistake to believe that this can be rationally overcome through logic. But clarifying, exploring, and establishing what groups focus on, what they perceive as value, their boundaries to thinking and fundamentally accepting a socially constructed reality, do assist strategists in establishing insights and opening up hidden aspects and attributes of group strategy sessions.

Post-chapter questions

- When starting a strategic process, what should I do first?
- Do I need to think about my preconceptions before I undertake strategic thinking?
- What is more influential, the way you do strategy or the prerequisites for thinking?
- Is what I observe an accurate interpretation of reality? Is my reality real?
- What would the strategic position look like from a different viewpoint?

References

Ackermann, F. & Eden, C. (2011). Strategic management of stakeholders: Theory and practice. *Long Range Planning*, 44, 179–196.

Andrews, K. R. (1971). *The Concept of Corporate Strategy*. United States: Homewood, IL: Dow Jones-Irwin.

Ansoff, H. I. (1965). *Corporate Strategy*. New York: McGraw-Hill.

Axelrod, R. M. (1976). *Structure of Decision: The Cognitive Maps of Political Elites*. Princeton: Princeton University Press.

Becher, T. & Trowler, P. (2001). *Academic Tribes and Territories: Intellectual Enquiry and the Culture of Disciplines*. New York: McGraw-Hill Education.

Berger, P. L. & Luckmann, T. (1966). *The Social Construction of Reality; A Treatise in the Sociology of Knowledge*. Garden City, NY: Doubleday.

Bettis, R. A. (1991). Strategic management and the straightjacket: An editorial essay. *Organization Science*, 2, 315–319.

Biglan, A. (1973). The characteristics of subject matter in different academic areas. *Journal of Applied Psychology*, 57, 195–203.

Boyne, G. A. (2002). Public and private management: What's the difference? *Journal of Management Studies*, 39, 97–122.

Bracker, J. (1980). The historical development of the strategic management concept. *Academy of Management Review*, 5, 219–224.

Brandenburger, A. M., Porter, M. E. P. & Siggelkow, N. (1996). *Competition and Strategy: The Emergence of a Field. McArthur Symposium*. Boston, MA: Harvard Business School.

Burr, V. (1996). *An Introduction to Social Constructionism*. London: Routledge.

Burrell, G. & Morgan, G. (1985). *Sociological Paradigms and Organisational Analysis: Elements of the Sociology of Corporate Life*. Aldershot: Gower.

Chandler, A. (1962). *Strategy and Structure: Chapters in the History of Industrial Enterprise*. New York: Doubleday.

Channon, D. F. (1983). Management policy and strategy, g. A. Steiner and j. B. Miner, cllier macmillan, london, 1982. No. Of pages: 357. Price: £14.25 ($15.95). *Strategic Management Journal*, 4, 294–295.

Chermack, T. J. & Kasshanna, B. K. (2007). The use and misuse of swot analysis and implications for HRD professionals. *Human Resource Development International*, 10, 383–399.

Christensen, C. R., Andrews, K. R., Bower, J. L., Hamermesh, G. & Porter, M. E. (1982). *Business Policy: Text and Cases*. Homewood, IL: Irwin.

Daft, R. & Buenger, V. (1990). Hitching a ride on a fast train to nowhere – the past and future of strategic management research. In J. W. Fredrickson (Ed.), *Perspectives on Strategic Management*. New York: Harper Business.

Dannenbring, D. G. & Starr, M. K. (1981). *Management Science: An Introduction*. Auckland: McGraw-Hill.

Dimaggio, P. J. & Powell, W. W. (1983). The iron cage revisited – institutional isomorphism and collective rationality in organizational fields. *American Sociological Review*, 48, 147–160.

Downing, S. (2005). The social construction of entrepreneurship: Narrative and dramatic processes in the coproduction of organizations and identities. *Entrepreneurship Theory and Practice*, 29, 185–204.

Drucker, P. (1946). *Concept of the Corporation*. New York: John Day.

Evered, R. (1980). Strategic management – a new view of business policy and planning – Schendel, D. E., Hofer, C. W. *Administrative Science Quarterly*, 25, 536–543.

Freeman, R. E. & Mcvea, J. (2001). *A Stakeholder Approach to Strategic Management*. Darden Business School Working Paper.

Ghemawat, P. (2002). Competition and business strategy in historical perspective. *Business History Review*, 76, 37–74.

Greiner, L. E., Bhambri, A. & Cummings, T. G. (2003a). Searching for a strategy to teach strategy. *Academy of Management Learning & Education*, 2, 402–420.

Greiner, L. E., Bhambri, A. & Cummings, T. G. (2003b). Searching for a strategy to teach strategy. *Academy of Management Learning & Education*, 2, 402–420.

Habermas, J. R. & Shapiro, J. J. (1972). *Knowledge and Human Interests*. London: Heinemann Educational.

Hambrick, D. C. (1994). What if the academy actually mattered. *Academy of Management Review*, 19, 11–16.

Harfield, T. (1997). *Competitive Strategies and Structures and Three New Zealand Industries Through a Postmodern Lens*. Canterbury: University of Canterbury.

Hax, A. C. & Majluf, N. S. (1984). *Strategic Management: An Integrative Perspective*. Englewood Cliffs, London: Prentice-Hall.

Hedley, B. (1976). Fundamental approach to strategy-development. *Long Range Planning*, 9, 2–11.

Hedley, B. (1977). Strategy and the "business portfolio". *Long Range Planning*, 10, 9–15.

Helms, M. M. & Nixon, J. (2010). Exploring swot analysis – where are we now? A review of academic research from the last decade. *Journal of Strategy and Management*, 3, 215–251.

Henderson, B. D. (1979). *Henderson on Corporate Strategy*. Cambridge, MA: Abt Books.

Henderson, B. D. (1979). *Henderson on Corporate Strategy*. New York; Scarborough, ON: New American Library.

Hill, T. & Westbrook, R. (1997). Swot analysis: It's time for a product recall. *Long Range Planning*, 30, 46–52.

Hirsch, P., Michaels, S. & Friedman, R. (1987). Dirty hands" versus "clean models. *Theory and Society*, 16, 317–336.

Hodgkinson, G. P. & Starkey, K. (2011). Not simply returning to the same answer over and over again: Reframing relevance. *British Journal of Management*, 22, 355–369.

Hogarth, R. M. (1987). *Judgement and Choice: The Psychology of Decision*. Chichester, Wiley.

Hollis, M. (1975). *Rational Economic Man*. Cambridge: Cambridge University Press.

Humphrey, A. (2005). *Sri Alumni Association Newsletter*. CA: SRI Association. Retrieved December 1, 2016 from www.sri.com/sites/default/files/brochures/dec-05.pdf.

Husserl E. (1970). *The Crisis of European Sciences and Transcendental Phenomenology: An Introduction to Phenomenological Philosophy*. Evanston, I: North Western University Press.

Jarzabkowski, P. & Kaplan, S. (2015). Strategy tools-in-use: A framework for understanding "technologies of rationality" in practice. *Strategic Management Journal*, 36, 537–558.

Jarzabkowski, P., Kaplan, S., Seidl, D. & Whittington, R. (2016). On the risk of studying practices in isolation: Linking what, who, and how in strategy research. *Strategic Organization*, 14, 248–259.

Jarzabkowski, P. & Whittington, R. (2008). A strategy-as-practice approach to strategy research and education. *Journal of Management Inquiry*, 17, 282–286.

Johnson, G. (2013). *Exploring Strategy*. Harlow, UK: Pearson.

Khurana, R. (2010). *From Higher Aims to Hired Hands: The Social Transformation of American Business Schools and the Unfulfilled Promise of Management as a Profession*. Princeton: Princeton University Press.
Koontz, H. & O'Donnell, C. (1976). *Management: A Systems and Contingency Analysis of Managerial Functions*. Canterbury: McGraw-Hill.
Leiss, W. (1975). Ideology and science. *Social Studies of Science*, 5, 193–201.
Mannheim, K. (1936). *Ideology and Utopia: An Introduction to the Sociology of Knowledge*, London: Routledge and Kegan Paul.
Marcuse, H. (1964). *One Dimensional Man: Studies in the Ideology of Advanced Industrial Society*. London: Routledge and Kegan Paul.
Mckinley, W. (2010). Organizational theory development: Displacement of ends? *Organization Studies*, 31, 47–68.
Mingers, J. (2003). A classification of the philosophical assumptions of management science methods. *Journal of the Operational Research Society*, 54, 559–570.
Mingers, J. (2006). Philosophical foundations: Critical realism. In *Realising Systems Thinking: Knowledge and Action in Management Science*. Boston, MA: Springer US.
Mintzberg, H. (1978). Patterns in strategy formation. *Management Science*, 24, 934–948.
Mintzberg, H. (1994). The fall and rise of strategic-planning. *Harvard Business Review*, 72, 107–114.
Mintzberg, H., Lampel, J. & Ahlstrand, B. W. (2001). *Strategy Safari: The Complete Guide Through the Wilds of Strategic Management*. Harlow: Financial Times Prentice Hall.
Mitroff, I. I. & Mason, R. O. (1982a). Business policy and metaphysics: Some philosophical considerations. *Academy of Management Review*, 7, 361–371.
Mitroff, I. I. & Mason, R. O. (1982b). Business policy and metaphysics: Some philosophical considerations. *The Academy of Management Review*, 7, 361.
Pettigrew, A. M. (2001). Management research after modernism. *British Journal of Management*, 12, S61–S70.
Pfeffer, J. (1993). Barriers to the advance of organizational science – paradigm development as a dependent variable. *Academy of Management Review*, 18, 599–620.
Porter, L. W. & Mckibbin, L. E. (1988). *Management Education and Development: Drift or Thrust into the 21st Century?* New York: McGraw-Hill Book Company.
Porter, M. E. (1980). *Competitive Strategy: Techniques for Analyzing Industries and Competitors*. New York: Free Press.
Porter, M. E. (1985). *Competitive Advantage: Creating and Sustaining Superior Performance*. New York: Free Press.
Porter, M. E. (1997). Response to letters to the editor. *Harvard Business Review*, March–April, 162–163.
Prahalad, C. K. & Bettis, R. A. (1986). The dominant logic: A new linkage between diversity and performance. *Strategic Management Journal*, 7, 485–501.
Rasche, A. (2008). *The Paradoxical Foundation of Strategic Management*. Berlin: Sage Publications Ltd.
Ratcliffe, J. W. (1983). Notions of validity in qualitative research methodology. *Knowledge-Creation Diffusion Utilization*, 5, 147–167.
Schoeffler, S. (1972). *Profit Impact on Marketing Strategy*. Marketing research institute internal memorandum.
Schoeffler, S., Buzzell, R. D. & Heany, D. F. (1974). Impact of strategic planning on profit performance. *Harvard Business Review*, 52, 137–145.
Shepherd, N. G. & Rudd, J. M. (2014). The influence of context on the strategic decision-making process: A review of the literature. *International Journal of Management Reviews*, 16, 340–364.
Shrivastava, P. (1986). Is strategic management ideological? *Journal of Management*, 12, 363–377.
Simon, H. A. (1957). *Models of Man. Social and Rational. Mathematical Essays on Rational Human Behavior in a Social Setting*. New York: Wiley.
Smircich, L. & Stubbart, C. (1985). Strategic management in an enacted world. *The Academy of Management Review*, 10, 724–736.
Spender, J.-C. (1989). Industry recipes: The nature and sources of managerial judgment. *Oxford, UK: Basic Blackwell. (1994)," Knowing, Managing and Learning," Management Learning*, 25, 387–412.

Standen, K. & Pretorius, M. (2016). The next step in the strategy – as – practice evolution: A comparative typology matrix. *Acta Commercii*, 16, e1–e11.

Starbuck, W. H. (2004). Vita contemplativa: Why I stopped trying to understand the real world. *Organization Studies*, 25, 1233–1254.

Suppe, F. (1977). *The Structure of Scientific Theories*. Urbana: University of Illinois Press.

Terry, G. R. (1977). *Principles of Management*. Homewood, IL: Irwin.

Tranfield, D. & Starkey, K. (1998). The nature, social organization and promotion of management research: Towards policy. *British Journal of Management*, 9, 341–353.

Von Neumann, J., Morgenstern, O., Kuhn, H. W. & Rubinstein, A. (1944). *Theory of Games and Economic Behavior (60th Anniversary Commemorative Edition)*. Princeton: Princeton University Press.

Weihrich, H. (1982). The tows matrix – a tool for situational analysis. *Long Range Planning*, 15, 54–66.

Whitley, R. (1984a). The fragmented state of management studies – reasons and consequences. *Journal of Management Studies*, 21, 331–348.

Whitley, R. (1984b). The scientific status of management research as a practically-oriented social-science. *Journal of Management Studies*, 21, 369–390.

Whittington, R. (2001). *What Is Strategy – and Does It Matter?* London: Thompson Learning.

Chapter 5

Influences on strategy development

Neo-institutional theory & organisational fields

Learning Outcomes

After reading this chapter you should be able to:

- identify neo-institutional and systemic forces
- assess institutional and systemic influences on strategic decision making
- explain and distinguish legitimacy drivers in your organisation
- establish current thinking in organisational fields and neo-insitutional theory
- to underpin and add theoretical reasoning as to why organisations may be undertaking strategy in similar ways within similar arenas, or differently across different organisational arenas

Pre-chapter questions

- Is strategic thinking influenced by my institutional setting and legitimacy drivers?
- What are the bounds of my organisational field?
- Does my organisation look similar to others in my field? If so why?

Key terms

- Neo-Institutionalism (NIT) – society is formed within institutionalised cultures, legitimising options formed groups, via the rules, norms, and beliefs of this institutional environment drive conformity and isomorphism
- Organisational field – a critical unit of analysis within NIT and can be defined as "a community of organizations that partakes of a common meaning system and whose participants interact more frequently and fatefully with one another than with actors outside the field" (Scott, 2014: 56)
- Isomorphism – becoming more similar or homogenous

DOI: 10.4324/9780429344305-9

5.1 Introduction

When we consider the widely accepted positivistic and generalisable forms of strategic analysis, it is easy to make the assumption that organisations with very different outlooks will undertake strategy (analysis/thinking) in a generic manner; but is that the case? Where it has been explored within the literature, authors propose very different strategic outlooks for different types of organisations and contexts (Whittington, 2001). Strategy theory can be considered as having two extremes. At one extreme it expounds general, almost universal frameworks (Daft and Buenger, 1990; Bettis, 1991; Rasche, 2008), for example the pervasive analysis, choice, and implementation framework utilised in the majority of strategy textbooks (Johnson et al., 2017). The more traditional positivistic/economics-based literature within strategy tends to overlook context (Greiner et al., 2003; Jarzabkowski and Whittington, 2008) and organisation type, arguing that a rational, economics-driven approach to analysis will be appropriate for every situation. At the other extreme, there are the more recent ideas emerging from the strategy as practice (SAP) perspective (Whittington, 1996; Johnson et al., 2007; Jarzabkowski and Whittington, 2008; Jarzabkowski and Spee, 2009; Whittington, 2010; Johnson, 2013), which tend to focus on micro-level behaviours in individual organisations. An approach that has been criticised for being overly fixed on the micro level (Vaara and Whittington, 2012; Elbasha and Wright, 2017) and does not raise the level up into a more generalisable and parsimonious group context or organisational field level.

The tension between the rational positivistic and the sociological subjectivist position raises questions as to what extent theories in strategy are universal. Further to this, to what extent are there differences in approaches to practiced strategy, across differing types of organisations and contexts (Smets et al., 2017)? Recent work within the SAP (Strategy as Practice) field explores the work of strategy within organisations at a micro-level of analysis (Vaara and Whittington, 2012; Elbasha and Wright, 2017) but fails to raise these insights to a higher, more generalisable level, negating studies on broader, more generalisable phenomena. Whittington (2001) explored this through his systemic or relativistic perspective wherein strategy-making depends on social context (Whitley, 1990; Shrivastava, 1986). The societal context of class, professions, countries, and cultures drive how actors and managers think operationally and strategically. This makes the act of strategy highly sociologically sensitive, where criteria other than profit or technical efficiency take priority. The main drivers for strategy become the cultural rules and the expected and operating routines within the culture. The history of the organisation and its "path dependency" becomes critical in understanding where the organisation has underpinned its social context. Neo-institutionalism, legitimacy, and isomorphism (Dimaggio and Powell, 1983) become critical concepts in exploring what is valued and prioritised within an organisational field.

This chapter focuses on this concept: neo-institutionalism and its critical unit of analysis, the organisational field. The chapter explores and evaluates institutional theory in order to apply its insights to the exploration of how strategy cognition may vary across differing organisational fields.

5.2 Neo-institutional theory

Prior to the rise of institutional theory in the late 1970s, organisations were assumed to function within Weberian-bounded rationality (Dimaggio and Powell, 1983). This describes the limited information available to actors upon which to interpret and make decisions as opposed to rationality, whereby all information is available and information is perfect (Fligstein, 1991). Within this assumption, agentic actors respond to circumstances, and managers analyse contexts and initiate actions to drive efficiency in order to compete and deliver technical and rational outcomes (Greenwood, 2008). Organisational structures are adapted to tasks (structural-contingency theory; Burns and Stalker, 1994); critical resources are managed logically (resource-dependence theory; Pfeffer and Salancik, 1978); and the organisation is modified, within a bounded rationality (Simon, 1957). Modifications are undertaken to satisfy prevailing market and performance environments (behavioural theory; Cyert and March, 1992), thus ensuring an appropriate fit to the business environment with senior managers fundamentally acting rationally (Greenwood, 2008).

From this rational standpoint, a typographical or taxonomic approach to explore organisations could be successfully undertaken through individual organisational dimensions (Daft, 2004; McKinley, 2010), analysing organisations through their functional and structural attributes in relation to their approach to strategic management.

The significant change that addressed gaps in these forms of organisational/environment models and defined NIT was that organisations are significantly influenced by their institutional level context. A context referred to as "the rules, norms, and ideologies of the wider society" (Meyer and Rowan, 1983: 84) in the structure of organisations or their inherent "normative and cognitive belief systems" (Scott, 1983a: 163). This institutional-level context also differentiated between old and new theories of intuitionalism in the scope of analysis. Within old institutionalism there was a focus on the community level, whereas NIT could include a wider range of actors: local, national, and international. NIT offers an approach to understanding organisational behaviours that in some cases moves away from any rational economic justification (Suddaby, 2013).

Although definitions of NIT can vary with some ambiguity (Wiseman and Baker, 2006), the original concept relies on the notion that society is formed within institutionalised cultures, which arrange and disperse models of organisations and individuals. Attention is drawn to forces external to the organisation, outside its organisational boundary, delimiting the infinite range of organisational choices and possibilities determined by internal economic divers. These forces are reduced to a limited and narrow range of legitimising options formed by the group's organisational field, via the rules, norms, and beliefs of their institutional environment (Dimaggio and Powell, 1983). This then drives a shared reality across the institution which culturally constrains actors within the institutions, as opposed to the individual agency of actors forming society independently (Wiseman and Baker, 2006).

Case study 4b An engineering school

This case study concerns a new form of school in the United Kingdom, partly sponsored by industry with a curriculum that is focused on that particular industry. These are referred to as university technical colleges and teach children from years 14 to 18. The college is similar to any normal school in the UK with a wide-ranging curriculum, but each college is unique with a focus on a particular vocational field. The views of employer stakeholders are directly used to influence curriculum and to ensure the best outcomes for the students.

All UK schools are inspected by a common inspection body. This body garners exceptional institutional legitimacy and weight; schools are judged by students and parents via a nationally understood rating and ranking. It is generally considered that this quality assurance framework is robust, thorough, and worthwhile but the senior leadership at the university technical college encountered a problem. The specific aims, insights, and principles of the university technical college clashed with some of the guidance, principles, and approach of the inspection body leaving the senior management team with a dilemma. Do they compromise what they believe is the right and correct set of actions and curriculum for the students, given the particular nature of their industrial field? Doing this would result in a lower ranking with the inspection body and reduce the organisation's legitimacy within the education or school's organisational field. Or, do they accept the inspection bodies approach and align more closely with national approaches to curriculum, thereby moving away from the unique purpose of the university technical college and potentially diminishing the unique positioning and advantages of being aligned with industry?

During a strategy-making session, the author observed that the senior leadership team chose to go with the former and breakaway from the standard institutional field legitimacy drivers. By doing this, they felt they had followed the correct the vision and mission of the organisation and the impact of not being aligned to national legitimacy drivers within education was a price worth paying.

Institutions in this context are not organisations but emerge as the building blocks of society including aspects of social, political, and organisational life, shaping behaviour perception, and choices (Berger and Luckmann, 1966). Institutions embody the scripts or packages of culture, both formal and informal, that defines a particular sector and with which they make sense of the world (Wiseman and Baker, 2006). For example, a local council would be referred to as an organisation; local councils as a whole could be viewed as an institution; similarly a single hospital would be an organisation, and the health care sector would be the institution. Social structures can acquire meaning, value, and significance (Selznick, 1949) outside of the purpose for which they are created. The structures, tasks, and functional elements develop new unintended meaning that can have no relation to their main function or organisational aims. For example, an organisation can develop an institutional attribute (for example, a charity) that emphasises its own survival, which was not an organisational aim initially (Selznick, 1949). The theory proposes that it is not economic drivers but social pressures on organisational fields, through rationalized myths (Meyer and Rowan, 1977), that become agreed standards or models of behavior; that, then, drives a pressure to conform to the institutional norms.

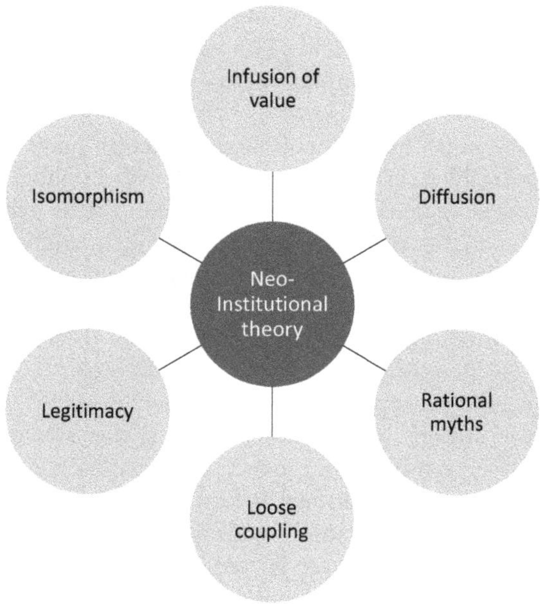

Figure 5.1 Six concepts defined within the neo-institutional theory

Organisations within a field become more similar, not because it is a more effective and efficient means of forming the organisation, but because the societal drivers of uncertainty and constraint generate isomorphic pressures, which then result in a level of homogeneity (Dimaggio and Powell, 1983). Underpinning these drivers is the need for organisations to survive, not primarily through technical efficiency but through legitimacy (Scott, 1983b). By seeming rational through the lens of the institution, the individual organisation can gain resources, reduce accountability, and be socially accepted within the context of that institution (Greenwood, 2008). Organisations seek legitimacy within groups of similar organisations by duplicating aspects of these organisations (Suddaby, 2013). The process, structures, and agency of the social actors is thereby constrained by social situations or the organisational context. Social actors move away from the initial drive to produce performance improvements and construct an environment that shapes and changes their ability to impact upon that environment (Dimaggio and Powell, 1983). All organisations in a field can seem to be one organisation or body with one central controlling mind, despite the autonomy or competitive relationship they have. This is illustrated in Figure 5.2.

Thus, groups of organisations in the same field tend towards similarity and tend to be similar. Institutionalisation is then both a process and an outcome (DiMaggio, 1988; cited in Wooten and Hoffman, 2016: 1). The impact of institutional-level forces can also be perceived to vary within differing contexts. The arena most significantly sensitive to these forces is the not-for-profit and governmental sectors, referred to as institutionalised organisations (Meyer and Rowan, 1977). However, in later works, the drivers of technical efficiency within less institutionalised settings were also fully encompassed into the model, with the technical or efficiency aspects being viewed as institutional constructs (Greenwood, 2008). We can see three drivers of conformity and isomorphism inFigure 5.3: the regulative, cognitive, and normative (Dimaggio and Powell, 1983).

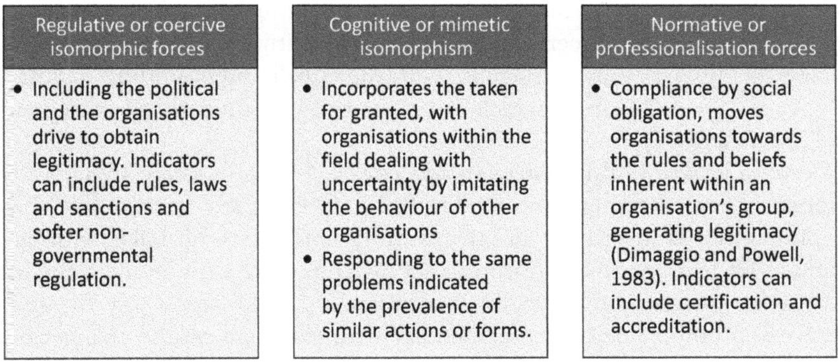

Figure 5.2 Drivers of conformity and isomorphism

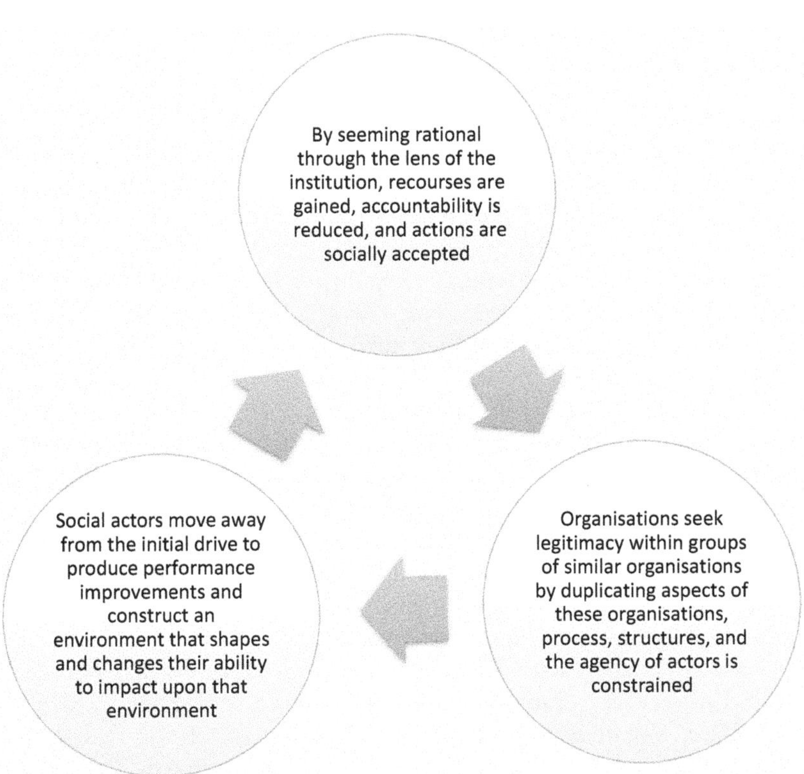

Figure 5.3 Rationality, legitimacy, and homogeneity

One critique of any visible homogeneous alignment may be that the compliance is merely a surface-level isomorphism (Zucker, 1987: 672). Here the pressure of technical efficiency and performance may contradict and outweigh any institutional isomorphic affects. The organisation may then decouple (Greenwood, 2008: 4) their actual modus operandi from the visible and institutionally acceptable version of the organisation. How far an organisation can decouple from their contexts or markets will in itself be delimited by the institutional- or field-level isomorphic drivers as the market itself is institutionally defined (Carroll, 1986). A further critique is the lack of attention paid to agency, which is a key concern of critics of neo-institutional theory, envisaging NIT as replacing the "hyper- muscular agent" with the equally preposterous "cultural dope" (Suddaby et al., 2013: 11) from which the notion of the institutional entrepreneur has emerged (Mutch, 2007).

The focus on isomorphism (Dimaggio and Powell, 1983) is incorrectly viewed as neo-institutional theory's defining concept (Hoffman, 1999). Early iterations of the theory can be summarised as describing an organisation's similarity with fields, with an excessive emphasis on legitimacy as a reason to act. Within these early models, the influence of agents or institutional entrepreneurs was minimised. NIT was overly focused on the "persistence and homogeneity of phenomena" with less focus on the changes over time or the strength or power of an institutional field (Dacin et al., 2002). However, this was then refined to help explain change in organisations and the agency of actors (in particular more marginal actors) (Suddaby, 2013) and adapted to include the influence and relationship actors have with the institutional environment.

Organisational fields

Organisational fields are the critical unit of analysis within NIT and can be defined as "a community of organisations that partakes of a common meaning system and whose participants interact more frequently and fatefully with one another than with actors outside the field" (Scott, 2014: 56). Following NIT, organisations share common logics and conceptual frameworks made up of normative and cultural-cognitive elements that guide organisational field member's behaviour, referred to as institutional logics (Friedland and Alford, 1991; Thornton et al., 2012; Scott, 2014). This enables organisations to both develop a common understanding of their field and offer varying or competing logics within subsets of the field.

As stated by Dimaggio "to understand the institutionalization of organizational *forms*, we must first understand the institutionalisation and structuring of organisational *fields*" (1991: 267 emphasis in original). The demarcation of an organisational field cannot be determined by any self-evident logic and can be defined by empirical investigation as they only exist in that they are themselves institutionally defined (Dimaggio and Powell, 1983). Figure 5.4 gives an example of organisational fields, the health field and local council field; note the author has deliberately overlapped the two fields as actors and organisations may be influenced by multiple and intricate institutions.

The notion of field approaches to understanding an object's behaviour was founded within early 19th-century studies of electromagnetism and fluid mechanics (Scott, 2014). The object was studied not just in isolation but in relation to external effects. An early proponent of field-based studies, Lewin (1946 reprinted 2009) proposed the notion of understanding organisations and the people and conditions encountered, as one

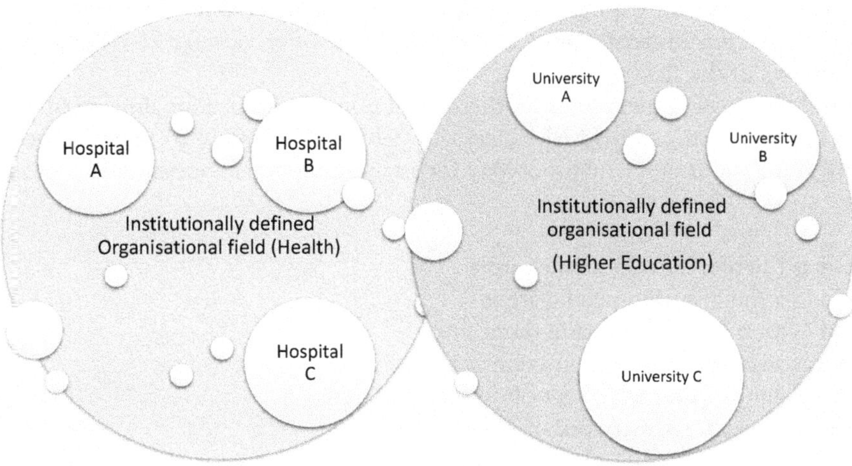

Figure 5.4 Example of organisational fields

interrelated constellation. His conception of field theory included all aspects of an individual's relationships, at a point in time, including the influence of behaviours. The aim was to observe and support the facilitation of change within organisations. This focus to a level of analysis that goes beyond individuals and individual organisations can be grouped into the following three categories: organisational set models, organisational population models and inter-organisational field models, (Scott and Meyer, 1991). The approaches are somewhat limited in perspective, either missing broad or supporting relationships, restricting the examination of relationships to a closed field or avoiding hierarchical influencers. As summaries of organisations in their environments, they retain a perception that organisations are primarily production systems with relationships and environment formed around technical flows, tasks information, and the sources necessary for delivering tasks (Scott and Meyer, 1991). Organisations are then viewed as forming structures that are shaped by technologies, technical aspects, and operational relationships (Perrow, 1967). Although a valid perspective, it is limited and does not recognise that organisations are not just a technical means of production existing in an economic vacuum. Organisations also have social and cultural aspects and influences within their institutional setting, which are more broadly referred to as relational and symbolic dimensions (Machado-da-Silva et al., 2006a) and the "regulative, normative and cultural-cognitive elements" (Scott, 2008) of their institutional setting.

Six perspectives on organisational fields

The shortcomings of the set model approaches are addressed within organisational field models, today firmly established by neo-institutionalism (NIT), now understood to be critical in linking the organisation and societal levels of analysis (DiMaggio, 1986). Following NIT, organisations also share common logics and conceptual frameworks made up of normative and cultural-cognitive elements that guide organizational field member's behaviour, referred to as institutional logics (Friedland and Alford, 1991; Thornton et al., 2012; Scott, 2014). An exploration of institutional logics enables organisations to both develop a common understanding of their field and offer varying or competing logics within subsets of the field.

The following section explores six theoretical post neo-institutionalism perspectives of analysis on organisational fields (Machado-da-Silva et al., 2006b) to review more recent thinking and to underpin a methodology for establishing organisational fields for strategic insight.

- field as the totality of relevant actors
- field as a functionally specific arena
- field as a centre of dialog and discussion
- field as an arena of power and conflict
- field as an institutional sphere of disputed interests
- field as a structured network of relationships

Field as the totality of relevant actors

A key component for this perspective on fields are the actors within the institutional sphere. Actors here are both individuals and the groups, social constructions, and forms that make up an influencing element. The types of actors include,

- individuals
- associations of individuals
- populations of individuals
- organisations
- associations of organisations
- populations of organisations

(Scott, 2014)

Organisational fields are defined to be a "recognised area of institutional life" Dimaggio and Powell (1983: 148) that is identifiable and encompasses the entirety of pertinent actors. This list can be expanded or reframed to include:

- similar groups of suppliers to an industry,
- producers of related services and products,
- consumers of related products or resources
- regulatory or controlling agencies

(Dimaggio and Powell, 1983: 148)

These collections of actors align with organisations as collections, with societal sectors working within the same area and offering comparable services, products, or functions (Scott and Meyer, 1991). The organisational field is a meaningful construct for the actors, with the perception of field boundaries being the defining characteristic which affect the practice and function of organisations in the field and the representation of that field. Actors then will "select models for emulation, where they focus information-gathering energy, which organisations they compare themselves with, and where they

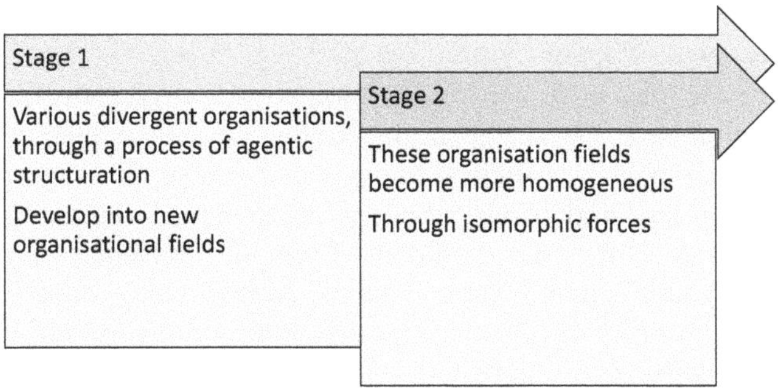

Figure 5.5 **Structuration of organisational fields**

recruit personnel" (Dimaggio, 1991: 267). The process of forming and defining an organisational field emerges through the process of structuration (Giddens, 1979). Structuration recognising the action of agents within structures and the forming of social practices and structures by these agents (Giddens, 1983). Broadly the process can be broken down into two stages, as shown in Figure 5.5.

Note: a key debate Giddens versus Archer:

It should be noted that the Giddens' (1984) structuration model is central to a key debate within sociocultural theory between Anthony Giddens and Margaret Archer. In brief, structuration is formulated on a process ontology, and the notion of the inseparability of the individual and society. Here practice and action are viewed as the critical aspects of sociocultural activity. These two key assumptions are rejected by Archer (1995) who recognises both: the individual as a separate entity and at the same time irreductable from the group and the group and its inherent interactions with the individual (King, 2010).

Field as a functionally specific arena

The field as a functionally specific arena is built on the concept of an industry but significantly also includes critical influences and organisations that impact on performance within a societal sector (Scott and Meyer, 1991), such as a common regulatory system. Included within this are those organisations that can influence performance of core domain organisations, and the concept broadens out from any localism into related and non-related organisations within the same functional arena, "similar and dissimilar interdependent organizations operating in a functionally specific arena together with their exchange partners, funding sources and regulators" (Scott, 2004: 9). Although not entirely encompassing the broader views of DiMaggio and Powell (1983) in capturing the totality of relevant actors, it has advantages in analysis by defining a more limited unit of analysis under the institutional lens. However, demarcating a 'line in the sand' for what is or is not, a relevant actor, such as the actors functional similarity or the scope of the fields the organisation may participate in, add methodological difficulties to this approach (Machado-da-Silva et al., 2006b).

The perspective includes both vertical and non-local linkages, organisations within a domain, and that domain's relevant economic elements, such as related products, functions, and services. Notably, as a societal view, it includes suppliers, customers, owners, regulatory agents, funders, and competitors, which then includes national and international relationships and actors. Also included within are interrelations, through product substitutability and shared demand, expanding the societal sector beyond that of a single industry. These communities of organisations may follow the same meaning systems and similar symbolic processes (Scott and Meyer, 1991).

In classifying sectors, Scott and Meyer (1991) explore three areas: use of product or function, substitutability, and diffusion of classes.

- Within product or function, the level of classification specification or the definition of boundaries is highlighted. As selection of classification variables limits or overtly influences research outcomes, which can lead to a restricted interpretation of any analysis conducted. The usefulness in defining sectors at differing hierarchical levels is addressed and viewed as useful, as is inherent within the SIC (Standard Industrial Classification) system. However, within a broader view of neo-institutionalism, this approach seems self-limiting and an arbitrary classification (Machado-da-Silva et al., 2006b).
- Substitutability is explored as domains stretching across products or services whilst fulfilling similar needs and may be entirely unrelated. The extent of the level of relationship is argued to be mitigated by the level of consensus of actors within a field.
- Lastly, diffusion, the notion that an organisation functions in one domain is limited, as many organisations diversify across multiple fields and are not limited to one single easily definable field.

The difficulties experienced by researchers in delineating an organisational field does give a functional level analysis within a domain some appeal (and has been revisited by some researchers (Scott, 1983b; Scott and Meyer, 1991). However, an industry-level classification with arbitrary delineation of a field is limited as it does not analyse its totality (Machado-da-Silva et al., 2006b).

Field as a centre of dialogue and discussion

The field as a centre of dialogue and discussion describes organisational fields as formed around a central issue or event surrounding or involving organisations in a shared thematic interest. Here organisations and agents in differing fields or domains undertake or become involved in the same central theme or debate. The field is then formed around common channels of dialogue around the important issues, reflecting the interests and goals of a group of organisations (Hoffman, 1999).

Rather than be bounded by SIC code classifications, Hoffman (1999) takes a view that it is the issues that the organisations encounter which define the field, establishing links that may not have been operationally present. The membership of the field is established through social interaction and may be time limited as the issue grows and depletes. The field is organised through the exchanges of information occurring within the debate, disputes and negotiation undertaken to achieve goals. Within more stable fields where an established legitimate logic prevails, there may be more limited and less intense debate over themes rendering the approach more difficult for analysis purposes (Zietsma and Winn, 2005). Institutionally, this perspective highlights institutions that are within a population of organisations within the field and the institutions that are at the heart of the shared issue, resulting in multiple institutional influences on organisational fields.

Hoffman (1999) used legal activity within a study of environmentalism to establish relevant actors within the organisational field under study. He recognised that the study deselected organisations that did not pursue litigious solutions but justified this as the level of meaning to the actors was demonstrated though the pursuit of legal action. To establish issues he utilised trade journals which institutionally framed the issues under study, reflecting the interests of the organisational field.

Using three pillars (Scott, 2014) of regulative (or legal), normative (or social) and cognitive (or cultural) Hoffman (1999) explores organisational field responses to issue-based, institutional drivers. From a regulatory perspective, the organisation will explore their interests within a given situation. In response to a normative institution, the organisation will need to make sense of their role and the expectations of their organisation within the situation (March, 1981). The cognitive-institutional drivers encompass the often unconscious (Zucker, 1983), taken-for-granted organisational paradigm that guides the actor's perception of the nature of reality and the form this then takes, thereby guiding both perception and reaction to the issue or event.

Field as an arena of power and conflict

Underpinned by Bourdieu, the field as an arena of power and conflict proposes that relationships between actors within social fields is based on power, power being a transient form of capital that is only ever field-specific. Bourdieu describes power as "economic capital (in its different kinds), cultural capital, and social capital as well as symbolic capital, commonly called prestige, reputation, fame, etc., which is the form assumed by these different kinds of capital when they are perceived and recognized as legitimate." (Bourdieu, 1991: 230). Fields become networks and systems of relations, in which social positions dictate power, and manoeuvres are undertaken by actors for resources (Everett, 2002). Fields are considered as a game with actors continually driving to accumulate capital, having stakes, investment, and trump cards (Bourdieu and Wacquant, 1992). The field will contain both the dominated and the dominant, who in action alter the mechanisms and outcomes of power within the field.

The fields are broadly separated into two: firstly, the field of "restricted production" (Bourdieu and Richardson, 1985) or "cultural production" (Bourdieu and Johnson, 1992). Within this type of field, organisations produce cultural goods for cultural goods producers, and the generation of cultural capital is the driver, cultural capital that is judged to have value by the field. Artists or musicians would be examples of actors within these fields; the field thus has significant influence on the organisation or actor. Secondly, there is more generalised production, (widespread/large-scale production) (Bourdieu, 1985). Here the field's production of cultural goods is for non-producers of cultural goods or the general public; the field then has less influence on the organisation and the organisational field. The two forms do not exist in isolation. For example, the generalised field can influence the restricted fields resulting in the restricted field lacking any independence and becoming "heteronomous" (Everett, 2002: 61). Measures of success may change within a heteronomous field and could move from a cultural capital-driven field to include economic capital, income or profit, and measures that may not normally exist in the field as the original measures based around field-specific legitimacy would have prevailed. In fact, within a truly autonomous restricted organisational field, a complete inversion of economic principles may dominate, with "charisma, aesthetic intention, and an interest in disinterestedness" (Everett, 2002: 61) driving the field. Actors within a field may not be best placed to recognise any heteronomous drift as their focus on legitimacy within a field, or the internal taboos of discussing this aspect of the field, may mask the fields changing nature (Everett, 2002).

Of note within cultural capital are further various forms of capital: embodied cultural capital (external wealth reengineering into the person, e.g. language skills), objectified cultural capital (ownership of cultural goods), institutionalised capital (that recognised ability as perceived by the institution to which the actor belongs). Others include linguistic capital (languages), social capital (relationships and networks), political capital, and most significantly for Bourdieu, symbolic capital, wherein the symbolic forms of capital become legitimate, arguably becoming the most valuable and giving the power to consecrate and legitimate capital forms (Bourdieu, 1989). Effectively a change in power can generate a change in the field. Actors can influence the field as they will attempt to generate value within the form of capital they recognise and discredit capital in disagreement with it. The apprach enables an understanding of the social actors (their objectives, ideologies, ideas, and behaviour) within a field, in particular those with power as defined by the field is essential to understanding and delimiting the field boundaries and undertanding the consituents of the field. The social actor's interests are located within a field of power which determines the actor's values and beliefs, implied within their actions and discourse (Leao, 2001 cited in Machado-da-Silva et al., 2006b).

Field as an institutional sphere of disputed interests

The key differentiator within the field as an institutional sphere of disputed interests is the less determinist and more active role of influential, incumbent actors influencing and changing the rules by which the field is structured (Machado-da-Silva et al., 2006b). Power and relationships, as supported by Bourdieu (Everett, 2002) underpins the perspective. By influencing the structural rules of the field, the powerful actors can change and improve their position within the field, thereby supporting their own interests (Fligstein, 2001). Fligstein (1991) argues that institutionalists have overstated the role of norms in the formation of organisational fields by undervaluing the comparative power of actors in field formation. In his view, organisations are influenced by three institutional spheres: their current strategies and structure, the other organisations within their organisational field, and the state within which rules, actions, and power relationships form. This is shown in Figure 5.6.

If rules determine action through constraint, the ability to develop and set rules will establish cognitive structures for actors within the field. This can then lead to powerful organisations, deliberately setting and establishing the nature of the organisational field itself (Machado-da-Silva et al., 2006b). An organisation's strategy will be a reflection of conflicts in pursuit of goals established within the constrained, institutionally

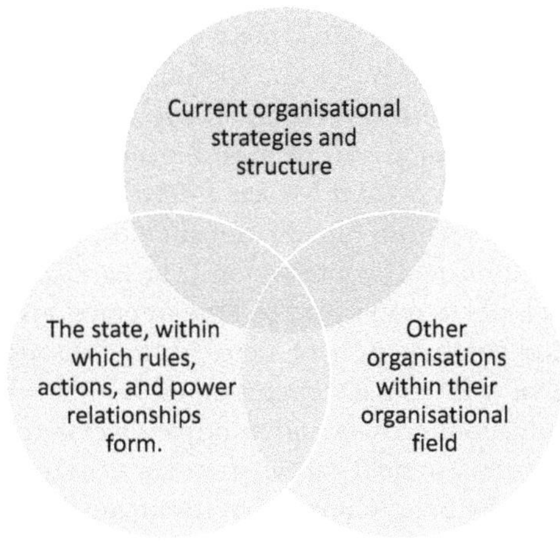

Figure 5 6 Field as an institutional sphere of disputed interests

driven, organisational field. So a change in a powerful organisational strategy will result in changes to the organisational field, and the weaker organisations will, through social or dependency links (including legitimacy, competition, and co-operation), be required to adapt to a field's changed position. The organisational field either legitimises actions or forms a reason for change in the organisation. The view argues that once key organisations have changed strategies and have seen supposedly superior results, then the actors with in field will change to match. The strategies may not be successful, but the institutional perception of these changes results in a perceived view that legitimises the change (Fligstein, 1991).

Stability of organisational fields is in direct relationship to stability within organisations; the more change in the field, the more change will be apparent in the organization, and vice versa (Fligstein, 1991). The level of stability or crisis in the field is viewed as a key element in field transformation and on the nature of member actions and strategies undertaken, crisis being frequently due to relationships breaking down or the invasion of other fields (Fligstein, 2001).

The role of skilled social actors in institution-building is emphasised, actors confronting one another during social interactions or "games". A process viewed as being critical in the formation and reproduction of organisational fields particularly when under crisis. "Skilled strategic actors provide identities and cultural frames to motivate others" (Fligstein, 2001: 4) through social skills, generating collective action and inducing cooperation and, therefore, approaching institutionalism from a more sociological perspective

In determining the scope of an organisational field, the point of view of the actors is sufficient in defining its nature, although it may be empirically difficult to specify which organisations exist in the field at any one point. The definition of the extent and form of the field will also be enforced by a powerful actor or the state; these organisations can then direct the actions of the field (Fligstein, 1991).

Fields as a structured network of relationships

The final perspective focuses on the social network being the sustaining force for an organisational field (Machado-da-Silva et al., 2006b). In referring back to the original interpretation of neo-institutionalism, actors not only engage in exchange relationships but also undertake social, structural, and relationship interactions, which act to delimit their actions (Dimaggio, 1991; Scott and Meyer, 1991). The approach explores the linkages across organisational types within organisational fields, introducing topological space as a metaphorical way of exploring the interaction (Machado-da-Silva et al., 2006b). Key research highlights the lack of attention paid to "the interactions of multiple, overlapping networks or the regulated reproduction of network ties through time" (Powell et al., 2005: 1134). Within the view there is a recognition of the emergent development of networks structures with multi-connectivity and multiple diverse connections giving central actors cumulative advantage in the field and, in a similar vein to the previous model, they can then set the agenda for the field. Cumulative advantage is achieved by new organisations joining the field having a preferential bias for attachment (generating links) with actors that have more or different links or ties. Powel et al. (2005) used citations within academic literature as an illustration of the process. Research on citation networks within academic papers showed the majority of articles having few citations with a select few having a very large number, the highly cited becoming more highly cited as high citation figures generate perceived credibility and are utilised more by emerging writers. Although an interesting finding, the writers caution that this approach may not be valid in all environments (Powell et al., 2005).

Institutional logics

The extent of the field determination through the field as a functionally specific arena perspective can be, to some extent, driven by "institutional logics" (Friedland and Alford, 1991: 248). The range and breadth of the institutional logics that drive a shared concept and behaviour will vary considerably in their form and in their "vertical depth" or the level of penetration (Krasner, 1988). At the meso-level, an organisation will be confronted with many and often contradicting logics (Friedland and Alford, 1991). This also ladders up to the institutional level and the effective choices an organisation makes and to which institutional-level logic it aligns.

Institutional logics can be critiqued as being conceived as exogenous to actors (Ibid). Goffman addresses this with a framework or "schemata of interpretation"(1974: 21) which can be seen as an active and impactful struggle into meaning (Lounsbury et al., 2003). Here the actors interpret events enabling them to actively find, understand, and effectively elicit meaning from events. Establishing their meaning and subsequent framing contributes to the construction of the actor's conception of reality (see chapter 4). This then supports the identification of issues and problems highlighting an approach for the organisation in its implementation or response (McAdam et al., 1996; Zald, 1996). Collectively held principles and interpretations of issues can become a "social heuristic" (Beamish and Biggart, 2012) or "rule of thumb", which enables a justifiable foundation for decisions based on a shared understanding of issues within the network, collective, or organisational field. This has been shown to lead to simplified decision-making, as there is a common set of decisions or approach, but it results in inhibited and conservative approaches (Ibid). Also included are disruptive and disorganised behaviours, as these actions or activities will take on a form that has a familiarity to the field, as the repertoire of actions is "surprisingly limited" (Tilly, 1977: 5–14). "In setting strategy and structure, firms may choose action from a repertoire of possible options. But the range of that repertoire is bound by the rules, norms, and beliefs of the organizational field" (Hoffman, 2001: 148), and although senor staff may feel they were developing autonomously, they are in fact following institutionally defined trends.

5.3 Chapter summary

Figure 5.7 offers a summary of the overall process of legitimacy and isomorphism.

The fundamentals of NIT detail a range of concepts that can be utilised to examine institutions (i.e. groups of organisations that become more homogenous through drivers of isomorphism [Hawley, 1968]), enabling analysis at a higher level than an individual organisation or that organisation's industry. The theory proposes that it is not economic drivers but social pressures on organisational fields (Machado-da-Silva et al., 2006b; Scott, 2014) through rationalised myths (Meyer and Rowan, 1977) that become agreed standards or models of behavior; this then drives a pressure to conform to the institutional norms. According to NIT actors seek legitimacy within groups of similar organisations by duplicating aspects of these organisations (Suddaby, 2013). Their institutions embodying the scripts or packages of culture, both formal and informal, defines a particular sector and with which, they make sense of the world (Wiseman and Baker, 2006). This results in organisations within an organisational field becoming more similar through a process of institutional isomorphism (Hawley, 1968).

So what can be made of this? If your organisation is significantly influenced by institutional legitimacy factors, is this a bad thing? If it enables the organisation to gain funds and approvals for activities then this surely could be good. That may be the case, but attempting to unpick drivers and activities that are undertaken for legitimacy versus activities and actions that may positively impact on the aims and objectives of the organisation may be worthwhile. The case study of the school inspection rankings is interesting in that the leaders of the organisation made a choice between what they feel is best for the individual participant of the school versus the institutional legitimacy drivers of certain levels of accreditation.

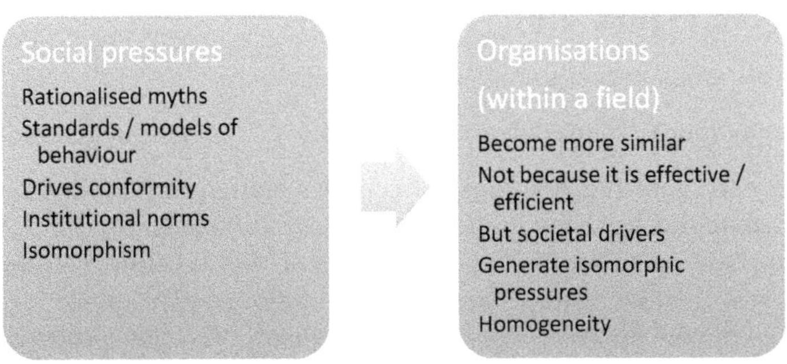

Figure 5.7 The overall process of legitimacy and isomorphism

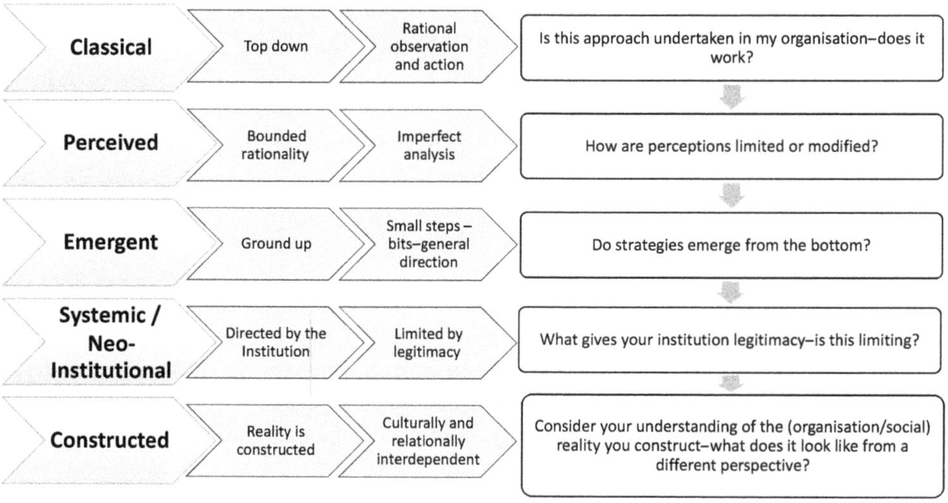

Figure 5.8 Self-assessment questions to explore influencing factors

The critical insight is understanding that activities and strategic goals may be heavily influenced by institutional legitimacy, and in accepting this, strategic choices can then be made in a more informed and enlightened manner. The institutionalist would argue that this cannot be done, as members of any institution can not necessarily see the institutional drivers in which they are immersed; a strategist would view institutional legitimacy as a resource or something to be considered, evaluated and used, or mitigated against. The truth is probably somewhere in between. A strategist can make every effort to understand institutional legitimacy, but it would be reasonable to assume that this can never be done completely or objectively. In considering your own organisation within the public sector, step back and consider what institutional legitimacy drivers influence your organisation and whether these are critical to what the organisation is trying to achieve.

Self-assessment questions to explore influencing factors (see Figure 5.8)

- Does your organisation follow a classical approach?
  - Is this approach limited/does this work?
- Are your (or your organisations) perceptions limited or bounded in any form, do the strategists have any limitations on their knowledge?
- Do you have an unwritten understanding of the direction you are going in which is in itself evident, or does it sometimes need explaining?
- What gives you or your organisation legitimacy? Do you prioritise this over what you believe would be the correct strategic action?

- Do you look like other organisations in your field, and why?
- If you considered your organisation or your understanding of your organisational environment from an entirely different perspective, what would it look like? Would you have the same priorities?

References

Archer, M. S. (1995). *Realist Social Theory: The Morphogenetic Approach*. Cambridge: Cambridge University Press.

Beamish, T. D. & Biggart, N. W. (2012). The role of social heuristics in project-centred production networks: Insights from the commercial construction industry. *Engineering Project Organization Journal*, 2, 57–70.

Berger, P. L. & Luckmann, T. (1966). *The Social Construction of Reality; A Treatise in the Sociology of Knowledge*. Garden City, NY: Doubleday.

Bettis, R. A. (1991). Strategic management and the straightjacket: An editorial essay. *Organization Science*, 2 315–319.

Bourdieu, P. (1989). Social space and symbolic power. *Sociological Theory*, 7, 14–25.

Bourdieu, P. & Richardson, J. G. (1986). *Handbook of Theory and Research for the Sociology of Education*. New York: Greenwood Press.

Bourdieu, P. (1991). *Language and Symbolic Power*. Cambridge: Oxford Polity Press, B. Blackwell.

Bourdieu, P. & Johnson, R. (1992). *Field of Cultural Production: Essays on Art and Literature*, Polity Press.

Bourdieu, P. & Wacquant, L. J. D. (1992). *An Invitation to Reflexive Sociology*. Chicago: University of Chicago Press.

Burns, T. & Stalker, G. M. (1994). *The Management of Innovation*. Oxford: Oxford University Press.

Carroll, V. P. (1986). Implications of salesforce productivity heterogeneity and demotivation: A navy recruiter case study. *Management Science: Journal of the Institute for Operations Research and the Management Sciences*, 32, 1371–1388.

Cyert, R. M. & March, J. G. (1992). *A Behavioral Theory of the Firm*. Cambridge, MA: Blackwell.

Dacin, M. T., Goodstein, J. & Scott, W. R. (2002). Institutional theory and institutional change: Introduction to the special research forum. *Academy of Management Journal*, 45, 45–56.

Daft, R. L. (2004). *Organization Theory and Design*. Ohio: South-Western College Publishing.

Daft, R. L. & Buenger, V. (1990). Hitching a ride on a fast train to nowhere – the past and future of strategic management research. In J. W. Fredrickson (Ed.), *Perspectives on Strategic Management*. New York: Harper Business.

Dimaggio, P.J. (1986). Structural analysis of organizational fields: A blockmodel approach. *Research in Organizational Behavior: An Annual Series of Analytical Essays and Critical Reviews*, 8, 335–370.

Dimaggio, P. J. (1988). Interest and agency in institutional theory. *Institutional Patterns and Organizations: Culture and Environment*, 1, 3–22.

Dimaggio, P. J. (1991). Constructing an organizational field as a professional project: Us art museums, 1920–1940. In Paul DiMaggio & Walter W. Powell (Eds.), *The New Institutionalism in Organizational Analysis*. London: University of Chicago Press.

Dimaggio, P. J. & Powell, W. W. (1983). The iron cage revisited – institutional isomorphism and collective rationality in organizational fields. *American Sociological Review*, 48, 147–160.

Elbasha, T. & Wright, A. (2017). Reconciling structure and agency in strategy -as-practice research: Towards a strong- structuration theory approach. *M@n@gement*, 20, 107–128.

Everett, J. (2002). Organizational research and the praxeology of pierre bourdieu. *Organizational Research Methods*, 5, 56–80.

Fligstein, N. (1991). The structural transformation of American industry. In Paul DiMaggio & Walter W. Powell (Eds.), *The New Institutionalism in Organizational Analysis*. London: University of Chicago Press.
Fligstein, N. (2001). Social skill and the theory of fields. *Sociological Theory*, 105–125.
Friedland, R. & Alford, R. R. (1991). *Bringing Society Back in: Symbols, Practices and Institutional Contradictions*. Chicago: The University of Chicago Press.
Giddens, A. (1979). *Central Problems in Social Theory: Action, Structure and Contradiction in Social Analysis*. London: Macmillan.
Giddens, A. (1983). Comments on the theory of structuration. *Journal for the Theory of Social Behaviour*, 13, 75–80.
Giddens, A. (1984). *The Constitution of Society: Outline of the Theory of Structuration*. Cambridge: Polity Press.
Goffman, E. (1974). *Frame Analysis: An Essay on the Organization of Experience*. Cambridge, MA: Harvard University Press.
Greenwood, R. (2008). *The Sage Handbook of Organizational Institutionalism*. London: Sage Publications.
Greiner, L. E., Bhambri, A. & Cummings, T. G. (2003). Searching for a strategy to teach strategy. *Academy of Management Learning & Education*, 2, 402–420.
Hawley, A. (1968). *Human Ecology*. New York: Macmillan.
Hoffman, A. J. (1999). Institutional evolution and change: Environmentalism and the U.S. Chemical industry. *The Academy of Management Journal*, 42, 351–371.
Hoffman, A. J. (2001). *From Heresy to Dogma: An Institutional History of Corporate Environmentalism*. Stanford: Stanford University Press.
Jarzabkowski, P. & Spee, A. P. 2009. Strategy-as-practice: A review and future directions for the field. *International Journal of Management Reviews*, 11, 69–95.
Jarzabkowski, P. & Whittington, R. (2008). A strategy-as-practice approach to strategy research and education. *Journal of Management Inquiry*, 17, 282–286.
Johnson, G. (2013). *Exploring Strategy*. Harlow, UK: Pearson.
Johnson, G., Whittington, R., Melin, L. & Langley, A. (2007). *Strategy as Practice Research Directions and Resources*, [Place of publication not identified]. Cambridge: Cambridge University Press.
Johnson, G., Whittington, R., Scholes, K., Angwin, D. & Regnér, P. (2017). *Exploring Strategy*, Harlow (England), Paris: Pearson.
King, A. (2010). The odd couple: Margaret archer, anthony giddens and british social theory. *The British Journal of Sociology*, 61, 253–260.
Krasner, S. D. (1988). Sovereignty: An institutional perspective. *Comparative Political Studies*, 21, 66–94.
Lewin, K. (1946). *Resolving Social Conflicts: And Field Theory in Social Science*. Washington, DC: American Psychological Association.
Lounsbury, M., Ventresca, M. & Hirsch, P. M. (2003). Social movements, field frames and industry emergence: A cultural – political perspective on us recycling. *Socio-Economic Review*, 1, 71–104.
Machado-Da-Silva, C. L., Guarido Filho, E. R. & Rossoni, L. (2006a). Organizational fields and the structuration perspective: Analytical possibilities. *BAR – Brazilian Administration Review*, 3, 32.
Machado-Da-Silva, C. L., Guarido Filho, E. R. & Rossoni, L. (2006b). Organizational fields and the structuration perspective: Analytical possibilities. *BAR – Brazilian Administration Review*, 3, 32–56.
March, J. G. (1981). Decisions in organizations and theories of choice. In: van de Ven, A. H. & Joyce, W. F. (eds.) *Perspectives on Organizational Design and Behavior*. New York: Wiley.
Mcadam, D., Mccarthy, J. D. & Zald, M. N. (1996). Introduction: Opportunities mobilizing structures and framing processes In Mcadam, D., Mccarthy, J. D. & Zald, M. N. (Eds.), *Comparative Perspectives on Social Movements: Political Opportunities, Mobilizing Structures, and Cultural Framings*. Cambridge: Cambridge University Press.
Mckinley, W. (2010). Organizational theory development: Displacement of ends? *Organization Studies*, 31, 47–68.
Meyer, J. W. & Rowan, B. (1977). Institutionalized organizations – formal-structure as myth and ceremony. *American Journal of Sociology*, 83, 340–363.

Meyer, J. W. & Rowan, B. (1983). The structure of educational organizations. *Organizational Environments: Ritual and Rationality*. Beverly Hills: Sage.

Mutch, A. (2007). Reflexivity and the institutional entrepreneur: A historical exploration. *Organization Studies*, 28, 1123–1140.

Perrow, C. (1967). A framework for the comparative analysis of organizations. *American Sociological Review*, 32, 194–208.

Pfeffer, J. & Salancik, G. R. (1978). *The External Control of Organizations: A Resource Dependence Perspective*. New York, London: Harper & Row.

Powell, W. W., White, D.R., Koput, K.W. & Owen-Smith, J. (2005). Network dynamics and field evolution: The growth of interorganizational collaboration in the life sciences. *American Journal of Sociology*, 110, 1132–1205.

Rasche, A. (2008). *The Paradoxical Foundation of Strategic Management*. Berlin: Sage Publications Ltd.

Scott, R. W. (1983a). The organization of environments. In R. W. Scott & J. W. Meyer (Eds.), *Organizational Environments: Ritual and Rationality*. Beverly Hills: Sage

Scott, W. R. (1983b). *Organizational Environments: Ritual and Rationality* (J. W. Meyer & W. R. Scott, Eds.). Beverly Hills: Sage.

Scott, W. R. (2004). Reflections on a half-century of organizational sociology. *Annual Review of Sociology*, 30, 1–21.

Scott, W. R. (2008). Approaching adulthood: The maturing of institutional theory. *Theory and Society*, 37, 427–442.

Scott, W. R. (2014). *Institutions and Organizations*. Beverly Hills: Sage Publications.

Scott, W. R. & Meyer, J. W. (1991). The organization of societal sectors: Propositions and early evidence. In W. W. Powell & P. Dimaggio (Eds.), *The New Institutionalism in Organizational Analysis*. Chicago: University of Chicago Press.

Selznick P. (1949). *Tva and the Grass Roots: A Study in the Sociology of Formal Organization*. Berkeley: University of California Press.

Shrivastava, P., 1986. Is strategic management ideological?. *Journal of management*, 12(3), pp. 363–377.

Simon, H. A. (1957). *Models of Man. Social and Rational. Mathematical Essays on Rational Human Behavior in a Social Setting*. New York: Wiley.

Smets, M., Aristidou, A. & Whittington, R. (2017). Towards a practice-driven institutionalism. In *The Sage Handbook of Organizational Institutionalism* (2nd ed.). London: Sage Publications.

Suddaby R. (2013). *Institutional Theory*. Thousand Oaks, CA: Sage Publications.

Suddaby R., Seidl, D. & Le, J. K. (2013). Strategy-as-practice meets neo-institutional theory. *Strategic Organization*, 11, 329–344.

Thornton, P. H., Ocasio, W. & Lounsbury, M. (2012). *The Institutional Logics Perspective: A New Approach to Culture, Structure, and Process*. Oxford: Oxford University Press.

Tilly, C. (1977). *From Mobilization to Revolution*. Ann Arbor, MI: University of Michigan.

Vaara, E. & Whittington, R. (2012). Strategy-as-practice: Taking social practices seriously. *Academy of Management Annals*, 6, 285–336.

Whittington, R. (1996). Strategy as practice. *Long Range Planning*, 29, 731–735.

Whittington, R. (2001). *What Is Strategy – and Does It Matter?* London: Thompson Learning.

Whittington, R. (2010). Giddens, structuration theory and strategy as practice. In *Cambridge Handbook of Strategy as Practice*, pp. 109–126. Cambridge: Cambridge University Press.

Wiklund, J., & Shepherd, D. (2003). Knowledge-based resources, entrepreneurial orientation, and the performance of small and medium-sized businesses. *Strategic Management Journal*, 24(13), 1307–1314.

Wiseman, A. W. & Baker, D. P. (2006). The symbiotic relationship between empirical comparative research on education and neo-institutional theory. In *The Impact of Comparative Education Research on Institutional Theory*. Bingley: Emerald.

Wooten M. & Hoffman, A. J. (2016). *Organizational Fields Past, Present and Future*. Ross School of Business Paper.

Zald, M. N. (1996). Culture ideology and strategic framing. In D. Mcadam, J. D. Mccarthy, & M. N. Zald (Eds.), *Comparative Perspectives on Social Movements: Political Opportunities, Mobilizing Structures, and Cultural Framings*. Cambridge: Cambridge University Press.

Zietsma, C. & Winn, M. I. (2005). *Reflections on Process and Process Theorizing: Revisiting Our Work "Organizational Field Power Dynamics and the 'War of the Woods'"*. Unpublished Manuscript, Presented at the the First Organization Studies Summer Workshop on Theorizing Process in Organization Research, Santorini: Greece.

Zucker, L. G. (1983). Organizations as institutions. *Research in the Sociology of Organizations*, 2, 1–47.

Zucker, L. G. (1987). Institutional theories of organization. *Annual Review of Sociology*, 13, 443–464.

Chapter 6

The psychology of decision-making

Learning outcomes

After reading this chapter you should be able to:

- define what "a strategic decision" is
- explain the difference between normative and behavioural decision-making models
- understand what cognitive heuristics are

Pre-chapter questions

- Is there a "right way" to make a decision?
- Think of a good decision that you have made. Why was this a good decision?
- Think of a bad decision that you have made or a bad decision that you have experienced. Why was this a bad decision?

Key terms

- Decision – a choice between two or more alternatives
- Strategic decision – decisions regarding the direction of the organisation or of a large part of the organisation. Also, decisions that affect large segments of society
- Normative decision-making – Use of a rational, logical process that consists of a series of steps to make a decision. How decisions "should" be made.
- Behavioural decision-making – use of experience, gut instinct, and non-rational means to make a decision. How decisions are "actually" made.
- Heuristics – cognitive shortcuts, or 'decision rules'. Fundamental to strategic decision-making

DOI: 10.4324/9780429344305-10

6.1 Introduction

This chapter explores the psychology of strategic decision-making. It explores the nature of decisions and offers a definition of what strategic decisions actually are, and these are distinguished from operational and administrative decisions.

We then discuss the various ways in which decisions can be made, and these are grouped into two schools of thought. Normative decision-making uses logical and rational approaches to undertake a series of steps to consider and evaluate the various options that present themselves and, in doing so, produces a final decision that is underpinned by robust analysis. Behavioural decision-making, on the other hand, uses experience and gut instinct to cut through the mass of data that managers are often confronted with, and the resulting decisions are fast but may be skewed by bias or other factors.

This is followed by an introduction to cognitive heuristics. These are shortcuts, or rules of thumb, that are inherent within everyone, and they can be used to make decisions. We show that strategy (the long-term big picture) is often based on a series of non-rational steps, and these ideas are introduced in this chapter prior to a fuller examination in the next chapter.

Throughout this chapter and the next, we have included illustrative quotes from public sector managers from different countries and disciplines. A total of 11 managers were interviewed for this chapter, and their experiences enrich the discussions and reveal how experienced managers make decisions in real life.

6.2 What is a "decision"?

This sounds like a simple question. Everyone knows what a decision is, right?

The reality is more complicated. It turns out that a "decision" is not easy to define. There is no universally-agreed definition of a decision, but it is generally agreed that some form of choice is involved (e.g. Akanbi, 2011; Eysenck and Keane, 2010). Indeed, Simon (1997: 3) argues that "the words 'choice' and 'decision' [can be] used interchangeably". In other words, they are the same thing. For the purposes of this chapter, we will use the following definition:

Key definition

- a "decision" is a choice between two or more alternatives

This definition assumes that there is always an alternative course of action – even if it is doing nothing as opposed to doing something. It also implies that a decision takes place at an instant: a choice is made at a point in time. However, Mintzberg and Waters (1990: 3) dispute this, arguing that decisions can evolve gradually or even "inadvertently". Case study 6a illustrates this point.

Case study 6a When was the decision made?

Ted was the manager of a large US local authority department that was responsible for building control. He was at a conference when he heard people discussing ISO9001. This is an internationally recognised quality management standard, and almost all private sector companies in the industry were accredited. This gave them the edge over the public sector, who were viewed by the construction industry as being less competitive. The conference delegates felt that if their organisations could gain the standard, this would level the playing field and could bring in lucrative new contracts. Ted had never previously heard of this standard and wanted to find out more.

Ted asked his deputy, Mary, to do some research. Unfortunately, he was involved in a car accident and had to take some time off work. When he returned six months later, the department had spent $1million. Ted was furious. He had not authorised this expenditure and wanted someone's head. He wanted to know what had happened and the name of the person who should be sacked. The subsequent investigation revealed the following:

> Ted asked Mary to do some research about ISO9001. Mary understood this to mean that this was the direction the department needed to go. She instructed her management team to undertake some research and use the results to reconfigure the department's strategy. Members of the management team took this as an instruction to change working practices. They would have to stop doing some tasks and undertake a number of new tasks. It was clear from the research that current data management practices were no longer appropriate and that a new IT system would be needed in order to manage the coming changes. The IT department was instructed to procure the system. In tandem, it was obvious that a new manager would need to be recruited to manage the new IT system; several new junior clerks would be needed to input the data; and a new manager would be needed to oversee the change in strategic direction that the department was now embarking upon. HR were instructed to begin the recruitment process.

And so it continued. All the way down the chain, people began taking on tasks as a result of the management decision to adopt ISO9001. The investigation concluded that, essentially, there had been a series of communication breakdowns. Everyone was at fault and nobody was at fault. Nobody should be sacked for what was, in essence, a series of misunderstandings.

Ted was powerless. All he had asked for was some research into whether or not ISO9001 was worth pursuing. Instead, his departmental strategy had changed; he had an IT system that he hadn't asked for; and several extra staff had been recruited to make it all work. To top it all off, it had cost the department $1million. However, nobody had actually made the decision to do any of this. The strategy had changed by accident.

Questions

1 What should the organisation have done to prevent this from happening?
2 What should they do now?

6.3 Typology of decisions

Task

- How many different types of decision are there?
- Working by yourself, make a list
- Then, compare notes with the person next to you and see if you can refine your list

How many did you come up with?

There are many different "types" of decisions but, as with most academic literature, there is no single list that everyone agrees upon. For example, Yao (2011) classifies decisions as being either immediate or delayed, whereas CSSP (2003) developed a typology for group decision-making, which analyses decisions into two main categories (structural characteristics and performance characteristics) with a further 20 subcategories, including power, legitimacy, stability, results-driven, and data-driven. In a medical context, several decision-making typologies have been proposed, which are typically risk-based (see for instance Sturmey, 1995; Whitney, 2003).

In a seminal series of studies known as the Bradford studies, researchers studied top strategic decisions in 30 organisations ranging in size from 100 to more than 50,000 employees. Five decisions were analysed from each organisation, making a total of 150 decisions (Hickson et al., 1986). Decisions were categorised in three ways: vortex-sporadic, tractable-fluid, and familiar-constricted.

- Vortex-sporadic decisions are controversial, complex, and involve ambiguity and uncertainty together with a need to manage conflicting viewpoints of many managers, and as a result they are often time-consuming (Cray et al., 1991).
- Tractable-fluid decisions are generally less complex, and because they are normally non-controversial, there is less likelihood of disagreement amongst decision-makers (Rowe, 1989).
- Familiar-constricted decisions are normal decisions which are straightforward and involve the smallest number of managers (Hickson et al., 1986).

It should be noted that the researchers stressed that these categories are merely approximations for what happens in practice (Rowe, 1989).

Table 6.1 highlights some other categories that have been proposed. Again, this list is intended to be representative rather than exhaustive.

Table 6.1 Illustrative typology of decisions

Type of decision	*Comments*
Routine	Involve the use of pre-established organisational procedures or rules (Miller et al., 2002).
Innovative	Made when a situation is confronted that has no precedent (Buchanan and Huczynski, 2019).
Significant	These decisions are highly consequential and have widespread and long-term impact (Miller et al., 2002).
Compromise	Making a decision that is acceptable to all requires "give and take". The decision is therefore rarely ideal (Drucker, 2001). This may not be a decision type in its own right, because all decision-making is a matter of compromise (Simon, 1997).
Complex	In general, the more complex a decision is, the harder it is to make (Watson, 1994), and complexity depends on factors such as the degree of familiarity, because topics which are unfamiliar to the decision-maker will not only require alternatives to be sought, but will also require the construction of mechanisms for search and evaluation (Cray et al., 1991).
Programmed	Decisions which occur frequently and can be made in a relatively straightforward fashion, and there are normally tried and tested protocols, formulae, or procedures for making them (Greenberg and Baron, 2008).
Non-programmed	Decisions which are unfamiliar, and for which there is no pre-specified course of action and no procedure to follow (Greenberg and Baron, 2008).

There is considerable overlap between these categories. For instance, programmed and routine decisions are very similar, as are non-programmed and innovative decisions.

One typology that has stood the test of time was developed by Igor Ansoff (1968). He identified three categories of decisions:

- Strategic – these are decisions "regarding the direction [an] organisation should take to achieve its mission" (Greenberg and Baron, 2008: 384). They may also have effects for large segments of society (Colignon and Cray, 1980). Examples include decisions relating to corporate objectives, which products/services should be offered, and where should they be marketed (Ansoff, 1968). Large-scale procurements are strategic decisions (Murray, 2011).
- Operational – these decisions are short-term and routine and comprise most of the decisions taken by managers. They seek to maximise the efficiency of resources. Examples include quality management, inventory control, and budgeting (Ansoff, 1968).
- Administrative – these decisions seek to ensure the smooth and effective collaboration of the strategic and operational decisions (Ansoff, 1968). Examples include decisions involving the organisation of people such as personnel and finance (Hicks, 1991).

This book is concerned with strategic decisions, as defined in this typology.

Strategic decisions

Senior managers who were interviewed during the preparation for this book gave the following examples of decisions what they regard as being strategic decisions.

> Strategic decisions are big decisions. They affect the whole organisation, or at least a large part of it.
>
> (Local authority, USA)

> Sometimes decisions are made that involve lots of different organisations working together. Some of my decisions involve the local council, national government, the Health Service, and private sector partners. They are strategic decisions because of the scale and reach that they have.
>
> (Health Service, UK)

> When we decide which services to offer and which ones to reduce, or stop altogether, they are strategic decisions because they impact the whole organisation and they can have a massive effect on the people we serve.
>
> (Local authority, USA).

> Our big procurements are strategic decisions because they commit the organisation to a course of action and set the policy for maybe the next decade or more.
>
> (Local authority, UK).

These examples have many similarities with the definition presented in Ansoff's (1968) typology above. Case study 6b outlines how managers made strategic decisions in the context of austerity.

Case study 6b Decisions made by managers

Following a major financial crisis, the UK government imposed a series of austerity measures. One local authority faced a large reduction in the amount of government grant that was paid to the organisation. This amounted to a 13% reduction of income in year one with a further reduction of 15% over the next two years. In order to set a legal budget, the organisation decided to reduce staff numbers by approximately 2,000 posts over the three-year period. A local government manager explained what she did.

> I had to take a decision to balance two fundamentally conflicting priorities. I had to balance the need to make savings with the need to protect frontlineservices. This is a moral issue. My staff have been loyal to me over the years under difficult circumstances. Now they need me to look after them. I need to repay them. I chose to protect existing staff, I deleted my vacant posts, got rid of overtime, supported early retirement for those who wanted to leave. I did everything I could because I felt it was the right thing to do.

However, in similar circumstances in the USA, three managers made the same decision (to protect existing staff), but for different reasons:

> This was a chance to streamline my service and get rid of people who were not performing, but I couldn't do it because of the unions. It's hard to do. They'd fight me all the way. There are too many hoops to jump through and it's not worth the effort. It was easier to keep my staff – even the bad ones – and lose the vacancies.
>
> (US local authority manager 1)

> The corporate procedure is that if I lose my current staff then I lose the post. I won't be able to fill it later. So, because I wanted to keep the post, I had to keep my staff. I couldn't keep functioning if I'd lost the posts forever.
>
> (US local authority manager 2.

> It's all about cost. It's cheaper to keep current staff than it is to try to recruit new staff.
>
> (US local authority manager 3)

Questions

1. The quotes in this case study suggest that the same decision can be made for different reasons. For each quote, what was the underlying reason for the decision?
2. Which reason for the decision do you most empathise with? Why?
3. For each of these managers, what are the implications of their decision-making approach for their organisations and their staff?

Although staffing decisions are normally regarded as administrative decisions (Ansoff, 1968), the UK manager in the case study felt that these are strategic decisions, at least in her case:

> Definitely strategic. I knew when I was making the decision cutting my vacancies was permanent. I was effectively saying that we can't deliver particular parts of the service in future. Quite consciously, I was setting out my service delivery priorities for the next few years. I was setting out the size and shape of my business unit for the next three years, but I was also making decisions about what I felt were my key services and setting out how I was going to deliver these with fewer staff. So, it's a strategic decision.

Clearly, this is not an exact science, since the manager in this example disagrees with Ansoff. Having identified a range of decision types, the following section explores some of the ways in which decisions can be made.

6.4 How are decisions made?

Introduction

There is a view that decision-making should be a normative (i.e. rational) process consisting of a sequence of steps that enhance the probability of attaining a desired outcome (Patton, 2003). A number of models have been developed that seek to prescribe the way in which decisions "should" be made. These include the rational economic model, Brunswik's lens model, the Vroom-Yetton decision-making model, and the Cynefin framework. These models are briefly outlined below.

In the opinion of some, the normative approach is an ideal rather than a description of how decision-makers actually function because people do not behave in a truly rational manner. For instance, the normative approach assumes that complete information is available to the decision-maker (Tarter and Hoy, 1998), whereas in reality, information may be needed which is difficult to collect and categorise (Miller et al., 2002). Furthermore, organisational goals are often complex and may conflict (Tarter and Hoy, 1998). Thus, it is rarely possible to consider all the alternatives, since there may be too many, or some alternatives may not occur to the decision-maker (Buchanan and Huczynski, 2019), and potential solutions may be hard to recognise and in turn create new problems (Miller et al., 2002).

Hence, an alternative to the normative approach has been developed, known as the behavioural approach. This avoids rationality and instead uses factors such as experience, gut instinct, and so forth to make decisions. An important point needs to be made here. The avoidance of rationality does not make behavioural methods wrong and does not result in inferior decisions. Thus, we do not refer to them as "irrational", because this has negative connotations. Instead, "non-rational" is a more appropriate description.

Once more, there are a number of models, but one thing they have in common is that they seek to describe the way in which decisions are actually made, regardless of their efficiency, wisdom, or practicality (Hill, 1979b). Examples of these models include bounded rationality, Incrementalism, naturalistic decision-making, and cognitive heuristics. Again, these models are briefly outlined in the following pages.

Normative models

Normative models seek to prescribe how decisions "should" be made in order to achieve the best possible outcome (Hutchinson and Gigerenzer, 2005). Indeed, Patton (2003: 993) argues that rational decision-making is "desirable", whilst Hill (1979a: 21) goes so far as to say that it is the "ideal decision-making process". Although there are many different tools used in normative decision-making, for instance decision trees and statistical techniques (Kahneman and Tversky, 1973), they typically possess certain common features which include a list of steps and a logical framework. It follows that two people, given the same skills, the same objectives and values, the same knowledge and information, can rationally decide only upon the same course of action (Simon, 1997). The following pages briefly outline the key features of some of these methods.

Rational economic model

This model assumes that decision-making is a rational process consisting of a series of steps. To arrive at a decision, a manager must define the purpose of the action, list the

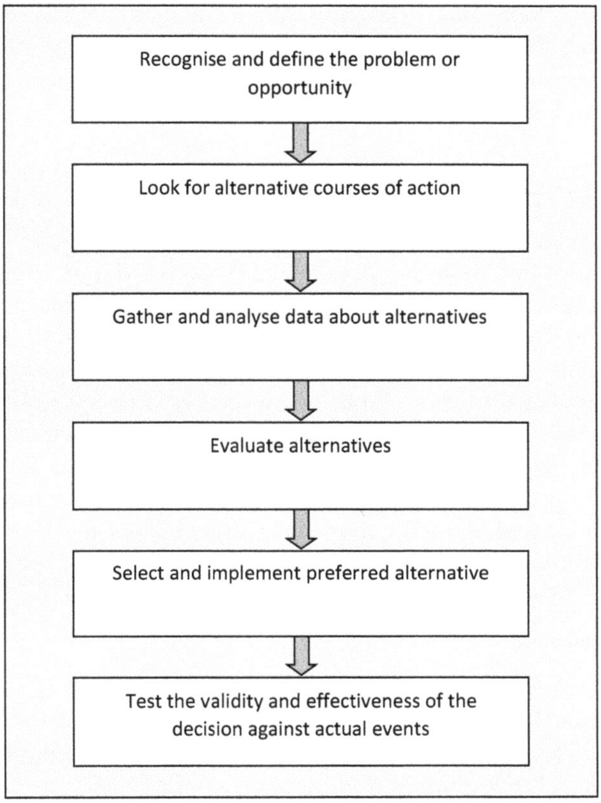

Figure 6.1 Rational economic model of decision-making

Source: Adapted from Buchanan and Huczynski (2019); Drucker (2001); Miller et al. (2002).

options available, choose between the options, and then turn that choice into action (Heller and Hindle, 1998). This can be illustrated by Figure 6.1, which is presented in full purely because it is, perhaps, the simplest example of a normative model owing to its straightforward, logical flow.

Since this diagram is derived from a combination of sources, it is rather generic. However, versions of the model have been studied in contexts as diverse as motivation (Rowley, 1996), strategic policy-making (Kørnøv and Thissen, 2000), fraud (McKeever, 2012), and energy management (Greene, 2011).

Brunswik's lens model

Egon Brunswik (1952, 1956) argues that people do not make decisions directly but view the environment and the object of the decision through a lens of factors and clues, each of which is assigned a statistical weighting. In this way, "stray" causes and effects are identified, and action can be taken accordingly. The important factors are "focused" via the lens (i.e. the effect of the different weights), and this determines the conclusion reached

(Brunswik, 1952, 1956). The model remains influential more than half a century after its creation (Wigton, 2008) and has been used in a range of contexts, including statistical correlation (Stewart, 1976), clinical judgment (Dana and Cocking, 1968), exploring the relationship between organisms and their environments (Petrinovich, 1979), and understanding non-verbal behaviour (Gifford, 1994).

Vroom-Yetton decision-making model

This model was developed by Victor Vroom and Phillip Yetton (Vroom and Yetton, 1973), and was later expanded by Vroom and Arthur Jago (Vroom and Jago, 1988). It is essentially a decision tree and seeks to help managers determine the degree to which they should involve their subordinates in the decision-making process (Vroom and Yetton, 1973). The model argues that effectiveness depends on managers' ability to adjust their decision-making method to the requirements of the situation. To help managers achieve this match, seven questions are asked in order. Answers to these questions lead along different routes, ultimately directing managers to the best decision-making method for that situation (Yukl, 2012). The relevance of the model in the present day is emphasised by Li (2011), who argues that future studies in decision-making and business management should adopt the Vroom-Yetton model, although much of the empirical research is several decades old (e.g. Field, 1982).

The Cynefin framework

In the late 1990s, Dave Snowden and colleagues developed the 'Cynefin' framework which attempts to determine how people perceive and make sense of situations in order to make decisions (Kurtz and Snowden, 2003). Cynefin views decisions as a process, and it seeks to assist decision-makers "to see things from new viewpoints; assimilate complex concepts; and address real-world problems and opportunities" (Snowden and Boone, 2007: 70). The framework links learning and knowledge (Cronjé and Burger, 2006) and comprises five contexts – simple, complicated, complex, chaotic, and disorder – and defines the leader's role in each of these domains (Snowden and Boone, 2007). For example, in complex situations managers should seek to increase the visibility of the underlying patterns before taking any action, and in chaotic situations managers should act quickly and decisively to reduce the turbulence and then rapidly respond to the reaction to that intervention (Snowden and Boone, 2007). The model is well-regarded (French, 2013). Indeed, in 2011, Snowden and Boone's (2007) paper has been used in a range of contexts including knowledge management (Kurtz and Snowden, 2003), the study of emergency situations (French and Niculae, 2004), and food-chain risk management (Shepherd et al., 2006).

Discussion 6.1 effectiveness of normative models

Suppose we were asked to explain why normative decision-making approaches might be effective in each of the following situations

- job interviews
- tender evaluation

- procuring a new IT system
- buying a house

In job interviews, candidates are typically rated against a series of predetermined criteria. Many of these criteria are matters of fact: either an applicant has a degree or they don't, either an applicant has previous experience or they don't. Other criteria are matters of opinion, but candidates are ranked against the "ideal" (presented in a person specification). Thus, by rating different candidates against the same criteria, it is possible to achieve a level of objectivity. If the different ratings are "scored", the person with the highest score will be given the job. This, it is argued, reduces bias because everyone is marked impartially against the requirements of the job. There is a series of steps that is followed, and there is a logic to the decision. Everyone presented with the same facts would make the same decision.

Tender evaluation is similar. The requirements of the contract are predetermined, and prospective bidders are assessed against these. Again, some of the requirements are matters of fact (either someone has five years' worth of accounts or they do not) but others are inherently subjective (can the applicant do the work?) but are rendered objective by a predetermined set of criteria that are shared with bidders early in the process to aid consistency and transparency. Again, bidders are scored, and whoever gets the highest score will be awarded the contract. There is a structure and logical flow to the decision-making process.

When procuring a new IT system, managers know what they want in advance. They establish a series of parameters upfront. The system needs to accommodate x concurrent users; it needs to address strategic issues y and z; it can't cost more than $xx; the system needs to interface with existing system yy, and so on. Various candidate systems are shortlisted against these parameters. Once more, there is a logic that is evident to all involved. No matter how affordable a system is, it will be rejected unless it meets all other parameters.

When people are buying a house, many factors must be considered. They do not simply buy the first house they see. One obvious factor is affordability. The buyer has a budget, and this effectively limits the number of choices – the house must fall within the budget. But this is not all. The condition of the house is important: perhaps the buyer wants a DIY project and is unconcerned about minor repairs, or perhaps they want somewhere they can move into immediately. There may be other considerations, such as parking, proximity to schools, and ease of access to local amenities. The buyer is likely to look at crime statistics and may also explore the surrounding area. All of these factors will shape the final decision. There is a process that means that each of the factors must be satisfied. If even one is found to be unsatisfactory, then the house will not be bought.

Normative decision-making theory also explains models such as five forces and VRIO. In these, there are a series of factors that must be considered. In Chapter 3, we saw that Porter and Barney argue that it is only by considering all factors that is it possible to form a holistic view. It is not possible to look at one or two aspects in isolation if one is to reach a proper decision. As we have seen, Barney actually mandates which combination of factors leads to sustained competitive advantage. There are steps to be followed, and there is a logic to the approach. Importantly, however, Rumelt (2011) recognises that strategic decisions are attempting to predict the future, or at least, they are attempting to shape the future. Both Porter and Barney use past behaviour as an indicator of future patterns. Is this possible? Rumelt argues that it is not. We cannot say for certain that a strategy WILL work. We can't even say that it WILL NOT work. We cannot predict the future. Thus, according to Rumelt, it is only possible to search for possible pitfalls and potential problems. All we can do is look for potential issues and do our best to act accordingly. Hence, normative models are not a guarantee of success in strategic decision-making, and other approaches need to be considered.

Behavioural models

Behavioural models refer to the way in which decisions are actually made (Hill, 1979b). They accept that factors such as emotional response, altruism, or prejudice may all be important in the decision-making process (Amaldoss et al., 2008). The following pages briefly outline some of these models.

Bounded rationality

As we have seen, normative decision-making requires the comparison of alternatives in order to select the best (Brown, 2004). However, in "real-world" decision-making, alternatives are often examined sequentially, and the first satisfactory alternative is likely to be the one actually selected (Fagan and Piquero, 2007). In other words, decision-makers look for the first workable option rather than trying to find the best possible option (Klein, 2008), so the decision neither maximises nor satisfies. It is said to "satisfice" (Simon, 1997). Once an option is found, decision-makers will look no further (Tarter and Hoy, 1998). This is bounded rationality and was proposed by Herbert Simon in the 1950s and 1960s (March and Simon, 1993; Simon, 1957; 1997).

Although more than half a century old, this is still among the most influential decision-making theories (Porac and Tschang, 2013). It recognises that most people do not think like computers, dispassionately assessing all of the known facts before reaching the optimal decision (Fagan and Piquero, 2007). It suggests that decision-makers tend to construct simplified mental models when dealing with complex problems. For instance, they may not have enough time to apply a normative approach (Gigerenzer and Selten, 2001), or the situation may be extremely complex (Simon, 1997). Therefore, decision-makers use bounded rationality to make decisions rather than a strict rigid rule of optimisation (Kahneman, 2003). Because of its pedigree and wide acceptance, bounded rationality has been studied in many contexts including health insurance (Korobkin, 2012), understanding political reasoning (Marcus and McKuen, 1993), organisational learning (Simon, 1991), and the adoption of new technology (Gounaris and Koritos, 2012).

Incrementalism

Incrementalism was developed by Lindblom (1959) and argues that decisions are rarely made at a fixed point in time. Instead, they slowly evolve in a series of small incremental steps (Tarter and Hoy, 1998). The outcomes of each change are monitored, and further changes are made as a result, and the process continues until a suitable solution is found

(Tarter and Hoy, 1998). McElhinney and Proctor (2005) suggest that this is a way of avoiding serious mistakes, although they argue that this approach means that decision-makers are unable to cope with problems presented by sudden or substantial paradigm shifts. This has been described as the "science of muddling through" (Lindblom, 1959: 79). It differs from the normative and bounded rationality models in a number of ways. For instance, setting objectives and generating alternatives are not separate (Tarter and Hoy, 1998). Furthermore, the direction is not fixed by the process; "in fact, the more complex the problem, the more likely that objectives will change as decisions evolve" (Tarter and Hoy, 1998: 215), whereas with both normative models and bounded rationality, alternatives are assessed sequentially in order (Simon, 1997). Indeed, incrementatlism can be seen as a "middle ground" lying between normative models and bounded rationality (Lindblom, 1959, 1977). Incrementalism has been researched in a number of contexts including strategic planning (Quinn, 1978), politics and governance (Lindblom, 1977), health care technology (Claxton et al., 2011), marketing (Wierenga, 2011), and crowd behaviour (Kameda et al., 2011).

Naturalistic Decision-Making (NDM)

There are many situations that occur in natural settings that are difficult to replicate artificially, such as stressful conditions, high stakes, danger, and varying levels of experience, and normative theories do not adequately explain how decisions are made under these circumstances (Klein, 2008). Researchers, therefore, began to use cognitive field research methods such as task analysis to observe and study skilled performers (Zsambok, 1997), and the results were used to develop models and theories that can then be tested in the real world (Klein, 2008). It was found that people behave differently in "real-world" situations than they do in "laboratory" conditions (Duggan and Harris, 2001), and thus naturalistic decision-making (NDM) was born.

NDM can have important practical implications. To quote a single example, although aircraft could be evacuated smoothly and rapidly when on the ground, when emergencies occurred for real, fatalities resulted because the aircraft were not evacuated as quickly as they "should" have been. NDM researchers sought to identify the reasons for this. They offered financial inducements to volunteers to evacuate quickly, and it was found that people began climbing over seats, pushing each other out of the way, and so forth. There was chaos, and evacuation took far longer than it should have done. It was established that the aircraft design could not cope under these conditions, and this helped to explain why lives were lost in real disasters. As a result, aircraft designs were modified; aisle lighting was introduced; and exits were improved. In short, lives were saved (Barreto and Ribeiro, 2012). Indeed, the importance of NDM can be illustrated by the range of contexts in which it has been studied. These include training delivery (Cannon-Bowers and Salas, 1998), production planning and scheduling (Gasser et al., 2011), military planning (Schmitt and Klein, 1999), outdoor adventure (Boyes and O'Hare, 2011), and software development (Moe et al., 2012).

Cognitive heuristics

Cognitive heuristics are the main focus of chapter 7 and are discussed in detail there, but this is a nice place to introduce them. They are behavioural models of decision-making and have been defined in the literature in many different ways, including "simplifying strategies" (Payne et al., 1993: 2), "rules of thumb" (Greenberg and Baron, 2008: 400), or even simply as "shortcuts" (LeBoeuf and Shafir, 2005: 126). Essentially, cognitive heuristics are general rules that are useful in guiding a search for a path to the solution of a problem.

As will be seen, these are extremely common and are widely used by managers when making strategic decisions. In view of this, the next chapter is devoted to cognitive heuristics. However, we can now return to the same questions we posed earlier in the chapter. We argued that in certain situations, decisions can be made in logical, rational, and normative ways. Is this actually true? Discussion 3.2 questions the earlier discussion.

Discussion 6.2 Do normative models really explain real life?

Suppose we were asked to explain why normative decision-making approaches might not be used in each of the following situations

- job interviews
- tender evaluation
- procuring a new IT system
- buying a house

Although we have argued above that each of the four situations can be understood in terms of normative theory, in reality, people do not behave in this way. They use behavioural models without realising it.

As we have seen, in job interviews candidates are supposed to be rated against a series of predetermined criteria. Candidates are ranked against the "ideal" (presented in a person specification). However, the reality is different. Suppose Mary is interviewed and does well, scoring 7/10. Then Mohammed comes in. Mohammed is clearly a better candidate than Mary. His answers are better than Mary's, and he is more attuned to what the interviewers are looking for. He scores 8/10. Tony is next to be interviewed. He is much weaker than Mohammed. Mohammed gave much better answers than Tony. Tony is the weakest candidate so far and scores 6/10. What has happened here? Mary was first and was compared to the criteria in line with the procedure. Mohammed was compared to Mary, not to the criteria. Tony was compared to Mohammed, not to the criteria. In other words, Mohammed has become the anchor point, and all subsequent candidates are compared to him. The organisation is not following its own procedures. Candidates are being compared to other candidates and not to the criteria. Moreover, the process is flawed – the first candidate can never be given 10/10 in case someone even stronger comes along later. What is actually happening is that cognitive heuristics are being used to simplify the decision-making process. This will be discussed later in this chapter.

Tender evaluation is similar. The requirements of the contract are predetermined, and prospective bidders are assessed against these. However, suppose I score the first tender bid as an 8 for the first requirement. Where does the figure 8 come from?

This is not an exact science. It is either plucked out of thin air or else it is based on my experience. Furthermore, as above, this becomes the anchor point for the next tender bid. Again, heuristics are used to make the decision.

When procuring a new IT system, managers generally base their requirements on what they currently have. They want to keep the bits of the current system that they like. In other words, the current system is an anchor point, and the final system is based upon this anchor. We have heuristics in action again.

When people are buying a house, it is undeniable that objective factors must be considered. If I can't afford a house, that is the end of the matter. However, this is actually the use a heuristic, which is discussed below. A single aspect (price) is used as the basis for the decision. Even if all of the objective factors are met in full, when I come to view a house, I might reject it because "it doesn't feel right" or I may choose it because "it feels welcoming". In other words, the final decision might come down to emotions or feelings. The final decision is based on a cognitive heuristic.

6.5 Chapter summary

This chapter has outlined the psychology of decision-making. The following key points were identified:

- A decision can be defined as making a choice between two or more alternatives.
- A strategic decision is one that impacts upon the whole organisation, or of a large part of the organisation. They might also affect large segments of society.
- There are two main schools of thought in decision-making theory. Normative decision-making uses a rational, logical process that consists of a series of steps to make a decision. Behavioural decision-making makes use of managers' own experience, gut instinct, etc, and uses non-rational means to make a decision.
- We have introduced the concept of cognitive heuristics. These are mental shortcuts, or "decision rules" that are part of everyone, and they are largely unavoidable. They are examined in detail in the next chapter.

Self-assessment questions

- Compare and contrast the normative and behavioural decision-making approaches identified in this chapter
- To what extent do you think that each of these approaches apply to strategic decision-making?
- Which decision-making approach might work best in your own experience in the workplace?
- Which decision-making approach might be best if you have a lot of time and have access to a lot of information?

- Following the financial crisis of 2008 and the subsequent implementation of austerity measures, and then subsequent issues such as the global pandemic, the world has been operating in conditions of considerable uncertainty. Which approaches to decision-making have been taken by politicians and big business? Were they effective? Why (or why not)?

References

Akanbi, P. A. (2011). Managerial decision-making in an organization: A theoretical framework. *Journal of Management and Corporate Governance*, 3, 39–52.

Amaldoss, W., Bettman, J. R. & Payne, J. W. (2008). Biased but efficient: An investigation of coordination facilitated by asymmetric dominance. *Marketing Science*, 27(5), 903–921.

Ansoff, H. I. (1968). *Corporate Strategy: An Analytic Approach to Business Policy for Growth and Expansion.* London: Penguin.

Barreto, M. M. & Ribeiro, S. L. (2012). Aircraft accident investigation: The decision-making in initial action scenario. *Work: A Journal of Prevention, Assessment and Rehabilitation*, 41, 4931–4935.

Boyes, M. A. & O'Hare, D. (2011). Examining naturalistic decision-making in outdoor adventure contexts by computer simulation. *Australian Journal of Outdoor Education*, 15(1), 22–34.

Brown, R. (2004). Consideration of the origin of Herbert Simon's theory of 'satisficing' (1933–1947). *Management Decision*, 42(10), 1240–1256.

Brunswik, E. (1952). *The Conceptual Framework of Psychology (International Encyclopedia of Unified Science, Volume 1, Number 10.).* Chicago: University of Chicago Press.

Brunswik, E. (1956). *Perception and the Representative Design of Psychological Experiments* (2d edn.). Berkeley, CA: University of California Press.

Buchanan, D. A. & Huczynski, A. (2019). *Organizational Behaviour: An Introductory Text* (10th edn), Harlow: Pearson Education.

Cannon-Bowers, J. A. & Salas, E. (1998). *Making Decisions Under Stress: Implications for Individual and Team Training*. Washington, DC: American Psychological Association.

Claxton, K., Paulden, M., Gravelle, H., Brouwer, W. & Culyer, A. J. (2011). Discounting and decision-making in the economic evaluation of health-care technologies. *Health Economics*, 20(1), 2–15.

Colignon, R. & Cray, D. (1980). Critical organizations. *Organization Studies*, 1, 349–366.

Cray, D., Mallory, G. R., Butler, R. J., Hickson, D. J. & Wilson, D. C. (1991). Explaining decision processes. *Journal of Management Studies*, 28(3), 227–252.

Cronjé, J. C. & Burger, D. (2006). Learning from a free-access digital information kiosk in Africa: An objectivist – constructivist investigation. *Aslib Proceedings: New Information Perspectives*, 58(3), 218–236.

CSSP. (2003). Typology of Group Decision Making: An Index of characteristics, dimensions and components. http://www.cssp.org/publications/constituents-co-invested-in-change/community-decision-making/collaborative-decision-making-typology.pdf.

Dana, R. M. & Cocking, R. R. (1968). Cue parameters, cue probabilities, and clinical judgment. *Journal of Clinical Psychology*, 24(4), 475–480.

Drucker, P. F. (2001). The effective decision. In Anonymous (Ed.), *Harvard Business Review on Decision-Making*. Boston: Harvard Business School.

Duggan, S. J. & Harris, D. (2001). Modelling naturalistic decision-making using an artificial neural network: Pilot's responses to a disruptive passenger incident. *Human Factors and Aerospace Safety*, 1(2), 145–166.

Eysenck, M. W. & Keane, M. T. (2010). *Cognitive Psychology* (6th edn). Hove: Psychology Press.

Fagan, J. & Piquero, A. R. (2007). Rational choice and developmental influences on recidivism among adolescent felony offenders. *Journal of Empirical Legal Studies*, 4(4), 715–748.

Field, R. H. G. (1982). A test of the Vroom-Yetton normative model of leadership. *Journal of Applied Psychology*, 67(5), 523–532.

French, S. (2013). Cynefin, statistics and decision analysis. *Journal of the Operational Research Society*, 64(4), 547–561.

French, S. & Niculae, C. (2004). *Believe in the Model: Mishandle the Emergency*. Proceedings of the 2004 ISCRAM conference: Brussels, May 3–4 2004, pp. 9–14. Retrieved June 27, 2020, from the ISCRAM Web Site: www.iscram.org/dmdocuments/ISCRAM2004_InvitedSF.pdf.

Gasser, R., Fischer, K. & Wäfler, T. (2011). Decision-making in Planning and Scheduling: A field study of planning behaviour in manufacturing. In J. C. Fransoo et al. (Eds.), *Behavioral Operations in Planning and Scheduling: Part 1*. Berlin: Springer Verlag, pp. 11–30.

Gifford, R. (1994). A lens-mapping framework for understanding the encoding and decoding of interpersonal dispositions in nonverbal behavior. *Journal of Personality and Social Psychology*, 66(2), 398–412.

Gigerenzer, G. & Selten, R. (2001). *Bounded Rationality: The Adaptive Toolbox*. Cambridge, MA: MIT Press.

Gounaris, S. & Koritos, C. D. (2012). Adoption of technologically based innovations: The neglected role of bounded rationality. *Journal of Product Innovation Management*, 29(5), 821–838.

Greenberg, J. & Baron, R. A. (2008). *Behavior in Organizations* (9th edn.). London: Pearson Education.

Greene, D. L. (2011). Uncertainty, loss aversion, and markets for energy efficiency. *Energy Economics*, 33(4), 608–616.

Heller, R. & Hindle, T. (1998). *Essential Manager's Manual*. London: Dorling Kindersley.

Hicks, M. J. (1991). *Problem Solving in Business and Management*. London: Thomson.

Hickson, D. J., Butler, R. J., Cray, D., Mallory, G. R. & Wilson, D. C. (1986). *Top Decisions: Strategic Decision-Making in Organizations*. Oxford: Blackwell.

Hill, P. H. (1979a). The decision-making process. In P. H. Hill (Ed.), *Making Decisions: A Multidisciplinary Introduction*. Reading, MA: Addison-Wesley.

Hill, P. H. (1979b). Introduction. In P. H. Hill (Ed.), *Making Decisions: A Multidisciplinary Introduction*. Reading, MA: Addison-Wesley.

Hutchinson, J. M. C. & Gigerenzer, G. (2005). Simple heuristics and rules of thumb: Where psychologists and behavioural biologists might meet. *Behavioural Processes*, 69, 97–124.

Kahneman, D. (2003). Maps of bounded rationality: Psychology for behavioral economics. *American Economic Review*, 93(5), 1449–1476.

Kahneman, D. & Tversky, A. (1973). On the psychology of prediction. *Psychological Review*, 80, 237–251.

Kameda, T., Tsukasaki, T., Hastie, R. & Berg, N. (2011). Democracy under uncertainty: The wisdom of crowds and the free-rider problem in group decision-making. *Psychological Review*, 118(1), 76–96.

Klein, G. A. (2008). Naturalistic decision-making. *Human Factors*, 50(30), 456–460.

Kørnøv, L. & Thissen, W. A. H. (2000). Rationality in decision-and policy-making: Implications for strategic environmental assessment. *Impact Assessment and Project Appraisal*, 18(3), 191–200.

Korobkin, R. B. (2012). *Bounded Rationality, Moral Hazard, and the Case for Relative Value Health Insurance*. UCLA School of Law, Law-Econ Research Paper No. 12–06. Retrieved June 30, 2020, from the UCLA Web Site http://dx.doi.org/10.2139/ssrn.1984937.

Kurtz, C. F. & Snowden, D. J. (2003). The new dynamics of strategy: Sense-making in a complex and complicated world. *IBM Systems Journal*, 42(3), 462–483.

LeBoeuf, R. A. & Shafir, E. (2005). Anchoring on the here and now: Insufficient adjustment in time and distance estimates. *Advances in Consumer Research*, 32(1), 126–127.

Li, C. (2011). Public reaction to large-scale projects in Chinese heritage sites and its impact on decision-making: Research framework, technological path and prospects. *International Journal of Services Technology and Management*, 15(1–2), 147–160.

Lindblom, C. E. (1959). The science of muddling through. *Public Administration Review*, 19, 79–99.

Lindblom, C. E. (1977). *Politics and Markets: The World's Political-Economic Systems*. New York: Basic.

McElhinney, D. & Proctor, T. (2005). Concept of entrapment and decision-making. *Management Decision*, 43(2), 189–202.

McKeever, G. (2012). Social citizenship and social security fraud in the UK and Australia. *Social Policy & Administration*, 46(4), 465–482.

March, J. & Simon, H. A. (1993). *Organizations* (2nd edn). Oxford: Blackwell.

Marcus, G. E. & McKuen, M. (1993). Anxiety, enthusiasm, and the vote. *American Political Science Review*, 87, 688–701.

Miller, S. J., Hickson, D. J. & Wilson, D. C. (2002). Decision-making in Organizations. In G. Salaman (Ed.), *Decision-Making for Business*. London: Sage.

Mintzberg, H. & Waters, J. A. (1990). Does decision get in the way? *Organization Studies*, 11(1), 1–7.

Moe, N. B., Aurum, A. & Dybå, T. (2012). Challenges of shared decision-making: A multiple case study of agile software development. *Information and Software Technology*, 54(8), 853–865.

Murray, J. G. (2011). Third sector commissioning and English local government procurement. *Public Money & Management*, 31(4), 279–286.

Patton, J. R. (2003). Intuition in decisions. *Management Decision*, 41(10), 989–996.

Payne, J. W., Bettman, J. R. & Johnson, E. J. (1993). *The Adaptive Decision-Maker*. Cambridge: Cambridge University Press.

Petrinovich, L. (1979). Probabilistic functionalism: A conception of research method. *American Psychologist*, 34(5), 373–390.

Porac, J. & Tschang, F. T. (2013). Unbounding the managerial mind: It's time to abandon the image of managers as 'small brains'. *Journal of Management Inquiry*, 22(2), 250–254.

Quinn, J. B. (1978). Strategic change: Logical incrementalism. *Sloan Management Review*, 20(1), 7–21.

Rowe, C. (1989). Analysing management decision-making: Further thoughts after the Bradford Studies. *Journal of Management Studies*, 26(1), 29–46.

Rowley, J. (1996). Motivation and academic staff in higher education. *Quality Assurance in Education*, 4(3), 11–16.

Rumelt, R. (2011). *Good Strategy/Bad Strategy: The Difference and Why It Matters*. London: Profile Books.

Schmitt, J. F. & Klein, G. (1999). How we plan. *Marine Corps Gazette*, 83(10), 18–26.

Shepherd, R., Barker, G., French, S., Hart, A., Maule, J. & Cassidy, A. (2006). Managing food chain risks: Integrating technical and stakeholder perspectives on uncertainty. *Journal of Agricultural Economics*, 57(2), 313–327.

Simon, H. A. (1957). *Models of Man, Social and Rational: Mathematical Essays on Rational Human Behavior in a Social Setting*. New York: Wiley.

Simon, H. A. (1991). Bounded rationality and organizational learning. *Organization Science*, 2(1), 125–134.

Simon, H. A. (1997). *Administrative Behavior* (4th edn). New York: Free Press.

Snowden, D. J. & Boone, M. E. (2007). A leader's framework for decision-making. *Harvard Business Review*, 85(11), 68–76.

Stewart, T. R. (1976). Components of correlation and extensions of the lens model equation. *Psychometrika*, 41(1), 101–120.

Sturmey, P. (1995). Diagnostic-based pharmacological treatment of behavior disorders in persons with developmental disabilities: A review and a decision-making typology. *Research in Developmental Disabilities*, 16(4), 235–252.

Tarter, C. J. & Hoy, W. K. (1998). Toward a contingency theory of decision-making. *Journal of Educational Administration*, 36(3), 212–228.

Vroom, V. H. & Jago, A. G. (1988). *The New Leadership: Managing Participation in Organizations*. Englewood Cliffs, NJ: Prentice Hall.

Vroom, V. H. & Yetton, P. W. (1973). *Leadership and Decision-Making*. Pittsburgh: University of Pittsburgh Press.

Watson, T. J. (1994). *In Search of Management: Culture, Chaos & Control in Managerial Work*. London: Routledge.

Whitney, S. N. (2003). A new model of medical decisions: Exploring the limits of shared decision-making. *Medical Decision-Making*, 23(4), 275–280.

Wierenga, B. (2011). Managerial decision-making in marketing: The next research frontier. *International Journal of Research in Marketing*, 28(2), 89–101.
Wigton, R. (2008). What Do the Theories of Egon Brunswik Have to Say to Medical Education? *Advances in Health Sciences Education*, 13(1), 109–121.
Yao, Y. (2011). The superiority of three-way decisions in probabilistic rough-set models. *Information Sciences*, 181(6), 1080–1096.
Yukl, G. (2012). *Leadership in Organizations* (8th edn.). Harlow: Pearson Education.
Zsambok, C. E. (1997). Naturalistic decision-making: Where are we now? In C. E. Zsambok & G. Klein (Eds.). *Naturalistic Decision-Making*. Mahwah, NJ: Lawrence Erlbaum.

Chapter 7

The use of cognitive heuristics in strategic decision-making

Learning outcomes

After reading this chapter you should be able to:

- define what a "cognitive heuristic" is
- explain the difference between different heuristics
- understand how senior managers use cognitive heuristics in their decision-making
- analyse your own use of cognitive heuristics

Pre-chapter questions

- Is it ever OK to use shortcuts to make a decision?
- Think of a good strategic decision that you have witnessed (in person or via other means). Why was this a good decision?
- Think of a bad decision you have witnessed (in person or via other means). Why was this a bad decision?

Key terms

- Decision – a choice between two or more alternatives
- Strategic decision – decisions regarding the direction of the organisation or of a large part of the organisation. Also, decisions that affect large segments of society
- Heuristics – cognitive shortcuts, or "decision rules". Fundamental to strategic decision-making

7.1 Introduction

This chapter builds upon the previous chapter that explored the psychology of strategic decision-making. In that chapter, we explored different types of decision and were able to

DOI: 10.4324/9780429344305-11

identify what we mean by "strategic decisions". We then explored the two main schools of thought in decision-making theory: normative and behavioural approaches. Normative decision-making uses logical and rational approaches to undertake a series of steps to consider and evaluate the various options that present themselves and, in doing so, produces a final decision that is underpinned by robust analysis. Behavioural decision-making, on the other hand, uses experience and gut instinct to cut through the mass of data that managers are often confronted with, and the resulting decisions are fast but may be skewed by bias or other factors. One of the behavioural models is cognitive heuristics, and we closed the previous chapter by introducing them in outline form.

Cognitive heuristics are shortcuts, or rules of thumb, that are inherent within everyone, and they can be used to make decisions. In this chapter, we again show that strategy (the long-term big picture) is often based on a series of non-rational steps, and many of these heuristics are examined in detail. Throughout this chapter, once more we have included illustrative quotes from public sector managers from different countries and disciplines. A total of 11 managers were interviewed for this chapter, and their experiences enrich the discussions and reveal how experienced managers make decisions in real life.

7.2 Cognitive heuristics

Introduction

This section examines some of the key cognitive heuristics. It will be remembered that these are shortcuts, or general rules, that are useful in guiding a search for a path to the solution of a problem. It is shown that they are used to make strategic decisions. Therefore, looking at how strategic decisions are "actually" made in the public sector offers a counterpoint to models such as Five Forces and VRIO, which suggest how these decisions "should" be made.

It is generally recognised that the "founding fathers" of heuristic research are Daniel Kahneman and Amos Tversky. They identified the three heuristics which have underpinned subsequent research (Hardin, 1999), namely anchor and adjustment, availability, and representative; but more recent research has expanded the list, and it now includes several dozen heuristics ranging from the general, such as the moral heuristic (Sunstein, 2005), to the very specific, for instance Apte and Hong's (1995) technical two-rule iteration. Whole books have been written about cognitive heuristics, and it is therefore beyond the scope of this book to address each of these in depth. Instead, we focus upon those that are commonly used in strategic decision-making. Table 7.1 outlines the heuristics that are examined further in this chapter.

Each of these heuristics is now addressed in turn.

Anchor and adjustment heuristic

This heuristic was first identified by Daniel Kahneman and Amos Tversky in the 1970s. As noted above, it can be defined as making "estimates by starting from an initial value that is adjusted to yield the final answer" (Tversky and Kahneman, 1982: 14). Individuals try to get "close" to the right answer and then make adjustments from the initial point by obtaining and using additional information as it becomes available (Presutti, 1995). To cite a single example, participants in an experiment were asked to estimate the percentage of African countries in the United Nations. Respondents gave different answers

Table 7.1 Cognitive heuristics explored in this chapter

Heuristic	*Definition*
Anchor and adjustment	Making "estimates by starting from an initial value that is adjusted to yield the final answer" (Tversky and Kahneman, 1982: 14).
Availability	The assumption that an event's probability is directly related to the frequency with which it has occurred in the past (Tversky and Kahneman, 1982). Hence, the easier something is to remember, the more important it seems (Greenberg and Baron, 2008).
Representative	A judgment of probability of the degree to which A resembles B (Tversky and Kahneman, 1972) or to situations in which people judge things on the basis of how well they match particular stereotypes (Buchanan and Huczynski, 2019).
Moral	"Decision rules that generate intuitions about fairness and justice, punitiveness and approval, right and wrong" (Cosmides and Tooby, 2006: 181).
Conjunctive	"Minimum cut-offs are established for each attribute. If an alternative does not exceed all the cut-offs for all attributes, it is rejected" (Lee and Geistfeld, 1998: 230).
Elimination By Aspects (EBA)	"The most important attribute is selected, and all alternatives not exceeding the cut-off with regard to this attribute are eliminated. The attribute that is second in importance is then selected and the elimination process continues until only one alternative remains" (Lee and Geistfeld, 1998: 230).
Weighted Additive (WADD)	This occurs where "good values on one attribute can offset bad values on another" (Payne et al., 1993: 29). This heuristic "considers the value of each alternative on all the relevant attributes and considers all the relevant importance or weights of the attributes to the decision-maker" (Payne et al., 1993: 24).

depending upon whether they given 10% or 65% as a "starting point" (Tversky and Kahneman, 1974). Because the initial value provided an anchor from which they could adjust, the estimated percentages were significantly higher when people were initially exposed to a high number rather than a low number. This example has been cited by several authors (see for instance LeBoeuf and Shafir, 2005; Simmons et al., 2010), and although this concept was first illustrated by Tversky and Kahneman (1974), it has been confirmed many times since (see for instance Chapman and Bornstein, 1996; Wong and Kwong, 2000).

Strategic decisions made using this heuristic

Development of strategy is often based on this heuristic. A US local government manager explained how she developed her five-year business plan.

> I know broadly where I need to be heading over the next five years, but I can't magic up a strategy from nothing. Imagine saying to taxpayers that I'm going to spend $100 million but I can't explain why I'm doing it. I am accountable. The strategy has to be based on something. I know what's worked and what hasn't worked. I have a

series of fixed points, and I base my plans on these. I know where my department's strengths are and I know where I am weaker. So, I need to build on my strengths and minimise or manage my weaknesses. I have a starting point and then I build on it.

(Local Government, USA)

The situation is similar in the UK, as the following comment illustrates:

You can't develop a business plan out of thin air. You need somewhere to start from. So what you do is look at your last plan and then use that as the basis for your new plan. You keep the bits that worked and you modify the things that didn't work.

(Family Support)

Target setting flows from the overall strategy.

Our targets set the strategy for the department. They tell us what we need to do, which direction we need to travel in, and how we're going to get there. We have long-term targets over five years, then we have annual targets so we can stay on course. They tell us what to do, not how to do it. They set the direction in broad brushstrokes, and then I get my managers to nail down the detail.

(Local authority, USA)

When setting annual targets for the coming year, managers developed their new targets by adjusting from a fixed anchor point. The following comments were typical:

Our income targets for the coming year are normally just last year's target plus 3% or so.

(Local authority, UK)

Performance targets for next year are based on this year's performance plus a few percent more.

(Local authority, UK)

Budget-setting follows from target setting. A UK health manager explained that "a budget is only a plan. That's all it is. It's a plan that's expressed in terms of money". Managers have to set long-term budgets over several years, but they also have to set annual budgets. "The process is the same. It doesn't matter if it's a five year plan or a one-year budget" (Health service, UK). In essence, these decisions were made in the same way as those relating to strategy development, as the following comments illustrate:

Suppose you have a savings target of 25% over five years. You start from your current budget and take slices off it a bit at a time until you get to your 25%. Then you look to see if the result is viable.

(Local Government, UK)

I make my [budget] decisions for next year based on the present position. This year is the starting point, and I adjust my savings target down from this until I get to the final target.

(Local Government, UK)

In these cases, managers deliberately start from the previous year's budget (i.e. the anchor point) and adjust accordingly to achieve the desired savings. The major difference from the strategy development process was that the objective was set externally (i.e. the final budget), not the anchor point, and it was up to decision-makers to determine how this would be achieved. In the case of strategy development, individual managers had much more freedom to operate.

Planning of large-scale civic events is common in local government contexts. These are strategic decisions because they fit into an overall plan and earmark significant funding and resources for many years, and they can impact upon many different organisations. Extreme examples might be the Olympic Games or Commonwealth Games. However, more common events are those such as July 4th parades in the US and the Lord Mayor's Parade in the UK. These form part of a larger programme of events that take place through the year, which include sporting events, pop concerts, and cultural activities. Again, the anchor and adjustment heuristic is used to make key decisions, and the following quote was typical:

> I'm planning years ahead. There might be a theme for a year. Maybe it's an anniversary – World War Two or something – and there will be a whole series of themed events around that. I'll be working with lots of different organisations . . . police, the government, health, maybe the military, all sorts. I have some fixed events too – Bonfire night. Others too. I'll schedule all the other events around these – making adjustments and modifications around this framework. I have my starting points and I then adjust from that.
>
> (Local authority, UK)

> The 4th of July is sacrosanct. That is fixed come rain or shine. There are a few events like that. Thanksgiving is another. Everything has to fit around these. I have my givens and then I adjust everything else around them. Gradually, more things become fixed – maybe a pop group is only available at a particular time. So that gets fixed, and I keep adjusting until the schedule is full.
>
> (Local authority, USA)

Once again, the strategy is planned around a number of fixed points, and then adjustments are made. The process is repeated and refined until the programme is completed. This iterative process is common in decisions such as these.

Availability heuristic

The availability heuristic can be defined as "the ease with which one can bring to mind exemplars of an event" (Folkes, 1988: 13). In essence, "people use the ease with which examples can be brought to mind as a cue for estimating the probability of [an event]" (Keller et al., 2006: 632). Thus, people may base their judgments on information that is readily available, even though it might not be accurate (Greenberg and Baron, 2008). Many instances of this heuristic in action are provided in the literature, but a single example is presented below as an illustration. In an often-repeated study, participants are given a list of well-known people containing both men and women and are asked to judge whether there are more men or women in the list. The actual numbers of men and women are identical but estimates are usually skewed in one direction or the other. The availability heuristic is suggested as the explanation, since the degree of fame (or infamy) of the people in the list influences the ease of recall, and hence distorts the estimates (See for instance Hertwig et al., 1999; Tversky and Kahneman, 1973, 1974).

Strategic decisions made using this heuristic

The use of this heuristic in strategic decision-making is relatively uncommon, but when it happens, the results can be significant. For example, in a UK local authority, the Head of Community Safety recalled how her entire department's strategy changed because of a single murder:

> I had developed a long-term strategy to improve the crime rate in the city. . . . It was all logical and planned, and it was based around facts and figures, and then it was derailed by a single incident. We had a 17-year-old mother who was stabbed to death. You remember things that have gone wrong more easily than things that worked well. They just pop into your head, and [they] influence how you develop your strategy. You arrange things to prevent the bad thing happening again – even if it was just a single case. Just because of that one incident, a task force was established to put measures in place to stop it happening again. Our whole strategy changed as a result. All your plans are forgotten about.

What was significant about this case, from the perspective of this heuristic, was the emotional impact it had on the decision-maker because this was instrumental in calling the incident to mind:

> You remember it because it affected you. . . . There's the whole debate around being a mother at 17. You can't fail to have an opinion on that one way or the other – so it affects you. Then you've got a young baby who's lost its mother. As a mother myself, that has an effect. . . . Logic tells you that you can't possibly prevent every single stabbing, but at the back of your mind, you can't help wondering whether there was something you could have done differently.

It is clear from this account that the availability heuristic was at work. An incident came to mind, and this incident caused the manager to change her plans.

When we were conducting research for this book, the only times we discovered this heuristic in strategic decision-making was where those concerned were involved in enforcement activity of some kind. The following account was typical:

> You only remember the bad things, and so you don't take account of things like frequency. A single event can make you blow things out of all proportion. I had neighbourhood officers patrolling the streets to help the police. It didn't occur to me that men and women would be treated differently by the public. The patrols had been going on daily for about four months, then one of my girls – a female officer – was attacked. She went to hospital and she was OK, but that one incident changed the whole strategy. I increased the number of patrols. I made sure that women never patrolled that area again. I made sure that women never patrolled alone. I gave

everyone panic alarms. That one incident was one too many. Logically, I should have looked at the fact that nothing had happened in four months, and I should have treated it as a blip . . . an anomaly. But all I could think about was this incident. It was in my mind constantly. It cost us a fortune, but it was worth it.

(Local authority, USA)

It is interesting that this heuristic was only found in enforcement-related situations, but we do not claim that this is the only time it occurs. What do you think?

Question

1 Can you think of any occasions where the availability heuristic might be used to develop strategic decisions?

Representative heuristic

The representative heuristic is based on the similarity of one thing to another. Indeed, Atkinson et al. (1996: 306) note that it is also known as the "similarity heuristic". It refers to a judgment of probability of the degree to which A resembles B (Tversky and Kahneman, 1972). Examples include judging the probability that an object or event A belongs to class or process B (Tversky and Kahneman, 1982); judging the probability that a sample A came from a population, B, or that A is an effect and B was the cause (Wickham, 2006); and judging the probability of an event on the basis of how well it represents the process that generated it (Wickham, 2003). This heuristic is used "whenever we judge the likelihood of something by intuitively comparing it with our preconceived ideas of a few characteristics that we believe represent a category" (Gross, 2001: 300)

A commonly cited example concerns 'Mrs Hill': "Mrs Hill is not in the best health and she has to wear glasses to see. Her hair is grey and she has wrinkles. She walks kind of hunched over" (Fisk et al., 2006: 498). In this case, research suggests that the representative heuristic is generally used to determine that it is more likely that Mrs Hill is old than that she works in a restaurant (Fisk et al., 2006). The representative heuristic has also been applied to real-life practical situations. To quote a single example, Garb (1996) argues that when making a diagnosis that a patient has schizophrenia a clinician is likely to use the representative heuristic because the patient can be compared to a typical patient with schizophrenia, or the typical symptoms of schizophrenia can be compared to the present case.

Strategic decisions made using this heuristic

Stereotyping is one form of this heuristic. The public are perceived to have certain expectations, and these are used to make strategic decisions. Once again, the planning of civic events is involved. These are regarded as strategic decisions because they involve setting the direction of many different organisations and involve substantial sums of money.

We plan for events months, or even years in advance. Stereotyping is fundamental. We assume that the public want to see the event, but we can't be sure. It's predicting

> the future. We stereotype the public. We make assumptions about which demographics might be most interested. How else can you do it?
>
> (Local authority, USA)

The same rationale was found in the UK:

> You use stereotypes. You make assumptions that the public will want to see such and such and thing and then you arrange it. You don't have time to consult properly so you have to make assumptions.
>
> (Local authority, UK)

On one such occasion, an event was planned in the UK which was based on a similar event that had happened in France some years earlier. This had involved a large display that wound its way through the city's streets.

> You remember how well the [event] went down with the French, and you stereotype on that basis. Because the [event] was popular over there, you assume that it will be popular here too, and so you make all the arrangements without any objective idea of what will really happen.
>
> (Local authority, UK)

However, this approach can have its problems. When the event in question took place in the UK, there was chaos. Traffic jams were caused; many arterial roads were blocked; the emergency services were severely hampered; and there was considerable public dissatisfaction.

> We made a big mistake. We looked at how the French public behave for this kind of event. They get there early and wait patiently for the [event] to pass by, and then they go home. We assumed that the British public would behave in the same way [but they didn't]. The British still arrived nice and early, but when the [event] came past, they started to follow it instead of going home like the French do. So, by the time we got to town, there were massive crowds everywhere and there was gridlock. We'd have been better off looking at how the British behave at big events and using that as our benchmark. We used the wrong crowd behaviour stereotype.
>
> (Local authority, UK)

Interestingly, although using this heuristic caused a problem, the manager felt that the issues were attributable to the wrong stereotype and not to a fundamental problem with the process. We have already encountered heuristics in event management (the anchor and adjustment heuristic), and therefore this demonstrates that multiple heuristics might be used in a single situation.

Moral heuristic

Moral heuristics can be defined as "decision rules that generate intuitions about fairness and justice, punitiveness and approval, right and wrong" (Cosmides and Tooby, 2006: 181). This can be illustrated by several examples, including:

- "Always keep your promise" (Bartsch and Wright, 2005: 546).
- "Avoid and punish betrayals of trust" (Koehler and Gershoff, 2005: 556).

- "Be honest" (Weirich, 2005: 564).
- "It is wrong to hurt some people for the benefit of others" (Hahn et al., 2005: 552).

These examples demonstrate that whereas other intuitive heuristics have been generalised (e.g. 'the' availability heuristic, 'the' representative heuristic), moral heuristics in the literature are very specific. Sunstein (2005) argues that moral heuristics are rules that lead decision-makers to jump to intuitive moral conclusions, and he presents two related hypothetical scenarios (originally formulated by Thomson, 1985), which are sometimes referred to as the "trolley versus footbridge" problem:

> The . . . trolley problem, asks people to suppose that a runaway trolley is headed for five people, who will be killed if the trolley continues on its current course. The question is whether you would throw a switch that would move the trolley onto another set of tracks, killing one person rather than five. Most people would throw the switch. The . . . footbridge problem, is the same as that just given, but with one difference: the only way to save the five is to throw a stranger, now on a footbridge that spans the tracks, into the path of the trolley, killing that stranger but preventing the trolley from reaching the others. Most people will not kill the stranger. But what is the difference between the two cases?
>
> (Sunstein, 2005: 540)

This problem has been researched extensively in many different forms (see for instance Greene et al., 2009; Waldmann and Wiegmann, 2010), and studies show that people are less opposed to throwing the switch than to pushing a bystander onto the tracks.

Strategic decisions made using this heuristic

The use of moral heuristics when setting future policy was especially common in areas such as bereavement, where there are rarely any 'right' answers. This is illustrated in case study 7a, with quotes from the Bereavement Manager.

Case study 7a Recycling heat from cremations

Background

Within the UK, there is a legal requirement for crematoria to install specialist equipment to remove mercury from cremation gases.

> The biggest piece of expenditure is the boiler unit. This doesn't act like a normal boiler, which heats things up from cold – this works the opposite way. It reduces the heat from the cremation emissions from 1300°C down to about 200°C, and only then are the emissions fed through the equipment. Now, all this heat has to go somewhere.

The manager had to make a decision to determine what would happen to this excess heat.

Decision

> I decided to recycle it and use it to heat the chapels. It was just a case of installing a heat exchange plate, and we've connected to the water from here and reuse the heat. Looking at the costings, it only cost around five or six grand to put the equipment in place, but on a normal day's operating at [the crematorium], we can now provide enough heat to heat a leisure centre – swimming pool, central heating, and water supply. That's how much heat we can reuse – huge savings. We don't have a choice with the mercury abatement. It's a legal requirement, but it's a change to the strategy of the council.

Justification for the decision

When the manager explained how he made this decision, it was clear that moral heuristics were key:

> I've had to make a moral decision. There are moral issues about recycling heat from cremations. Some would argue that we're saving money from the dead, and that it's gruesome. But there is another moral aspect too. We're living in a green and environmental age. There's a moral argument that we should be conserving energy and recycling whatever we can – other morality comes into play. Then there's a third argument. If we could save this amount of money it would mean that we can keep our charges down. It could be argued that morally we shouldn't charge the earth for our services at a time when families are at their lowest ebb. You can't reconcile all sides of the argument. I've tried. I've spent ages going over the arguments in my mind, and I can't find a way to satisfy all extremes. So, I've done what I believe to be morally right. I've installed the plant.

The consequences of the decision are unclear

> I realise that this is one of those situations where there isn't a 'right answer' and that plenty of people will disagree with me, and I'm expecting a lot of criticism. I can take that so long as I feel that it's the right thing to do in my own mind.

Questions

1 Do you think the Bereavement Manager was right to take the action he did?
2 Why do you feel this way?

In this case, there is no "right or wrong" answer. The manager had to make the decision on the basis of what he believed to be right.

Thus far, we have looked at heuristics in isolation. However, we have seen with event management that more than one heuristic may be used within a single situation. The following pages explore large-scale public procurements. As will be seen, these involve the use of three heuristics in combination.

Discussion 3.3 Potential issues in using cognitive heuristics

By definition, cognitive heuristics use shortcuts and do not consider all possible factors. If I am only using part of the information, how do I know that I am using the right part? How do I know that I am not missing out something important? If I am making decisions drawn from my personal experience (for instance), then does this leave me open to bias and distortion? Issues such as these have led to a considerable debate in the literature, and two schools of thought have emerged.

The first of these is the **heuristics and biases** school. This is associated with Daniel Kahneman and Amos Tversky. Their research focused on the effectiveness of heuristics, the errors that resulted from their use, and how these errors might be overcome, or at least managed (Tversky and Kahneman, 1972, 1973, 1974). Since then, many others have taken a similar position (e.g. Greenberg and Baron, 2008; Slovic et al., 2004), and the fact that these decisions are sometimes regarded as flawed has resulted in a considerable effort to find ways to improve heuristic decision-making (Bryant, 2007; De Neys and Feremans, 2013). Essentially, the argument is that:

- Heuristics exist.
- Heuristics only use part of the available information. Thus, they are inherently flawed.
- Heuristics lead to error.
- The use of heuristics should be avoided, or at least minimised, because normative models give better decisions.

The second school of thought is the **fast and frugal** school. This is particularly associated with Gerd Gigerenzer. This suggests that people make rapid decisions (i.e. "fast") using only part of the available information (i.e. "frugal") (Gigerenzer, 2008). This research seeks to understand how heuristics operate (Katsikopoulos, 2009), and "rules" have been proposed that seek to explain how heuristics are used when searching for a solution. These include starting rules (i.e. what triggers the search?), searching rules (i.e. how is the search conducted?), and stopping rules (i.e. what causes the search to end?) (Goldstein and Gigerenzer, 2009). Essentially, the argument is that:

- Heuristics exist.
- Heuristics only use part of the available information. This makes them efficient because they are a good use of time, knowledge and resources.

- Heuristics do not inherently lead to error.
- The use of heuristics should be encouraged because they are at least as effective as normative models.

In other words, there is general agreement about the existence of heuristics, and there is a broad consensus about how they operate. Beyond this, however, there is considerable disagreement.

Cognitive heuristics in the strategic procurement process

Large procurements are the most complex type of public sector procurement and typically take more than a year to complete. There are many legal and regulatory constraints built into the process. By law, procurements for contracts that exceed specified values must be advertised in the Official Journal of the European Union (OJEU) and follow a series of prescribed stages. At the time of writing, the threshold relevant to this book was €5,350,000 for public sector and utility works contracts or contracts involving civil engineering activities. As shown above, large-scale procurements are regarded as being strategic decisions because they set the course of action for the organisation for perhaps the next 10–25 years (Murray, 2011; Walker, 2007).

First we will present an outline of three heuristics which are commonly used in strategic procurement, and then we illustrate the use of these heuristics in a case study, which contains quotes from several public sector managers to illustrate their thinking.

Conjunctive heuristic

The conjunctive heuristic is defined as: "minimum cut-offs are established for each attribute. If an alternative does not exceed all the cut-offs for all attributes, it is rejected" (Lee and Geistfeld, 1998: 230. In other words, it consists of a series of must-have or must-not-have criteria, all of which must be met. If all of the must-have and all of the must-not-have rules are satisfied, the alternative will be considered further (Hauser, 2014). For example, a house that is unaffordable will be rejected regardless of its features or location. In other words, it fails to meet a minimum level of desirability for at least one of its attributes (Elrod et al., 2004). Some authors regard this heuristic as a variation on bounded rationality (Johnson et al., 1989) because for a given alternative to be selected, it must be "good enough" on the key attributes (Gilbride and Allenby, 2006).

This heuristic can have different forms. The above definition states that values must be "exceeded" in order for a given alternative to be considered further, and this implies a "maximum" value (Zhu and Givan, 2005). For instance, the requirement might be the number of years' work experience above a certain point (Elrod et al., 2004). However, the converse might also be true, with a "minimum" value being important, such as only alternatives with prices below a certain threshold being considered (Zhu and Givan, 2005).

Elimination By Aspects (EBA) heuristic

Alternatives are described by the attributes or aspects that they possess. The decision-maker places different levels of importance on each of these aspects (Gilbride and Allenby,

2006). This heuristic is defined as occurring when: "the most important attribute is selected, and all alternatives not exceeding the cut-off with regard to this attribute are eliminated" (Lee and Geistfeld, 1998: 230). An alternative interpretation of this heuristic is that the decision-maker selects an aspect and eliminates all alternatives that do not have that aspect (Hauser, 2014). A slight refinement is offered by Yee et al. (2007), who suggest that eliminating an aspect is effectively the same as accepting its complement. As an example, when shopping, people typically have a set of brands that they will consider buying from a product category. This set is derived by eliminating certain aspects. For instance, all coffees below a certain price might form the consideration set, with those above this price being eliminated (Fader and McAlister, 1990).

Weighted additive (WADD) heuristic

The WADD heuristic considers the value of each alternative on all the relevant attributes and considers the relevant importance of the attributes to the decision-maker. The relative importance, or weight, reflects "the extent to which one is willing to trade attribute values" (Payne et al., 1993: 24), and the weighted 'scores' "are summed to yield the overall value" (Shah and Oppenheimer, 2008: 207). As an example, when purchasing a car, a customer could consider range of factors relating to several cars, including price, fuel efficiency, reliability, and so forth. Each factor could be weighted by the consumer to reflect their relative importance to him/her. Suppose that reliability was felt to be the most important attribute, with a low price also being desirable: in this case, reliability would receive the highest weighting, and trade-offs could be made so that high reliability could compensate for a high price (Cimarosti, 2009).

This strategy involves substantial computational processing of the information. The decision-maker needs to assess the importance of each attribute and assign a subjective value to each possible attribute level. Then, the decision-maker considers one alternative at a time, evaluates each of the attributes of the alternative in question, multiplies each attribute's subjective value by its weight, and sums these products across all of the attributes to obtain an overall evaluation for each alternative. Finally, the alternative with the highest value is selected (Cimarosti, 2009).

The combination of these heuristics is illustrated in case study 7b.

Case study 7b UK local authority contract procurement

Background

The decision was made to let a contract to procure a contract. This would include highways design and maintenance, lighting maintenance, traffic signal maintenance, and street cleansing. The contract would have a ten-year duration and would cover the whole city. The total contract value was approximately £380m, and this put the contract well above the *de minimis* threshold required by the EU. Therefore, there was a legal requirement to follow the prescribed procedures and timescales, and the total procurement took 18 months to complete.

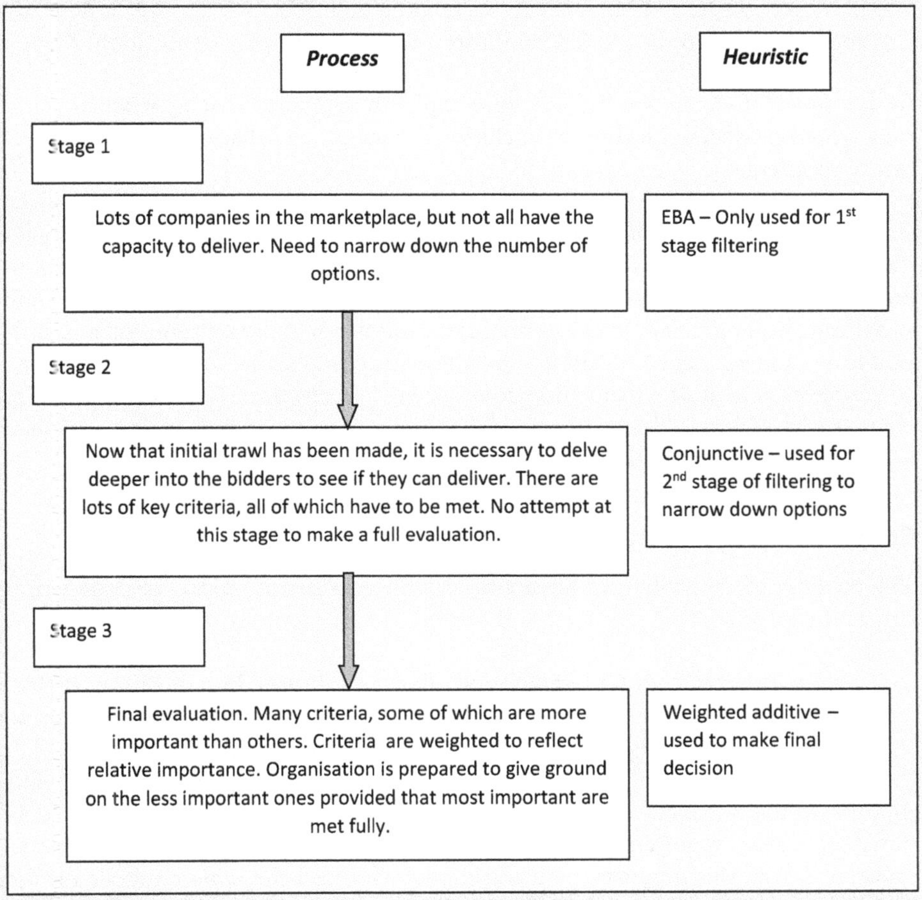

Figure 6.2 Conceptual model of strategic procurement process

When the procurement process is analysed, it can be seen that there are three main stages. Figure 6.2 offers a conceptual model of the procurement, and it illustrates that each of these stages is linked to a particular heuristic.

Stage 1: Elimination By Aspects (EBA) heuristic

The purpose of this stage of the procurement was the need to reduce the number of applications that need to be assessed in detail. This supports the literature, which offers the same rationale for the use of this heuristic (Shah and Oppenheimer, 2008). The following quote from a senior manager was typical:

> You don't physically have the time to go into detail with all bidders. You need a quick way to get the numbers to a more manageable level. When we got the

> bids back, we had 63 bidders who were interested. We couldn't look at them all, and so we had to do a 'quick and dirty' trawl to try to get the numbers down.

In the case of the contract, bidders were explicitly informed that a particular criterion would be deemed to be an "exclusion" criterion and that it was vital to meet this to progress.

The choice of which criterion is essential is determined by the nature of the contract, and a number of factors are typically used as EBA cut-off criteria. Capacity was used where contracts were so large or so diverse that it would be difficult to provide a common standard of service with a series of small contracts, such as adult social care. Strategic fit was an essential criterion where contract required a significant level of investment and had significant political implications, such as in the case of the development of a major shopping centre. Perhaps the most common option is a financial appraisal. Essentially, if a bid does not meet this criterion, it is excluded regardless of how strong the rest of the bid might be.

Stage 2: Conjunctive heuristic

The purpose of this stage is to further reduce the number of bidders. As one senior manager explained:

> We'd started off with 63 bidders, and after the first weeding out [using EBA], we still had 32 companies who'd made it through. That's still far too many to deal with, and so we put all the bids through a second stage.

Apart from the single cutoff criterion outlined above, there were a number of additional mandatory requirements – all of which had to be met in order for the bid to proceed. Again, this supports the literature, which offers the same rationale for the use of this heuristic (Zhu and Givan, 2005). Examples of such criteria were given by a senior manager

> Did the company have good references? Did they have the appropriate insurances? . . . Did they have experience of doing this kind of work before on this kind of scale? Did they have the capacity to deliver, or were they too small? Were the directors bankrupt or barred from running a company. Failure against any one of these things meant that the company was out.

Again, bidders had been notified of these mandatory criteria upfront and were, therefore, able to take this into account in their planning. A senior manager highlighted the impact of the measures taken thus far:

> After we'd been through the two stages, we only had 11 bids who'd got through all the hurdles out of the 63 we started with. That was still a bit large, but it wasn't unmanageable. We decided to invite them all to tender.
>
> (Corporate Performance)

Up to this point, in the contract "quick and dirty" methods had been used to reduce the number of bids being assessed. However, now that the organisation was in a position to invite the successful bidders to submit a formal tender, the WADD heuristic was used to make the final decision, and this is discussed below.

Stage 3: WADD heuristic

The purpose of this stage is to drill down into the detail of the remaining bids.

A range of documentation was issued as part of the Invitation to Tender, which provided bidders with details of the evaluation process and how the scoring of tenders would be undertaken. The following weightings were applied (Figure 6.3):

Subject	*Weighting*
Business continuity and quality management	5%
Equal opportunities	20%
Details of 'key persons' and management	5%
Health and safety	20%
Method statement	50%
Total	**100%**

Figure 6.3 Weightings applied to the contract

The method statement outlines how services will be delivered "on the ground": Senior managers emphasised its importance.

> It sets out how a company plans to deliver the contract. How they plan to do it], how performance will be measured. Things like that. It looks at the practicalities. How much will it cost? How will they work alongside us and our other partners? What innovation will they bring? How will they physically do the work? How many people? What equipment?

This was felt to be the most important part of the bid, and it therefore carried 50% of the total mark. However, even if a company was perfect on this aspect, which is unlikely, they'd still only score 50%, so they need to be good on the other sections too if they want to win the contract. Thus, the weightings seek to balance financial and non-financial factors in order to achieve value for money.

Each of the weightings contained sub-elements which where themselves weighted, but the precise details are not necessary for this chapter. It is sufficient to say that the calculation is both onerous and complex. The different parts of the bid were graded separately, and the weightings were applied to arrive at a final mark for the overall bid. The bid with the highest weighted score was deemed to be the preferred bidder and was called in for detailed clarification discussions before being awarded the contract.

Questions

1 Do you feel as though this decision-making process is appropriate for a decision of this type?
2 Are there any other processes that might require the use of multiple heuristics?
3 Why might this decision be made differently in the private sector?

It can be seen from the foregoing that "procurement heuristics" are different from the other heuristics presented earlier in this chapter. They are structured and have a series of predefined steps that are applied consciously and logically, whereas those such as representative and availability are more intuitive and more likely to be applied unconsciously. There are indeed different categories of heuristics in the literature, but a full discussion is outside the scope of this book. Interested readers might wish to read the work of Daniel Kahneman and Gerd Gigerenzer to more fully explore some of the debates in this field.

7.3 Chapter summary

This chapter has outlined the use of cognitive heuristics in strategic decision-making. The following key points were identified:

- Strategic decisions are not always based on a logical and analytical assessment of the situation. Instead, they are often made using cognitive heuristics. These are mental short-cuts, or "decision rules" that are part of everyone, and they are largely unavoidable.
- There are many different heuristics that are used by managers – largely unconsciously on many occasions. These include anchor and adjustment, availability, representative, and moral heuristics.
- Some heuristics can be used consciously. Examples include EBA, conjunctive, and WADD – all of which are often used in strategic procurement decisions.
- We do not argue that heuristics are "good" or "bad". In this chapter, we merely show that they are prevalent, and therefore need to be understood.

Self-assessment questions

- Compare and contrast the different cognitive heuristics identified in this chapter – anchor/adjustment, availability, representative, moral, EBA, conjunctive, WADD
- To what extent do you think that you use cognitive heuristics yourself? Can you think of any times where you might have used heuristics?
- In which situations do you think normative models might be more appropriate and in which situations do you think that heuristics might be more appropriate? Why?
- Which heuristics might you be likely to find in health services? Why?
- Given that strategy is effectively trying to predict the future, by definition, there is uncertainty. In what ways do you think heuristics might be able to reduce the level of uncertainty? How? Why?

References

Apte, C. & Hong, S. J. (1995). Predicting equity returns from securities data. In *Advances in Knowledge Discovery & Data Mining*. Palo Alto, CA: AAAI Press.

Atkinson, R. L., Atkinson, R. C., Smith, E. E., Ben, D. J. & Nolen-Hoeksema, S. (1996). *Hilgard's Introduction to Psychology* (12th edn.). Fort Worth: Harcourt Brace.

Bartsch, K. & Wright, J. C. (2005). Towards an intuitionist account of moral development. *Behavioral and Brain Sciences*, 28(4), 546–547.

Bryant, E (2007). Self-regulation and decision heuristics in entrepreneurial opportunity evaluation and exploitation. *Management Decision*, 45(4), 732–748.

Buchanan, D. A. & Huczynski, A. (2019). *Organizational Behaviour: An Introductory Text* (10th ed.). Harlow: Pearson Education.

Chapman, G. B. & Bornstein, B. H. (1996). The more you ask for, the more you get: Anchoring in personal injury verdicts. *Applied Cognitive Psychology*, 10, 519–540.

Cimarosti, A. (2009). *Survey Answering Behavior in Conjoint Analysis*. University of Bern: Masters Thesis.

Cosmides, L. & Tooby, J. (2006). Evolutionary psychology, moral heuristics and the law. In G. Gigerenzer & C. Engel (Eds.), *Heuristics and the Law (Dahlem Workshop Report 94)*. Cambridge, MA: MIT Press, pp. 181–212.

De Neys, W. & Feremans, V. (2013). Development of heuristic bias detection in elementary school. *Developmental Psychology*, 49(2), 258–269.

Elrod, T., Johnson, R. D. & White, J. (2004). A new integrated model of noncompensatory and compensatory decision strategies. *Organizational Behavior and Human Decision Processes*, 95, 1–19.

Fader, P. S. & McAlister, L. (1990). An elimination by aspects model of consumer response to promotion calibrated on UPC scanner data. *Journal of Marketing Research*, 27, 322–332.

Fisk, J. E., Bury, A. S. & Holden, R. (2006). Reasoning about complex probabilistic concepts in childhood. *Scandinavian Journal of Psychology*, 47, 497–504.

Folkes, V. S. (1988). The availability heuristic and perceived risk. *Journal of Consumer Research*, 15, 13–23.

Garb, H. N. (1996). The representativeness and past-behavior heuristics in clinical judgment. *Professional Psychology: Research and Practice*, 27(3), 272–277.

Gigerenzer, G. (2008). Why heuristics work. *Perspectives on Psychological Science*, 3(1), 20–29.

Gilbride, T. J. & Allenby, G. M. (2006). Estimating heterogeneous EBA and economic screening rule choice models. *Marketing Science*, 25(5), 494–509.

Goldstein, D. G. & Gigerenzer, G. (2009). Fast and frugal forecasting. *International Journal of Forecasting*, 25(4), 760–772.

Greenberg, J. & Baron, R. A. (2008). *Behavior in Organizations* (9th edn.). London: Pearson Education.

Greene, J. D., Cushman, F. A., Stewart, L. E., Lowenberg, K., Nystrom, L. E. & Cohen, J. D. (2009). Pushing moral buttons: The interaction between personal force and intention in moral judgment. *Cognition*, 111, 364–371.

Gross, R (2001). *Psychology: The Science of Mind and Behaviour* (4th edn). London: Hodder and Stoughton.

Hahn, U., Frost, J.-M. & Maio, G. (2005). What's in a heuristic? *Behavioral and Brain Sciences*, 28(4), 551–552.

Hardin, W. III. (1999). Behavioral research into heuristics and bias as an academic pursuit: Lessons from other disciplines and implications for real estate. *Journal of Property Investment & Finance*, 17(4), 333–352.

Hauser, J. R. (2014). Consideration-set heuristics. *Journal of Business Research*, 67, 1688–1699.

Hertwig, R., Hoffrage, U. & Martignon, L. (1999). Quick estimation: Letting the environment do the work. In G. Gigerenzer & P. M. Todd (Eds.), *Simple Heuristics That Make Us Smart*. New York: Oxford University Press, pp. 209–234.

Johnson, E. J., Meyer, R. J. & Ghose, S. (1989). When choice models fail: Compensatory models in negatively correlated environments. *Journal of Marketing Research*, 26, 255–270.

Katsikopoulos, K. (2009). The conceptual connection between lens models and fast and frugal heuristics: A process approach. *Theory and Psychology*, 19(5), 688–697.

Keller, C., Siegrist, M. & Gutscher, H. (2006). The role of the affect and availability heuristics in risk communication. *Risk Analysis*, 26(3), 631–639.

Koehler, J. J. & Gershoff, A. D. (2005). Betrayal aversion is reasonable. *Behavioral and Brain Sciences*, 28(4), 556–557.

LeBoeuf, R. A. & Shafir, E. (2005). Anchoring on the here and now: Insufficient adjustment in time and distance estimates. *Advances in Consumer Research*, 32(1), 126–127.

Lee, J. & Geistfeld, L. V. (1998). Enhancing consumer choice: Are we making appropriate recommendations? *The Journal of Consumer Affairs*, 32(2), 227–251.

Murray, J. G. (2011). 'Third sector commissioning and English local government procurement. *Public Money & Management*, 31(4), 279–286.

Payne, J. W., Bettman, J. R. & Johnson, E. J. (1993). *The Adaptive Decision-Maker*. Cambridge: Cambridge University Press.

Presutti, A. H. (1995). Anchor and adjustment heuristic effect on audit judgement. *Managerial Auditing Journal*, 10(9), 13–21.

Shah, A. K. & Oppenheimer, D. M. (2008). Heuristics made easy: An effort-reduction framework. *Psychological Bulletin*, 134(2) 207–222.

Simmons, J. P., LeBoeuf, R. A. & Nelson, L. D. (2010). The effect of accuracy motivation on anchoring and adjustment: Do people adjust from provided anchors? *American Psychological Association*, 99(6), 917–932.

Slovic, P., Finucane, M. L., Peters, E. & MacGregor, D. G. (2004). Risk as analysis and risk as feelings; some thoughts about affect, risk and rationality. *Risk Analysis*, 24(2), 311–322.

Sunstein, C. R. (2005). Moral heuristics. *Behavioral and Brain Sciences*, 28(4), 531–542.

Thomson, J. J. (1985). The trolley problem. *Yale Law Journal*, 94, 1395–1415.

Tversky, A. & Kahneman, D. (1972). Subjective probability: A judgment of representativeness. *Cognitive Psychology*, 3(3), 430–454.

Tversky, A. & Kahneman, D. (1973). Availability: A heuristic for judging frequency and probability. *Cognitive Psychology*, 5(2), 207–232.

Tversky, A. & Kahneman, D. (1974). Judgment under uncertainty: Heuristics and biases. *Science*, 185, 1124–1131.

Tversky, A. & Kahneman, D. (1982). Judgement under uncertainty: Heuristics and biases. In D. Kahneman, P. Slovic, & A. Tversky (Eds.), *Judgement Under Uncertainty: Heuristics and Biases*. Cambridge: Cambridge University Press, pp. 3–22.

Waldmann, M. R., & Wiegmann, A. (2010). A double causal contrast theory of moral intuitions in trolley dilemmas. In S. Ohlsson & R. Catrambone (Eds.), *Proceedings of the 32nd Annual Conference of the Cognitive Science Society*. Austin, TX: Cognitive Science Society.

Walker, N. (2007). The strategic commissioner's box of tricks. *Housing, Care and Support*, 10(4), 32–38.

Weirich, P. (2005). Regulation of risks. *Behavioral and Brain Sciences*, 28(4), 564–565.

Wickham, P. A. (2003). The representativeness heuristic in judgements involving entrepreneurial success and failure. *Management Decision*, 41(2), 156–167.

Wickham, P. A. (2006). How to become an effective – bias-free – decision-maker in an increasingly global economy. *Handbook of Business Strategy*, 7(1), 57–62.

Wong, K. F. E. & Kwong, J. Y. Y. (2000). Is 7300 m equal to 7.3 km? Same semantics but different anchoring effects. *Organizational Behavior and Human Decision Processes*, 82, 314–333.

Yee, M., Dahan, E., Hauser, J. R. & Orlin, J. (2007). Greedoid-based noncompensatory inference. *Marketing Science*, 26(4), 532–549.

Zhu, L. & Givan, R. (2005). Simultaneous heuristic search for conjunctive subgoals. *Proceedings of the 20th National Conference on Artificial Intelligence*, 3, 1235–1241.

Section 4

Strategic tools in practice

Chapter 8

Current debates within strategy as practice, neo-institutional theory, and workshops

Learning outcomes

After reading this chapter you should be able to:

- define "strategy as practice"
- develop an appreciation of **social constructionist theory**
- appreciate the nature and affordances of a strategy workshop

Pre-chapter questions

- Does strategy always work in the real world the way it is supposed to according to the literature? Can you think of any examples of when it doesn't?

Key terms

- Workshop – "arrangement whereby a group of people learn, acquire new knowledge, perform creative problem-solving, or innovate in relation to a domain-specific issue" (Ørngreen and Levinsen, 2017: 72).
- Strategy as practice – the study of the practice of making or undertaking strategy

8.1 Introduction: strategy as practice

A critical and recent arena of research, strategy as practice (SAP), addresses the limitations of mechanistic traditional strategy (Farjoun, 2002) as outlined in chapter 2. Within SAP is something that people do (Jarzabkowski et al., 2007; Jarzabkowski and Whittington, 2008; Jarzabkowski and Spee, 2009), a social practice (Whittington, 1996) which pays attention to how strategy practitioners act and interact. As this field has developed, the definition has widened to incorporate the development of strategy and its implementation

DOI: 10.4324/9780429344305-13

(Jarzabkowski, 2004; Whittington, 2006). SAP aims to move strategy away from being the preserve of the senior manager and incorporates the wider range of actors and influencers (Johnson et al., 2007). The field has grown to include a range of critical strategic arenas including:

- strategy tools in use (Jarzabkowski, 2004)
- the processes involved within strategy (Maitlis and Lawrence, 2003)
- discourse (Samra-Fredericks, 2003; Samra-Fredericks, 2005)
- identity (Laine et al., 2016)
- narrative analysis (Vaara et al., 2016; Kryger, 2017)
- sense-making (Balogun and Johnson, 2004)

SAP draws on the social theory of agency and structure being interconnected (Giddens, 1984) and acknowledges that the practitioner, their practice (the activities) and praxis (the reasoning behind action and thought) are interconnected (Marcuse, 1964; Habermas and Shapiro, 1972). Practitioners are viewed as being embedded within their organisational or cultural context (Vaara and Whittington, 2012), and the perspective thus contributes to understanding how context may influence strategy. SAP's focus on "technologies of rationality" (Jarzabkowski and Kaplan, 2015: 1) examines the models, frameworks, and tools used to develop strategy in context, critiquing the oversimplification of decision-making when observed at the practical micro level (Jarratt and Stiles, 2010).

As SAP includes a broad range of activity, the unit of analysis spreads to include almost any activity within the organisation being considered as strategy activity (Johnson et al., 2007). Taking this idea to the extreme, if strategy "is everything, maybe it's nothing" (Wildavsky, 1973: 1). This critique can be addressed by focusing on specific strategic episodes and observing operational routines and patterns which consistently occur in the production of strategy, such as the strategy workshop (Hendry and Seidl, 2003).

8.2 Strategy within different contexts

The production of strategy within different contexts has been explored from a variety of different perspectives. Some examples consist of the longitudinal works on individual organisations by Mintzberg, including a study of an entrepreneurial firm (Mintzberg and Waters, 1982), the public sector National Film Board (Mintzberg and McHugh, 1985), and a study of realised strategies at McGill University (Mintzberg and Rose, 2003). Spender developed the notion of industry recipes to "guide strategic thinking" (Spender, 1989: 10) through a study of iron founders, dairymen, and the forklift truck industry, defining the industry through an interpretive or phenomenological approach. Institutional industry constraints and the regulatory nature of societal drivers in theorising an industry's approach to alliances or mergers has also been explored (Yin and Shanley, 2008).

Of particular interest is Whittington (2001) in his exploration of strategy and contexts at a typographical level within the four perspectives of "Whittington's Cross". Here he positions four different contexts for organisations linked to four broad approaches to strategy formulation, namely profit versus pluralistic and deliberate versus emergent.

Whittington (1996: 731). Within his "systemic view" strategy depends on the "particular social system in which the strategy-making takes place" (Whittington, 2001: 4). Through the systemic lens he challenges the universality of any particular approach to strategy and recognises the plurality of how differing organisations approach strategy within their institutional (Dimaggio and Powell, 1983) settings. The perspective gives managers an insight into how they could use the perspective as an approach to evaluating the rules and social characteristics of their circumstances, but does not explore what actually happens within organisations. Whittington raises for further study the question: how do the practitioners of strategy really act and interact?

Institutionalism and strategy

Strategy as practice (SAP) and neo-institutional theory (NIT) both emerged as a reaction to assumptions of economic rationality within organisations, organisations acting in ways that contradict purely economic responses and the rational actor myth held within strategic decision-making (Suddaby et al., 2013). Although SAP continues to have some critique in its micro-level focus and lack of generalisability (Vaara and Whittington, 2012; Elbasha and Wright, 2017), being overly focused on detailed micro activities, without engaging with broader meaning or how actor perceptions are entrenched in wider cognitive schemes (Johnson et al., 2007). Many SAP studies falling into a descriptive trap, undertaking micro-level studies, too contextualised to enable any generalisability (Suddaby et al., 2013; Smets et al., 2015).

Conversely, NIT research has focused on broad recipes and norms and have often overlooked the coalface (Barley, 2017) and the detailed activities that sustain them (Whittington, 2006). The main focus of research has comprised of geographically related actors such as US art museums and the big five accounting firms (Greenwood and Suddaby, 2006; Smets et al., 2017). The research unrealistically categorises the organisational actor as an "institutional 'dope'" (Suddaby et al., 2013: 11) who cannot escape the social structures within which they are embedded, diminishing the actor's agency.

More recent research bridging these theoretical arenas has grown (Suddaby et al., 2013; Smets et al., 2015) and been explored within the concept of practice-driven institutionalism (PDI) (Smets et al., 2017), bridging the gaps within both theories. For example, an SAP approach addresses the some of the focus of NIT in that it is concerned with what people do in the making of strategy and how the organisational and institutional context influence these approaches to the practice of strategy (Johnson et al., 2007). Johnson et al. (2007) go further and describe four broad theoretical starting points for further research within SAP research: The Carnegie tradition of sense-making and routines, situated learning, actor-network theory, and institutional theories (see Figure 8.1). These are mapped on the vertical axis against micro or macro phenomena, micro being focused on detailed activity and macro broader focused on patterns across society. The horizontal axis exploring the process of how strategy is done versus the content of strategies.

The approach taken by this book aligns with the institutional position on Figure 8.1, exploring micro–strategy-making within a more macro-organisational field setting. A combination of the two theoretical strands address blind spots within both theories (Suddaby et al., 2013; Smets, Greenwood et al., 2015; Smets, Aristidou et al., 2017). The SAP perspective explores new micro-level analysis linked to institutional level insights (Johnson et al., 2007; Elbasha and Wright, 2017; Smets et al., 2017).

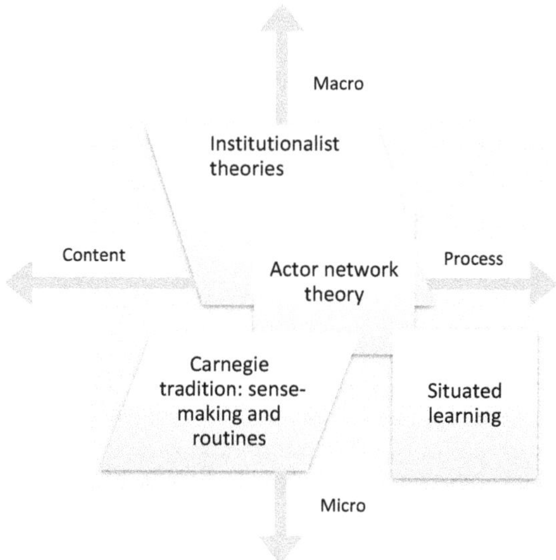

Figure 8.1 Four theoretical resources for SAP research

Note: social constructionist principles underpinning the workshop

Before beginning the discussion on strategy workshops as a method for developing strategic insight, there follows a brief explanation of the positioning of this approach within the social constructionist philosophy. A fundamental tenant of social constructionism is that it does not perceive the individual or group as having any definable or discoverable nature. This anti-essentialism describes a view that there is nothing within things or people defining what they are or their nature. Their perception of reality is not based on objective facts, but knowledge is derived through construction of reality within a cultural society, between and because, of social interaction (anti-realism). All knowledge is interdependent upon history and culture of the participants and groups performing activities in understanding their truth.

Language, within social constructionism, is viewed as a precondition of thought. Social interaction within a culture is reproduced and transmitted through language, and that language and framework preconditions thought. Language is also seen as a form of social action; people interact through language and, through this interaction, understanding of the world is developed and constructed. The language used by actors is full of action and not a passive vehicle for the transmission of knowledge and thought.

The focus of social constructionism is interaction and social practice; it is something people do together, rather than an emphasis on the individual. It has the group and their interaction with each other as the creators of a constructed reality. It is centred on the dynamics of social interaction or on how phenomena form when people are interacting (Burr, 1996). These features of social constructionism, anti-essentialism, anti-realism, culture and historical specificity, language and social practice, and interaction can be accommodated and explored effectively through social practice activities and cognitive mapping. The social practice is a strategy workshop, utilising strategic options, decision analysis, and cognitive strategy-making processes to develop strategic insight and actions.

8.3 Workshops

A key element of this text book is to appreciate strategic cognition, causality, and attention within an individual organisation and gain an appreciation for the socially constructed reality within a public sector organisation or field. In order to support practitioner "on the ground" undertaking strategy development, the tactic of a strategy workshop was selected as a workable way of developing strategy. Workshops are commonly undertaken by public sector organisations for the development of their actual organisational strategy. By aligning with a standard approach, the workshop retains legitimacy and avoids the method driving the strategy, which can be critiqued as a form of "methodolatry" (Janesick, 1994: 215). Within the workshop the strategy process will be enacted through the strategy-making or SODA (Ackermann et al., 1992; Eden, 1992; Bryson et al., 1995; Eden, 1995), technique founded on cognitive causal mapping (Axelrod, 1976; Huff, 1990; Laukkanen, 1994).

A strategy workshop can be considered as a "strategic episode" (Hendry and Seidl, 2003) wherein actors separate themselves from their daily routines to undertake focused group work on strategic planning. They are a widespread, recognised, and frequently formal part of an organisation's strategic development processes (Hodgkinson et al., 2006). Although widely used, there is limited current research on strategy workshops (Healey et al., 2015), with little detail available on regularity, participation, impact, and effectiveness (Hodgkinson et al., 2006) or on how the workshop and the affordances (Jarzabkowski and Kaplan, 2015) (Oliver, 2005) of the strategy tools utilised generate strategy knowledge (Paroutis et al., 2015). Recent studies have addressed this and focused on design characteristics and cognitive outcomes (Healey et al., 2015), highlighting the limited number of case studies used in the generation of data.

One definition of workshops is stated as an "arrangement whereby a group of people learn, acquire new knowledge, perform creative problem-solving, or innovate in relation to a domain-specific issue" (Ørngreen and Levinsen, 2017: 72). The form is directly linked to creative problem-solving (CPS) frequently referred to by the now redundant term "brainstorming" (Osborn, 1953) and also draws upon mind mapping, later refined into the causal mapping process (Eden, 1988; Ackermann et al., 1992; Eden, 1994).

Arguably a formal strategy workshop leans towards a planning and design style of strategic development which can be viewed as ineffective, "formulaic and ritualistic" (Hodgkinson et al., 2006: 480). Strategy workshops are deemed an important area for further investigation with a specific research gap emerging on the generalisability of strategy workshop research across sectors with differing systems and differing approaches to governance (Hodgkinson et al., 2006).

Within the SAP field “off-site awaydays” and “meetings” are defined as a form of strategy tool. From an SAP perspective, strategy meetings are so common across varying types of organisations that they may be collectively referred to as institutional practices (Suddaby et al., 2013). In considering the affordances (Jarzabkowski and Kaplan, 2015) of the strategy workshop from an institutional perspective, the institutionally defined organisational field may also restrict and direct the input into this strategy tool. The institutionally defined properties of the actor environment system or circumstance (Faraj and Azad, 2012) offers different possibilities of action within a strategy workshop. Research within this perspective is viewed as limited (Jarzabkowski and Kaplan, 2015) with recommendations that strategy workshops need to be explored and understood as institutional phenomena influenced by their institutional and organisational contexts (Johnson et al., 2007). As of yet, no studies have explored the strategy workshops with the NIT lens.

Current research within SAP explores the shaping and adaptation of strategy tools in use (Jarzabkowski and Kaplan, 2015). The key tool used in this text is based on the ‘Making Strategy’ (Eden and Ackermann, 1998) approach, a variation of revealed causal cognitive mapping (Laukkanen, 1994; Montibeller and Belton, 2006; Laukkanen, 2012; Nelson et al., 2000 [#892]) within a strategy awayday or workshop.

Key discussion: strategy workshop

Using this tactic (Robson, 1993) to explore strategy, representatives from an organisation will go through a standardised process of strategy workshop facilitation. A facilitated process enables individuals within the group to express ideas, resulting in a mutual and agreed consensus. The justification for this recommended tactic is that a strategy workshop is a recognised endemic construct for strategy-making that public sector organisations understand and use. It is common practice for organisations to use strategy awaydays to discuss the long-term direction and scope of their organisation (Hodgkinson et al., 2006; Johnson et al., 2010; Healey et al., 2015).

8.4 Chapter summary

In summary, by exploring, these insights expandthe research expands the arguably positivistic strategy literature, by exploring more accurate theory through the use of micro-level SAP insights. Further, the restrictions highlighted within a purely micro-level analysis, currently dominating SAP research, are addressed by utilising a macro lens derived from NIT. The NIT field further extends insights through analysis of micro, actor-level agency, addressing the field’s key gap. Lastly a more detailed understanding of strategy workshops will further develop knowledge within this area of practice.

There is clearly a need for strategy to explain the actions of actors and bring more accuracy to theory by utilising more sociologically informed approaches, which include institutional theory, to support accuracy within existing strategy theory (Jarzabkowski and Whittington, 2008). Smets et al. (2017) argue that the combination of the two theoretical strands address blind spots within both theories. A contextual reference for practice is achieved by an institutional eye. The field of strategic decision-making has explored a range contextual variables that may influence strategic decisions, but existing studies are fragmented, inconsistent, and limited in range and highlight the need for more detailed work (Shepherd and Rudd, 2014). By addressing functional practice but relating it to institutional phenomena and practices across institutionally defined organisational fields. This combination of perspectives "can open each other's eyes to new phenomena and start looking at familiar phenomena in new ways" (Smets et al., 2017: 283). Acknowledging practice-driven institutionalism will enable the close-up "zooming in" scrutiny of strategy-making workshops within organisations, then zooming out to the broad societal logics embedded within institutionally defined organisational fields of study.

Within the practice lens, a quest for rationality is viewed as a social convention that pre-prescribes sets of values for actors, the strategy tools symbolising "rational strategic processes" (Meyer and Rowan, 1977; Jarzabkowski and Kaplan, 2015: 551), very much neo-institutional views. Research recommendations are put forward by Jarzabkowski and Kaplan (2015) to explore the strategic management consultancy field, individuals, teams, and projects, but this reveals a gap as there are no recommendations or discussion on comparative studies across organisational fields and how actors within differing organisational fields may utilise strategy tools in ways that may be defined by the institutionalism within those fields.

References

Ackermann, F., Eden, C. & Cropper, S. (1992). *Getting Started with Cognitive Mapping*. London: Banxia Software.

Axelrod, R. M. (1976). *Structure of Decision: The Cognitive Maps of Political Elites*. Princeton: Princeton University Press.

Balogun, J. & Johnson, G. (2004). Organizational restructuring and middle manager sensemaking. *The Academy of Management Journal*, 47, 523–549.

Barley, S. R. (2017). Coalface institutionalism. In R. Greenwood, C. Oliver, T. B. Lawrence, & R. E. Meyer (Eds.), *The Sage Handbook of Organizational Institutionalism*. London: Sage.

Bryson, J., Ackermann, F., Eden, C. & Finn, C. (1995). Using the 'oval mapping process' to identify strategic issues and formulate effective strategies. In *Strategic Planning for Public and Nonprofit Organisations* (pp. 257–275). San Francisco, CA: Jossey Bass.

Burr, V. (1996). *An Introduction to Social Constructionism*. London: Routledge.

Dimaggio, P. J. & Powell, W. W. (1983). The iron cage revisited – institutional isomorphism and collective rationality in organizational fields. *American Sociological Review*, 48, 147–160.

Eden, C. (1988). Cognitive mapping. *European Journal of Operational Research*, 36, 1–13.

Eden, C. (1992). On the nature of cognitive maps. *Journal of Management Studies*, 29, 261–265.

Eden, C. (1994). Cognitive mapping and problem structuring for system dynamics model-building. *System Dynamics Review*, 10, 257–276.

Eden, C. (1995). *Strategic options development and analysis (Soda)*. In *Rational Analysis Revisited*. Birmingham: Operational Research Society.

Eden, C. & Ackermann, F. (1998). *Making Strategy: The Journey of Strategic Management*. Thousand Oaks, CA, London: Sage.

Elbasha, T. & Wright, A. (2017). Reconciling structure and agency in strategy -as-practice research: Towards a strong- structuration theory approach. *M@n@gement*, 20, 107–128.

Faraj, S. & Azad, B. (2012). The materiality of technology: An affordance perspective. In *Materiality and Organizing: Social Interaction in a Technological World* (pp. 237–258). Oxford: Oxford University Press.

Farjoun, M. (2002). Towards an organic perspective on strategy. *Strategic Management Journal*, 23, 561–594.
Giddens, A. (1984). *The Constitution of Society: Outline of the Theory of Structuration*. Cambridge: Polity Press.
Greenwood, R. & Suddaby, R. (2006). Institutional entrepreneurship in mature fields: The big five accounting firms. *The Academy of Management Journal*, 49, 27–48.
Habermas, J. R. & Shapiro, J. J. (1972). *Knowledge and Human Interests*. London: Heinemann Educational.
Healey, M. P., Hodgkinson, G. P., Whittington, R. & Johnson, G. (2015). Off to plan or out to lunch? Relationships between design characteristics and outcomes of strategy workshops. *British Journal of Management*, 26, 507–528.
Hendry, J. & Seidl, D. (2003). The structure and significance of strategic episodes: Social systems theory and the routine practices of strategic change. *Journal of Management Studies*, 40, 175–196.
Hodgkinson, G. P., Whittington, R., Johnson, G. & Schwarz, M. (2006). The role of strategy workshops in strategy development processes: Formality, communication, co-ordination and inclusion. *Long Range Planning*, 39, 479–496.
Huff, A. S. (1990). *Mapping Strategic Thought*. Chichester: John Wiley & Sons.
Janesick, V. J. (1994). The dance of qualitative research design: Metaphor, methodolatry, and meaning. In *Handbook of Qualitative Research*. Thousand Oaks, CA: Sage Publications, Inc.
Jarratt, D. & Stiles, D. (2010). How are methodologies and tools framing managers' strategizing practice in competitive strategy development? *British Journal of Management*, 21, 28–43.
Jarzabkowski, P. (2004). Strategy as practice: Recursiveness, adaptation, and practices-in-use. *Organization Studies*, 25, 529–560.
Jarzabkowski, P., Balogun, J. & Seidl, D. (2007). Strategizing: The challenges of a practice perspective. *Human Relations*, 60, 5–27.
Jarzabkowski, P. & Kaplan, S. (2015). Strategy tools-in-use: A framework for understanding "technologies of rationality" in practice. *Strategic Management Journal*, 36, 537–558.
Jarzabkowski, P. & Spee, A. P. (2009). Strategy-as-practice: A review and future directions for the field. *International Journal of Management Reviews*, 11, 69–95.
Jarzabkowski, P. & Whittington, R. (2008). A strategy-as-practice approach to strategy research and education. *Journal of Management Inquiry*, 17, 282–286.
Johnson, G., Prashantham, S., Floyd, S. W. & Bourque, N. (2010). The ritualization of strategy workshops. *Organization Studies*, 31, 1589–1618.
Johnson, G., Whittington, R., Melin, L. & Langley, A. (2007). *Strategy as Practice Research Directions and Resources* [Place of publication not identified]. Cambridge: Cambridge University Press.
Kryger, A. (2017). Strategy development through interview technique from narrative therapy. *Journal of Organizational Change Management*, 30, 4–14.
Laine, P.-M., Meriläinen, S., Tienari, J. & Vaara, E. (2016). Mastery, submission, and subversion: On the performative construction of strategist identity. *Organization*, 23, 505–524.
Laukkanen, M. (1994). Comparative cause mapping of organizational cognitions. *Organization Science*, 5, 322–343.
Laukkanen, M. (2012). Comparative causal mapping and cmap3 software in qualitative studies. *Forum: Qualitative Social Research*, 13.
Maitlis, S. & Lawrence, T. B. (2003). Orchestral manoeuvres in the dark: Understanding failure in organizational strategizing*. *Journal of Management Studies*, 40, 109–139.
Marcuse, H. (1964). *One Dimensional Man: Studies in the Ideology of Advanced Industrial Society*. London: Routledge and Kegan Paul.
Meyer, J. W. & Rowan, B. (1977). Institutionalized organizations – formal-structure as myth and ceremony. *American Journal of Sociology*, 83, 340–363.
Mintzberg, H. & Mchugh, A. (1985). Strategy formation in an adhocracy. *Administrative Science Quarterly*, 30, 160–197.
Mintzberg, H. & Rose, J. (2003). Strategic management upside down: Tracking strategies at mcgill university from 1829 to 1980. *Canadian Journal of Administrative Sciences/Revue Canadienne des Sciences de l'Administration*, 20, 270–290.

Mintzberg, H. & Waters, J. A. (1982). Tracking strategy in an entrepreneurial firm. *Academy of Management Journal*, 25, 465–499.
Montibeller, G. & Belton, V. (2006). Causal maps and the evaluation of decision options: A review. *The Journal of the Operational Research Society*, 57, 779–791.
Nelson, K. M., Nadkarni, S., Narayanan, V. K. & Ghods, M. (2000). Understanding software operations support expertise: A revealed causal mapping approach. *Mis Quarterly*, 24, 475–507.
Oliver, M. (2005). The problem with affordance. *E-Learning and Digital Media*, 2, 402–413.
Ørngreen, R. & Levinsen, K. (2017). Workshops as a research methodology. *Electronic Journal of E-learning*, 15, 70–81.
Osborn, A. F. (1953). *Applied Imagination, Principles and Procedures of Creative Thinking*. New York: Charles Scribner's Sons.
Paroutis, S., Franco, L. A. & Papadopoulos, T. (2015). Visual interactions with strategy tools: Producing strategic knowledge in workshops. *British Journal of Management*, 26, S48–S66.
Robson, C. (1993). *Real World Research*. Oxford: Blackwell Publishing.
Samra-Fredericks, D. (2003). Strategizing as lived experience and strategists' everyday efforts to shape strategic direction*. *Journal of Management Studies*, 40, 141–174.
Samra-Fredericks, D. (2005). Strategic practice, 'discourse' and the everyday interactional constitution of 'power effects'. *Organization*, 12, 803–841.
Shepherd, N. G. & Rudd, J. M. (2014). The influence of context on the strategic decision-making process: A review of the literature. *International Journal of Management Reviews*, 16, 340–364.
Smets, M., Aristidou, A. & Whittington, R. (2017). Towards a practice-driven institutionalism. In Royston Greenwood, Christine Oliver, Tom Lawrence, Renate Meyer (Eds.), *The Sage Handbook of Organizational Institutionalism* (2nd ed.). London: Sage.
Smets, M., Greenwood, R. & Lounsbury, M. (2015). An institutional perspective on strategy as practice. *The Cambridge Handbook of Strategy as Practice*, 2, 283–300.
Spender, J.-C. (1989). *Industry recipes: The nature and sources of managerial judgment*. Oxford, UK: Basic Blackwell.
Suddaby, R., Seidl, D. & Le, J. K. (2013). Strategy-as-practice meets neo-institutional theory. *Strategic Organization*, 11, 329–344.
Vaara, E. Sonenshein, S. & Boje, D. (2016). Narratives as sources of stability and change in organizations: Approaches and directions for future research. *The Academy of Management Annals*, 10, 495–560.
Vaara, E. & Whittington, R. (2012). Strategy-as-practice: Taking social practices seriously. *Academy of Management Annals*, 6, 285–336.
Whittington, R. (1996). Strategy as practice. *Long Range Planning*, 29, 731–735.
Whittington, R. (2001). *What Is Strategy – and Does It Matter?* London: Thompson Learning.
Whittington, R. (2006). Completing the practice turn in strategy research. *Organization Studies*, 27, 613–634.
Wildavsky, A. (1973). If planning is everything, maybe it's nothing. *Policy Sciences*, 4, 127–153.
Yin, X. & Shanley, M. (2008). Industry determinants of the "merger versus alliance" decision. *The Academy of Management Review*, 33, 473–491.

Chapter 9

Revealed cognitive causal mapping

Theoretical underpinning and approaches to analysis

Learning Outcomes

After reading this chapter you should be able to:

- summarise the research informed depth in underpinning the causal cognitive mapping process
- undertake empirical analysis of a developed cognitive map.
- describe the philosophical underpinnings of revealed cognitive causal mapping
- justify the benefits and critique the affordances of causal mapping

Pre-Chapter Questions

- Can an individual or group's mind map be expressed in an accurate manner?
- Can you evaluate the dominant logic of your organisation?
- How do you make sense of complexity with strategic analysis?

Key terms

- Workshop – "arrangement whereby a group of people learn, acquire new knowledge, perform creative problem-solving, or innovate in relation to a domain-specific issue" (Ørngreen and Levinsen, 2017: 72).
- Cognitive map – a physical map or representation on the actors mind or cognition regarding a subject or domain.
- RCCM (revealed cognitive causal mapping) – cognitive map produced by those involved
- Dominant logics – socially constructed truth, or the cultural norms and beliefs of an organisation.
- Causality – a relationship between cause and effect.

DOI: 10.4324/9780429344305-14

9.1 Introduction

This chapter adds a research-informed depth in underpinning the causal cognitive mapping process detailed in the previous chapter. The guide to undertaking a strategy workshop can be accessed and utilised without the deeper knowledge and underpinning that supported its development. However, strategists may be interested to explore its underpinning processes and justifications.

The second part of this chapter explores analysis of a developed cognitive map. Again, this is not necessary for undertaking a strategy workshop within an organisation but may be of interest for the reader in developing a deeper insight into the focus of strategic attention and any approaches or limitations that may be present within a cognitive map. When undertaking a strategy-making workshop, actors, representing their organisations, generate 'ideas' (namely; issues, goals, unique capability and statement of strategic intent) through a cognitive mapping process (Eden, 1988a; Ackermann et al., 1992; Eden, 1994). The strategy-making process enabled participants to express issues, goals, core competence, and a statement of intent (Eden, 1995; Eden and Ackermann, 1998; Eden and Ackermann, 2000) that summarises their position and approach to strategy based on "deliberate emergent" strategic principles (Eden and Ackermann, 1998: 6). The nature of this approach enables organisational actors to express what they perceive as issues of importance, from their personal, organisational, and institutional reality. These ideas thus constitute a data set that can be utilised both for strategy analysis and gives the reader an approach to analysis that may scratch below the surface of a strategy workshop enabling exploration of groups thinking at a far deeper and empirical level.

9.2 Background and description of cognitive causal mapping

Causal cognitive maps can be seen as a group of processes that systematically represent an actor or group's cognition concerning what they know or believe about phenomena within a domain or arena (Hodgkinson et al., 2004). A causal cognitive map however is not just a representation of an actor's assertions within a domain, it also captures its causal structure, generating consequences derived from these assertions (Axelrod, 1976). In a similar vein to mind mapping (Buzan and Buzan, 1996), causal cognitive maps are a depiction of the structure and influence of causal relationships as perceived by actors and represented within a map of ideas; a visual illustration of relationships between elements within a system (Burgess et al., 1992). Topologically a causal cognitive map is a set of concepts connected together with directional indicators forming a hierarchical means-end's structure, which represents a person's discourse (Montibeller and Belton, 2006).

Causal mapping has a long history in the exploration of individuals and organisations idiosyncratic belief systems (Markóczy and Goldberg, 1995) and are widely used in problem structuring interventions where they can generate rich models representing chains of argument in complex networks (Montibeller and Belton, 2006). They can be employed to represent and explore subjective knowledge of phenomena, formed into a discourse or map of the causes, effects, and links between ideas (Eden, 1992).

Examples of the use of causal mapping for the investigation of managers and decision-makers can be traced back to Axelrod (1976) in analysing and describing political decision-maker's beliefs, with Huff (1990), Eden (1992), and Laukkanen (1994) prominent in the field. Axelrod's (1976) seminal text utilised the term "cognitive mapping", later, "(cause or) causal mapping" became the more dominant term. However, the literature inconsistently refers to either or both interchangeably, regardless of whether the researcher is referring to internal mental models or the revealed external mapped representations of these models (Laukkanen, 2012). For clarity the author will refer to **revealed cognitive causal mapping** (Nelson et al., 2000) **(RCCM)**, as the key terminology for the approach being used within this book. This clarification of the method explicitly states that the cognitive map produced is one that is revealed (or asserted [Axelrod, 1976]) by the actors, and may not actually represent the true cognitive map experienced or understood by the actors. The actor's assertion, or what they reveal, may be different to the true nature of their internal cognitive map, as this only exists in the mind of the actor and cannot be realistically captured. The revealed causal map, however, is in the public domain and is visible (Nelson et al., 2000). The correlation between what is true and what is revealed will be imperfect and affected by mitigating factors such as awareness or group dynamics (Nelson et al., 2000) or, potentially, institutional and organisational field drivers.

Broadly, causal cognitive mapping has a focus on social and individual cognition, exploring the formation of social actors beliefs and knowledge and their formation and influence within a setting (Laukkanen, 2012). The map is a process that reveals the mental model that actors create in understanding their environment (Johnson-Laird, 1983). Parallel concepts such as industry recipe (Spender, 1989) and dominant logic (Prahalad and Bettis, 1986) have similar underpinnings. From a cognitive psychology perspective, a symbolic representation of the world is one of the key elements in understanding action by actors. This cognitive symbolic representation builds a scaffolding around which to build solutions and actions. A mental map is useful in understanding the development of actions, actions which have causation within the mental model. Causation is, therefore, critical in understanding how actors develop strategic choices and consequences (Axelrod, 1976). Causal mapping, therefore, enables a systematic elicitation for comparison and analysis (Markóczy and Goldberg, 1995). As an empirical method, cognitive causal mapping can indicate an actors cognitive operations as the model corresponds to the actor's behaviour.

The key benefit of RCCM is that it enables a causal inference analysis through an interconnected network topology. There is only one form of relationship between concepts or ideas, the causal relationship. The concepts or ideas being connected through a means to ends structure where ideas or concepts have two poles. One connection is where the idea is derived from, and the second connection relates to what the idea may causally link to further up the hierarchy. Concepts are represented as points or ideas and the links between these points are causal arrows (Axelrod, 1976; Montibeller and Belton, 2006). See Figure 9.1.

Figure 9.1 Simple causal linkage

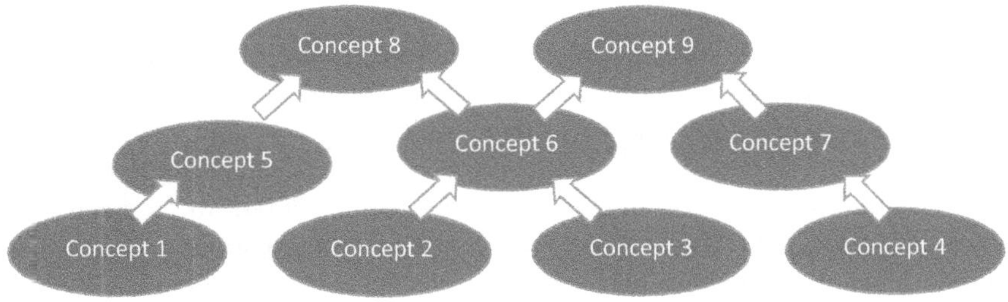

Figure 9.2 Causal map

One of the key aspects of the method is "causal inference", the effect of one idea or concept on other ideas and concepts within the map. Actors/participants can trace the path of concepts that are connected to the final head of the map. The eventual level or impact of this effect can be calculated by adding the causal links along a path (Montibeller and Belton, 2006). Causal maps are effectively directed graphs characterised by a hierarchical structure forming a means-end diagram (Figure 9.2). The map is drawn up through representative short pieces of text linked by unidirectional arrows. In general (and within the approach used within this text) the statement is referred to as the "idea" (Brightman, 2003; di Gregorio, 2006) with the idea at the tail of the arrow taken to "cause" the idea at the head of the arrow (Eden et al., 1992). Generally causal maps are depicted as visual graphs in nature but can also be presented in numeric form in a square matrix (Laukkanen, 2012).

Types of causal and cognitive map

A number of approaches in the collection of data and construction of a causal map are available in the literature. These include analysis of organisational members statements (Axelrod, 1976), interviewing (Weick and Bougon, 1986), and questionnaires (Montazemi and Conrath, 1986). One example is comparative causal mapping (CCM) which draws upon causal statements through interviews, which are then constructed into causal maps by the researcher (Laukkanen, 2012). This approach can be either unstructured where the researcher develops causal statements through interviews (Laukkanen, 2012) or "structured" where a pool of constructs is used to develop the causal map, referred to as the "pairwise" (Hodgkinson et al., 2004) approach. With the "unstructured" approach, the researcher undertakes the mapping process following an in-depth interview; the researcher then translates the data into a causal map by decoding the text (Axelrod, 1976). The pairwise cognitive mapping approach is more structured. Here the facilitator presents research participants with a preformatted set of variables, for example marketing, engagement, recruitment, etc. Participants then consider the influence and causation of these variables producing the causal map. Causality is directional with arrowheads and may include positive or negative causality as well as levels of degree. Although clearly thorough in its approach with advantages for comparison across causal maps from differing organisations/actors, one key critique of these method is its time-consuming nature and the limited number of variables. Further to this, the focus leans towards a cognitive map of causal relationships within an organisation and not a specific consideration of strategic cognition within organisations for comparative purposes.

A more direct form of data collection is the idiographic or "freehand" (Hodgkinson et al., 2004) approach. Here a group directly creates a single composite causal map, agreeing concepts, ideas, and causal linkages as they are developed (Eden, 1988a; Eden, 1992; Eden and Ackermann, 1998). This is referred to as primary or direct method to elicit cognitive insights directly from actors in situ (Hodgkinson et al., 2004). In the freehand format the participants construct the map themselves, with a facilitator supporting the process of map generation rather than interpreting interviews in order to generate a map. Nelson et al. (2000) further explores a range of causal mapping approaches within the literature and highlighted the idiographic Strategic Options Development and Analysis or SODA (Eden, 1995) approach as being particularly appropriate in facilitating decision-making. The approach taken within here follows the "freehand" method wherein participants self-generate content and causality, directly into a causal map. The approach aligns closely with causal "influence diagrams" (Coyle, 1977) drawn from the management systems literature and developed into a strategy workshop. The participants both create variables/ideas and position them in an order that represents their cognitive understanding of the issue under study. A "decision-making" (Eden, 1988a) approach to causal mapping generates a means-end's chain of argument in a cause-and-effect structure, heads having no further outgoing arrows and bottom nodes having only out arrows (Montibeller and Belton, 2006). Single direction arrows are used to denote causality. This approach is seen to have a lower cognitive demand on participants and is potentially quicker to administer and less demanding, ensuring that participants fully engage with the activity. This is particularly useful where a sustained engagement is required to complete the strategy mapping task; any lowering of motivation will be detrimental to the process and less effective (Hodgkinson et al., 2004). Engagement is further enhanced by the nature of the activity being a strategy workshop for the organisation, which is then used for organisational development.

RCCM's can also include a number of properties, the first being an influence relationship that is either positive or negative. Within fuzzy causal maps this includes a level of strength, usually numerical, placed on the causation arrow, although these are not a critical part of the definition of a causal map (Markóczy and Goldberg, 1995). Network maps have also been referred to as "signed diagraphs" (Axelrod, 1976; Laukkanen, 2012) which attributed a positive or negative sign to the causal interaction rather than a single positive relationship between issues or assertions.

Although the model utilised within this text formally aligns with the freehand approach, the method does have some elements of structure (by following SODA [Eden, 1995]), the approach brings in some influence from a pairwise method as actors/participants are prompted to think within certain structures, namely: issues, goals, core competence, actions, and statements of strategic intent.

Philosophical underpinnings of revealed cognitive causal mapping

Cognitive causal mapping is drawn from a number of fields:

- psycho-logic – the idea that the persons cognitive processes can be mapped within a mathematical system
- causal inference – utilises statistics to describe a body of data with causal variables

- graph theory – enables the conceptualisations of paths and complex interconnections
- evaluative assertion analysis – encodes documents to explore relationships between concepts and decision theory, analysing decision-making and structures leading to outcomes through choice

(Axelrod, 1976)

It must be noted that this cognitive representation of the world is not necessarily rational or accurate from a positivistic standpoint, but is based on the beliefs, knowledge, and isomorphic drivers of the actors environment (Laukkanen, 2012) and their mutually agreed socially constructed reality. Actors may have strong institutional (Scott, 2008) pressures to align with existing beliefs, knowledge, and understanding of their organisational environment. Objectively developing a cognitive understanding of an environment from ground zero, prior to any workshop or analysis would be difficult, stressful, and unfeasible. There are social drivers and isomorphic (Dimaggio and Powell, 1983) pressures to align to a social groups understanding or interpretation of an issue or environment. A social group interpretation of cognition implies that the mental map will exhibit a tendency towards coherence and stability within the setting (Laukkanen, 2012).

Within this approach the attention is placed on the mental models or belief systems of specific social or organisational groups/fields, a specific focus differentiated from a broader general approach to cognition within the cognitive sciences. Huff (1990) describes five approaches to mapping, of which influence and causality of elements are of particular interest and popularity with the strategy field.

Dominant logics and causal maps

The process of developing a social dialogue through cognitive causal mapping has been used to explore and compare dominant logics (Prahalad and Bettis, 1986) within organisations (Schraven et al., 2015). The neo-institutional (Dimaggio and Powell, 1983; Alvesson and Spicer, 2019) insight on the development of structures, norms, and behaviours (Scott, 2004) encourages researchers to explore the institutional logics enacted by actors. Institutional logics become apparent through practice (Lindberg, 2014) yet may compete and coexist for dominance with a range of institutional logics across organisational actors (Schraven et al., 2015). Empirical studies on establishing the organisations dominant mindset or institutional logics perspective is lacking (Schraven et al., 2015). Cognitive causal mapping has addressed this and been used successfully to explore dominant logics within enterprises (Crilly and Sloan, 2012), directly clarifying the apparency of the dominant institutional logics through the agreed, group cognitive mapping process.

The method allows the researcher to go further than an individual organisation or group and compare social cognition patterns and dominant logics across a population, exploring any conformity to shared logics (Schraven et al., 2015). As a method for capturing cognitive patterns within organisations or groups, causal cognitive mapping is a well-suited and justified method (Laukkanen, 2012).

By undertaking a group cognitive mapping process the participating groups are articulating their language and understanding of the situation. Then by developing an understanding of a socially constructed truth, they formulate action. Within discourse analysis, observations of what is explicitly stated need also to be evaluated against positions and content that is not expressly stated. When deconstructing accounts, or in this case cognitive maps, looking at what has been written needs to be supplemented with what has been implied or rejected, elements which have not been included.

This aligns with discourse analysis which approaches the analysis of data by identifing subjects 'ways of talking' to establish themes or discourse (Burr, 1996). Once these themes or discourse are established, what are the implications? What are the effects; what is implicitly stated; and whose interests do these themes of discourses operate for or reject? Causal cognitive mapping has enabled academics with an interest in strategic cognition to explore the mental representations of actors within organisations, in particular the representations of strategic phenomena (Hodgkinson et al., 2004).

9.3 Benefits and affordances of causal mapping

Communication of complexity

One of the advantages to utilising revealed causal cognitive mapping is its ability to break down obstacles to the communication process. If we accept that humans develop a schema initially based on prior experiences, environment, and information, but also modified and reinforced by the participant (Hogarth, 1987). Then simply asking users for information about their perception is likely to lead to an incomplete or incorrect set of insights (Daft and Lengel, 1986). The limited information processing capabilities of the mind and its effect on judgement can be encapsulated as four main limitations to processing capability.

1 Short-term memory is limited in its ability to hold a number of different concepts at once, (Lloyd et al., 1960). Causal mapping enables the participant to systematically store ideas and concepts on the map for later use and recall. Thus, maps assist in the perception of large scale environments which are difficult to encapsulate (Weick and Bougon, 1986). The freehand approach to cognitive causal mapping does appear to have certain affordances (Jarzabkowski, 2004) and depend predominantly on the recall of causal relationships by participants. The approach also assumes and that belief systems, or revealed assertions, can actually be modelled through this mechanism (Axelrod, 1976).
2 There is a tendency for actors to bias more recent information that is more frequently used than information that, although concrete, could be less frequently used. By using causal mapping within the workshop environment with multiple actors, a richer picture of phenomenon can be developed with a higher likelihood of incorporating a wider range of concepts, beyond those that are recent or often considered.
3 The tendency of humans to tend towards sequential information processing limits focus to one cognitive frame at any particular time, thereby missing any wider and more complex causal relationships across concepts. The causal nature of the mapping approach enables the group to thoroughly consider and connect ideas and concepts in a way that captures interrelated concepts, thereby extending the cognitive frame.
4 The use of a wider workshop also assists in breaking down established decision rules or rules of thumb (Hogarth, 1987) and individual biases and learned routines (Laukkanen, 2012). Approaches that may be employed by participants to reduce effort and cognitive strain. A cognitive causal map also relies on the language and stated beliefs

of an individual or group. The manner in which the map is elicited can be highly influential on the nature and content of the map (Markóczy and Goldberg, 1995). By developing the map with several organisational members, a richer picture of phenomena is developed, and the impact of heuristic biases reduced. (Burgess et al., 1992).

Obstacles between actor and facilitator

Causal mapping can also be successfully used to overcome obstacles between the user/participant and the facilitator, as both parties can effectively speak a different language and build their thinking within differing frames of reference (Burgess et al., 1992). The actors and facilitators schema or schemata (Hogarth, 1987) will be a construction and simplification of organisational phenomena. The actor reflects their organisational and managerial interpretation, whilst the facilitator may lean towards the technical. Further to this, the difference will not just be between the group of participants and the facilitator but also between the participants themselves. Each individual possessing their own unique schema and interpretation of organisational phenomena. These differences can be further compounded by language differences within the actor's specialisations. This could include technical, normative, shorthand, and acronyms common within the setting, which can act as a barrier to a common understanding between parties. Developing a shared meaning of issues through mutual discussion and exposition via the mapping process can enable "cryptic constructs" (Bougon, 1992) to be clarified though the conversations implicit in developing a shared map. The causal map, by nature, forces parties towards common agreement on terminology and language. The causal mapping process, with its inherent visual and iterative nature, supports and directs a consensual agreement between actors, eventually producing clear agreed descriptions of organisational issues and overcoming the differences between actors.

Making sense of complex environments

RCCM can assist in making sense of complex environments whilst retaining a level of complexity. In order to understand complex environments actors move towards simplification and parsimony. This can be difficult, but the nature of the map enables a cognitive bottleneck of complexity to be articulated, expressed, and understood by both actors and researchers (Axelrod, 1976). It is the final visible map that makes this form of analysis powerful, as actors can engage with the causal model in a visible overall structure that retains its complexity; and the simple, single form of relationship and causation supports reliability in measurement of these relationships (Axelrod, 1976).

On the other hand, RCCM can lack some richness in depth as the map is, by nature, a group compromise of the organisation and actors (revealed) cognitive understanding (Nelson et al., 2000). Also cognitive mapping assumes an understanding of organisational context by the actor. This understanding may only exist at a tacit level, as causal mapping's purpose "is to develop rich understandings of complex situations" (Burgess et al., 1992: 144)

Given that the causal map is founded on the schema of the participating actors (Eden, 1988b), there will be a tendency for participants to focus on their day-to-day operations and less on the higher level macro or holistic view of the issue under study, in this case the strategic position of the organisation. A recommendation for mitigating this focus is to ensure that as many participants with diverse perspectives are included as possible, potentially including those no longer with the organization. However, the issue of participation from a single organisational level or from mixed organisational levels remains a dilemma (Burgess et al., 1992). One response to this has been to adapt the original SODA ([Eden, 1995] model to include a range of more classical strategic analysis tools, thereby raising macro industry and wider organisation ideas and perspectives.

Cognitive maps can also grow to be too complex for the participants to interpret the range and quantity of information contained within. One approach to mitigating this is to strive for visual symmetry of the map. The facilitator then aims to develop a symmetrical causal structure to manage the maps complexity. In doing so, a paradox emerges between the development of a detailed and valid map, versus one that captures the true complexity of the issue under study. The recommendation in balancing this paradox is to develop a composite compromise map that reflects collective understanding of all the participants (Burgess et al., 1992).

The structural complexity of actors cognitive mental representations of strategy vary. Actors are reliant on recall for the freehand mapping approach, which is not a systematic method and can produce errors of memory and causation either from omission or choice. The freehand mental representation of the actor strategic cognition may then be a limited or a restricted representation of their mental model and, therefore, have errors (Hodgkinson et al., 2004).

Contradictory statements

A further benefit within the use of causal mapping is the ability for the development of the map to address contradictory statements or elements highlighted by participants. The iterative and group process of developing the map assists in the expression of contradictions and opens the debate to resolving these. The visual nature of the map clearly expressing contradictions for initiating discussion (Burgess et al., 1992). Further to this, if contradiction does occur and remains on the map, its importance can be evaluated by a measure of centrality (Eden, 1988a) of concepts and frequency of causal links. An area with few causal connections can be seen as having a lower importance within the map, multiple causal links implying a higher level of importance.

Related to contradictions are causal loops. These occur when a chain of means and ends loops back on itself in circularity. Although effectively breaking away from the hierarchical nature of a causal map, these loops can be interpreted as containing ideas which can be collapsed to a single node within the map. The ideas within the loop can then be explored at this hierarchical status level (Eden, 1992).

9.4 Analysis of causal mapping

Analysis of causal cognitive maps requires that all information within the maps is utilised in as objective a manner as possible. Subjective elements are required to be made explicit, as maps are open to wide and varying interpretation. Approaches within how causal maps are compared and the techniques for systematically undertaking this is limited (Markóczy and Goldberg, 1995) and dispersed, with a focus within strategy towards supporting strategic analysis and decision-making, rather than utilising them as a research tool (Montibeller and Belton, 2006; Abuabara and Paucar-Caceres, 2021). Methods for coding vary between researchers and are dependent on the aims and purpose of the mapping (Eden et al., 1992). The approach taken here follows an open "freehand" (Hodgkinson et al., 2004) structure underpinned by personal construct theory (Kelly, 1955; Bannister and Fransella, 1971).

Initial stages in analysis

Organising the map

Causal maps have two specific properties: a property of hierarchy and a property of linkages. Complex maps with multiple idea statements can be analysed in a number of ways that enable the properties of the map to be more clearly visible. Firstly, organising the map into a more symmetrical pattern or shape by manoeuvring aligned concepts close together and reducing overlapping links enables the map to take on a useful layout for analysis (Eden et al., 1992). Karl Weick's (1995) insight that we do not really know what we know until we see it said is particularly pertinent to cognitive causal mapping. The researcher's ability to allow an open approach to the development of ideas and causation will enables participants to express more complexity. A clear map structure then can assist in expressing the emerging characteristics of the groups collaboratively developed cognitive causal thinking. The key benefit of organising the map in this way is that themes and areas of interest are easy to see due to the nature of the diagrammatic form of the causal map.

Arranging the cognitive causal map acts as an initial stage in analysis.

- The first part of the organisation of the map is to redraw the map to enable a flow in a direction (Axelrod, 1976). In general the researcher will use a bottom up flow following the strategy-making approach (Eden, 1995).
- Second, an attempt is made to reduce the number of crossing points of causal linkages (Axelrod, 1976).

The organisation of the map will reveal areas of high interconnectivity, clusters, central concepts, and islands of unconnected groups.

Clusters

The most common technique for analysis of a causal map is cluster analysis, which explores distance or similarity in the data (Markóczy and Goldberg, 1995). A cluster (see Figure 9.3) is a group of nodes and ideas which have identifiable separation from other elements of the map. A cluster can be identified as having tight linkages across a range of nodes or ideas and more limited or minimised linkages to other elements of the map. This is referred to as the "robust" elements of the cognitive causal map (Eden et al., 1992). Any small changes to these groups would not significantly change the overall nature of the map.

Islands

If the map is found to be made of relatively unconnected clusters there is an implication of lower complexity than a map that is far more interconnected. This suggests that the

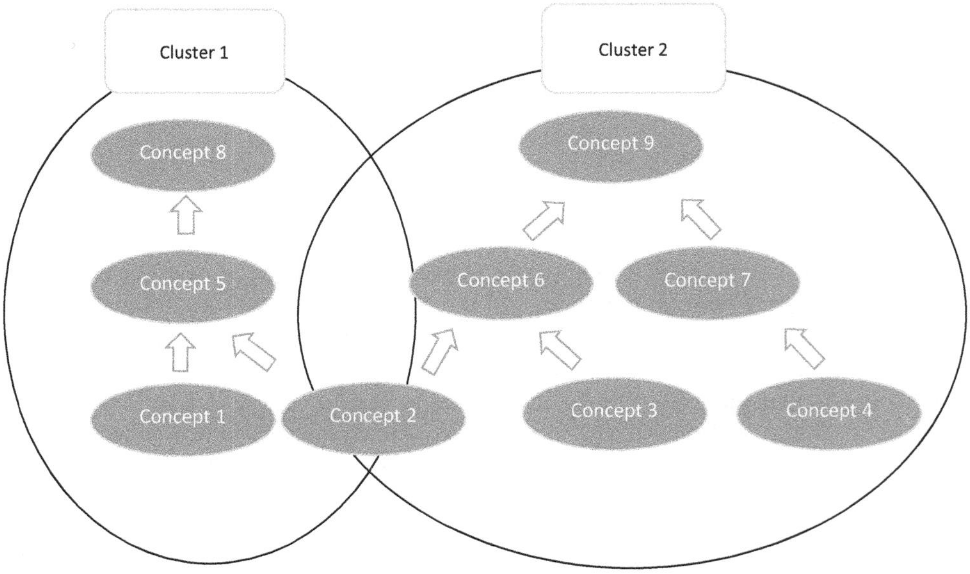

Figure 9.3 Clusters

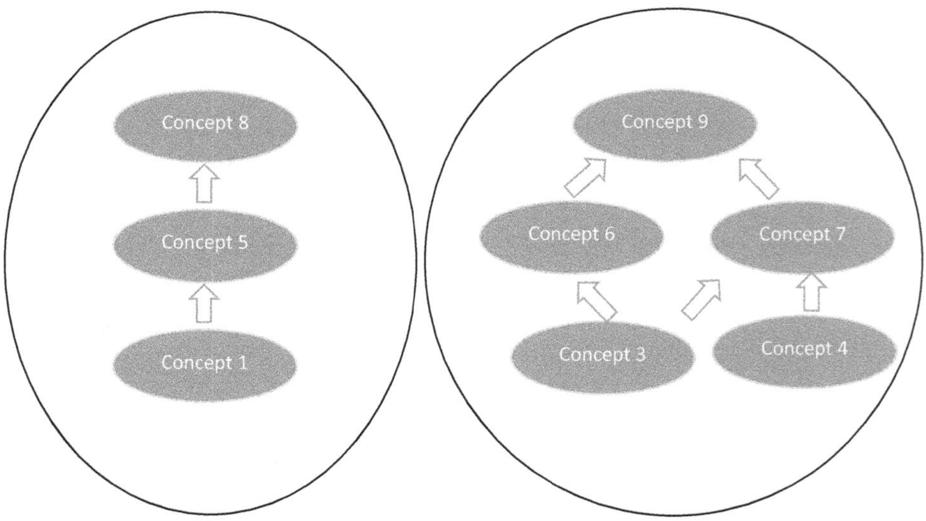

Figure 9.4 Islands

participants have potentially simplified the complexity of the issue under study (Ibid). Not all ideas are interconnected across the causal map; islands of nodes and ideas that are disconnected from other elements of the map emerge. Unconnected clusters are referred to as "islands". Where nodes are interconnected, the extent of that interconnectivity can indicate the strength of linkages across themed areas and conform a basis for the identification of clusters (Figure 9.4).

Heads

Bringing hierarchy back into the analysis alongside clusters and analysis considering "core constructs" can be identified, comprising of nodes that are both central and act as heads within the map. This approach to analysis is structural in nature as the heads or central constructs are identified in relation to the content of the subordinate ideas or notes. The core constructs are then explained by these subordinate ideas or nodes clarifying and describing their nature. Nodes that have multiple linkages across the map and, thereby, appear in a range of groups are clearly important to the participants (Figure 9.5). The level of linkage is referred to as "potent", and the idea or node can also be considered as a core construct.

Core constructs

The more highly connected ideas can be referred to as "core constructs" (Eden et al., 1992: 313) that have a particular depth or significance for actors and are critical to establishing an organisation's recipe (Spender, 1989) or dominant institutional logic (Prahalad and Bettis, 1986). They may also demonstrate any homogeny across organisations or organisational fields (Figure 9.6).

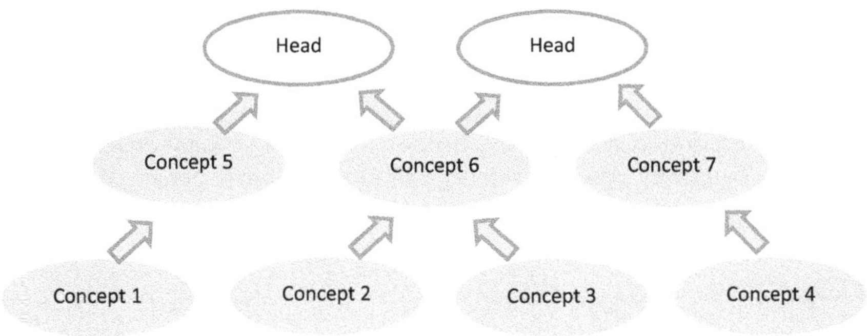

Figure 9.5 Causal map

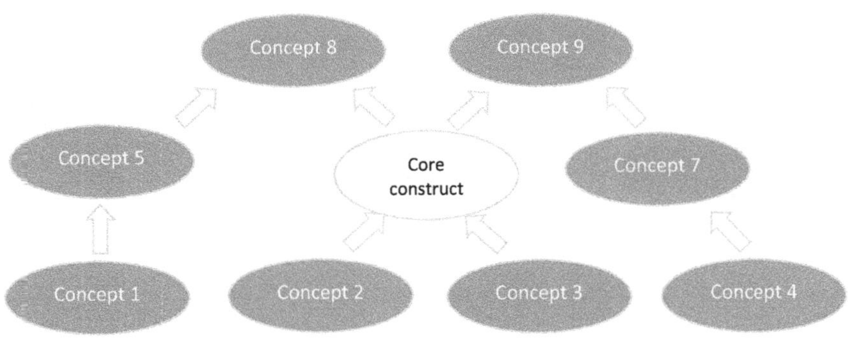

Figure 9.6 Core construct

Analysis of complexity

In order to establish the level of cognitive complexity of the map, a straightforward evaluation of how many nodes or ideas exist and the level of connectivity across all of these nodes or ideas can be performed. These findings will of course be influenced by the nature of the construction of the causal map and the length of workshop and number of participants contributing to ideas and connectivity.

A critical part of the analysis then is to frame analysis complexity against the numbers of participants, the length of time allocated to causal mapping workshop, and the willingness of participants to be open within the process. (Eden, 1992) A further more robust approach would be to consider ideas and causal links as a ratio, allowing comparison across differing maps. A densely connected map would have a higher complexity ratio than one that is less well connected, regardless of the number of ideas within the map. One limitation within the process will be the facilitator, otherwise referred to as the Mapper. The ability of the Mapper to elicit ideas linkages from the group will directly impact on the complexity of the map.

Idealised thinking

A refinement of this approach is an analysis of the ratio of the number of heads and number of tales versus the total number of ideas within the map. Where maps demonstrate a proportionally small number of heads, the map could be considered as cognitively simple or idealised thinking, as the complexity has been reduced to a small number of key ideas. A large number of heads within a map demonstrates the detail of complexity within an area and could be viewed as more cognitively complex (Eden, 1992). The author is cautious of this assumption as striving for parsimony within a strategy development workshop may be a cognitively complex activity and not necessarily perceived as a beneficial outcome for a strategy mapping session.

Causal loops

Causal loops can be defined as a circularity argument of idea causing, through the mapping hierarchy, a second idea which in turn then loops back to the original idea. These can be viewed as a mistake in coding, or they imply the existence of a dynamic interaction

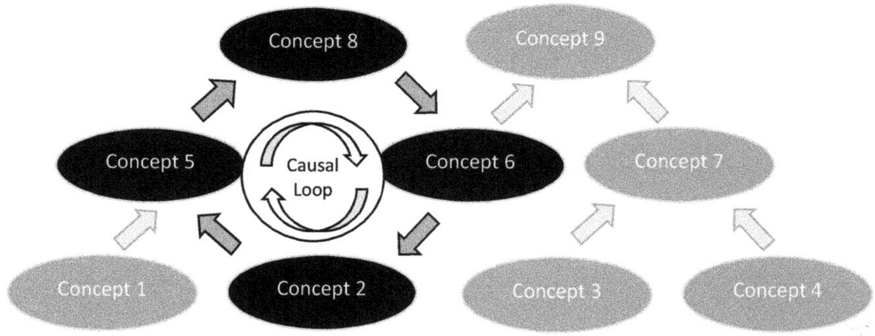

Figure 9.7 Causal loops

between two areas. A hierarchical map implies a simplicity of cause and effect which in reality may not be as easy to separate. Where causal loops occur this will be analysed and discussed, but it is essential for the researcher to identify these as they can affect the analysis software in undertaking domain and centrality analysis (Figure 9.7).

9.5 Comparative causal/cognitive mapping within a workshop setting

Critically this form of mapping is linked to goal structures and aimed at actions (Brightman, 2003). More specifically the form used is a "team map" (Eden, 1988a), which makes sense of the emergent strategic perspective of the organisation. Within this format, actors, representing their organisations, will generate "ideas" (namely; issues, goals, unique capability, and statement of strategic intent) through a cognitive mapping process (Eden, 1988a; Ackermann et al., 1992; Eden, 1994). The strategy-making process will enable participants to express issues, goals, core competence, and a statement of intent (Eden, 1995; Eden and Ackermann, 1998; Eden and Ackermann, 2000) that summarises their position. This is an approach to strategy based on "deliberate emergent" strategic principles (Eden and Ackermann, 1998: 6). The nature of this approach will enable organisational actors to express what they perceive as issues of importance, from their personal, organisational, and institutional reality.

Influencing constructs

The main forms analysis discussed focus on clusters and hierarchy. For a more accurate comparison of these rich subjective maps methods are required for establishing their emergent properties. An exploration of whether groups who selected one construct went on to link this to be similar or different construct, evaluating the correlation between various constructs or ideas and how influential or not they are within domains. This can be referred to as influencing constructs. This approach is recommended for open approaches to mapping (being where constructs are predetermined by the researcher as opposed to developed openly by the participant) (Markóczy and Goldberg, 1995).

Simplification

The causal map generated with a group will, by nature, have a significant level of detail embedded within it. In the pursuit of parsimony, it is necessary to strip out and collapse the map into clusters with higher levels of connectivity. The aim is to focus on the main emergent characteristics of the map for a higher level of analysis (Eden et al., 1992).

A deeper level of analysis can be undertaken using Decision Explorer software. Here a map can either be developed in Decision Explorer or transferred to the software upon completion. This then enables varying levels of coding and analysis of linkages. Two useful analysis functions include:

- Cent – (Centrality)
    - This analysis tool examines the centrality of a concept or set of concepts based on its linkages, implying a level of criticality of the strategic issue as perceived by the

participants. Centrality analysis is an approach to identifying "nub of the issue" (Eden, 1988a: 11).

- Domain
  - This analysis tool explores the density of direct links to an idea and analysis.

(Please note that Decision Explorer offers a much wider range of analysis tools than are detailed here).

Centrality analysis

Exploration of concept centrality, using centrality analysis within Decision Explorer which analyses individual concept linkages to its directly linked concepts and wider linkages. This highlights ideas which have a high density of links and are further elaborated or supported by other ideas within the cognitive mapping process.

Percentages of concept centrality within each of the idea sections, namely issues, core competence, goals, actions, and statement of strategic intent. Percentages section derived factor of all ideas generated, comparative analysis.

The centrality score derived from Decision Explorer (DE) represents the collectively of concepts with links immediately around each concept, the second figure being the wider range of concepts linked to the central concept. This identifies busier concepts developed by the workshop actors (Eden, 2004). Higher number of connections around an issue indicates the centrality and importance of that issue; this approach is based on the assumption that actors will discuss issues of importance more frequently (di Gregorio, 2006). (Jones, 2002: 67) summarises the scoring thus:

> The analysis uses a scoring system for calculation. For each level away from the central concept, the score attached to the number of concepts is reduced. Those concepts immediately linking into the central concept score 1, those concepts that link into them score 0.5, those that link into them score 0.33, and so on up to 7 levels out.

Interconnectivity domain

One approach to the analysis of specific ideas or nodes within the map is domain analysis. This is a calculation of which ideas/nodes have the highest number of causal links, and indicates which ideas are more cognitively central to the map. This analysis does not consider the complexity of the map as a whole, but does effectively rank the cognitive importance of each idea.

Interconnectivity centrality analysis central concepts

Analysis of the immediate connectivity of an idea or node ignores any wider context and broader connectivity across the map as a whole. Centrality analysis is founded on the same principle as Domain but adds additional layers of connectivity giving a broader understanding of the importance of the idea within the cognitive causal map. The analysis counts direct links to the idea, then the links to this second level and then on to a defined level. A further refinement of this broader connectivity is through the weighting of the connected links diminishing with distance from the central idea or node. Effectively each concept ring of connectivity having a reduced waiting up to a maximum. This is referred to as centrality analysis and is conveniently undertaken through specialist software (Jones, 2002; di Gregorio, 2006). A higher number indicates more important cognitive centrality of an idea. Key ideas with higher centrality can then be compared across differing maps for analysis.

9.6 Chapter summary

This chapter has explored the background and approaches to causal mapping. One thing a strategy practitioner should always bear in mind is that organising the map is in itself a form of analysis. By just organising and reducing crossing lines and bringing ideas together into logical groups will reveal useful information. This may feel more of a craft than a formal analysis, but it does enable group thinking, priorities, and the key cognitive areas of attention and interest to be displayed. Our advice when first attempting analysis of any cognitive map is first to organise the map, then just look at it, establish where elements of density appear, what groupings are most populated, and what the central constructs are. Does the map keep emphasising a single set of themes? Doing this first can help reduce the background noise of a complex map and help the strategist focus on the key areas for attention and discussion.

References

Abuabara, L. & Paucar-Caceres, A. (2021). Surveying applications of strategic options development and analysis (soda) from 1989 to 2018. *European Journal of Operational Research*, 292, 1051–1065.

Ackermann, F., Eden, C. & Cropper, S. (1992). *Getting Started with Cognitive Mapping*. Cumbria, UK: Banxia Software.

Alvesson, M. & Spicer, A. (2019). Neo-institutional theory and organization studies: A mid-life crisis? *Organization Studies*, 40, 199–218.

Axelrod, R. M. (1976). *Structure of Decision: The Cognitive Maps of Political Elites*. Princeton: Princeton University Press.

Bannister, D. & Fransella, F. (1971). *Inquiring Man: The Theory of Personal Constructs*. Harmondsworth: Penguin.

Bougon, M. G. (1992). Congregate cognitive maps – a unified dynamic theory of organization and strategy. *Journal of Management Studies*, 29, 369–389.

Brightman, J. (2003). *Mapping Methods for Qualitative Data Structuring (qds)*. Strategies in qualitative research: Methodological issues and practices using QSR NVivo and NUD* IST conference, London, UK.

Burgess, G. M., Clark, T. D., Hauser, R. D. & Zmud, R. W. (1992). The application of causal maps to develop a collective understanding of complex organizational contexts in requirements analysis. *Accounting, Management and Information Technologies*, 2, 143–164.

Burr, V. (1996). *An Introduction to Social Constructionism*. London: Routledge.

Buzan, T. & Buzan, B. (1996). *The Mind Map Book: How to Use Radiant Thinking to Maximize Your Brain\'S Untapped Potential*. New York: Penguin.

Coyle, R. G. (1977). *Management System Dynamics*. London: John Wiley & Sons Australia, Limited.

Crilly, D. & Sloan, P. (2012). Enterprise logic: Explaining corporate attention to stakeholders from the 'inside-out'. *Strategic Management Journal*, 33, 1174–1193.

Daft, R. L. & Lengel, R. H. (1986). Organizational information requirements, media richness and structural design. *Management Science*, 32, 554–571.

Di Gregorio, S. (2006). *Introduction to Decision Explorer*. A short course note. Retrieved August 8, 2018, from https://banxia.com/pdf/de/DEIntro1.pdf.

Dimaggio, P. J. & Powell, W. W. (1983). The iron cage revisited – institutional isomorphism and collective rationality in organizational fields. *American Sociological Review*, 48, 147–160.
Eden, C. (1988a). Cognitive mapping. *European Journal of Operational Research*, 36, 1–13.
Eden, C. (1988b). *Strategic Decision Support Through the Use of Computer Based Analysis and Presentation of Cognitive Maps*. Strathclyde: University of Strathclyde, Department of Management Science.
Eden, C. (1992). On the nature of cognitive maps. *Journal of Management Studies*, 29, 261–265.
Eden, C. (1994). Cognitive mapping and problem structuring for system dynamics model-building. *System Dynamics Review*, 10, 257–276.
Eden, C. (1995). Strategic options development and analysis (Soda). In Reinhold, A. J. (Ed.), *Rational Analysis Revisited: Proceedings of a One-Day Event on Problem Structuring Methods Organised by the Operational Research Society and Laseors*. Birmingham: Operational Research Society.
Eden, C. (2004). Analyzing cognitive maps to help structure issues or problems. *European Journal of Operational Research*, 159, 673–686.
Eden, C. & Ackermann, F. (1998). *Making Strategy: The Journey of Strategic Management*. Thousand Oaks, CA, London: Sage.
Eden, C. & Ackermann, F. (2000). Mapping distinctive competencies: A systemic approach. *The Journal of the Operational Research Society*, 51, 12–20.
Eden, C., Ackermann, F. & Cropper, S. (1992). The analysis of cause maps. *Journal of Management Studies*, 29, 309–324.
Hodgkinson, G. P., Maule, A. J. & Bown, N. J. (2004). Causal cognitive mapping in the organizational strategy field: A comparison of alternative elicitation procedures. *Organizational Research Methods*, 7, 3–26.
Hogarth, R. M. (1987). *Judgement and Choice: The Psychology of Decision*. Chichester: Wiley.
Huff, A. S. (1990). *Mapping Strategic Thought*. Chichester: John Wiley & Sons.
Jarzabkowski, P. (2004). Strategy as practice: Recursiveness, adaptation, and practices-in-use. *Organization Studies*, 25, 529–560.
Johnson-Laird, P. N. (1983). *Mental Models: Towards a Cognitive Science of Language, Inference, and Consciousness*. Cambridge, MA: Harvard University Press.
Jones, M. (2002). *Decision Explorer User's Guide Version 3.2.3.2 Ed*. Kendal: Branxia Software Ltd.
Kelly, G. (1955). *The Psychology of Personal Constructs*. New York: W.W. Norton.
Laukkanen, M. (1994). Comparative cause mapping of organizational cognitions. *Organization Science*, 5, 322–343.
Laukkanen, M. (2012). Comparative causal mapping and cmap3 software in qualitative studies. *Forum: Qualitative Social Research*, 13.
Lindberg, K. (2014). Performing multiple logics in practice. *Scandinavian Journal of Management*, 30, 485–497.
Lloyd, K. E., Reid, L. S. & Feallock, J. B. (1960). Short-term retention as a function of the average number of items presented. *Journal of Experimental Psychology: General*, 60, 201–207.
Markóczy, L. & Goldberg, J. (1995). A method for eliciting and comparing causal maps. *Journal of Management*, 21, 305–333.
Montazemi, A. R. & Conrath, D. W. (1986). The use of cognitive mapping for information requirements analysis. *Management Information Systems Quarterly*, 10, 45–56.
Montibeller, G. & Belton, V. (2006). Causal maps and the evaluation of decision options: A review. *The Journal of the Operational Research Society*, 57, 779–791.
Nelson, K. M., Nadkarni, S., Narayanan, V. K. & Ghods, M. (2000). Understanding software operations support expertise: A revealed causal mapping approach. *Mis Quarterly*, 24, 475–507.
Nelson, K. M., Nelson, H. J. & Armstrong, D. (2000). *Revealed Causal Mapping as an Evocative Method for Information Systems Research*. Proceedings of the 33rd Annual Hawaii International Conference on System Sciences, January 7–7, 2000, p. 10, vol. 2.
Ørngreen, R. & Levinsen, K. (2017). Workshops as a research methodology. *Electronic Journal of E-learning*, 15, 70–81.

Prahalad, C. K. & Bettis, R. A. (1986). The dominant logic: A new linkage between diversity and performance. *Strategic Management Journal*, 7, 485–501.

Schraven, D., Hartmann, A. & Dewulf, G. P. M. R. (2015). Resuming an unfinished tale: Applying causal maps to analyze the dominant logics within an organization. *Organizational Research Methods*, 18, 326–349.

Scott, W. R. (2004). Reflections on a half-century of organizational sociology. *Annual Review of Sociology*, 30, 1–21.

Scott, W. R. (2008). Approaching adulthood: The maturing of institutional theory. *Theory and Society*, 37, 427–442.

Spender, J.-C. (1989). Industry recipes: The nature and sources of managerial judgment. *Oxford, UK: Basic Blackwell. (1994), "Knowing, Managing and Learning," Management Learning*, 25, 387–412.

Weick, K. E. (1995). *Sensemaking in Organizations*. London, Thousand Oaks, CA: Sage Publications.

Weick, K. E. & Bougon, M. G. (1986). Organizations as cognitive maps: Charting ways to success and failure. In H. P. Sims & D. A. Gioia (Eds.), *The Thinking Organization*. London: Jossey-Bass Publishers.

Chapter 10

Running a strategy workshop – a practical guide

Learning outcomes

After reading this chapter you should be able to:

- facilitate and conduct a strategy-making workshop that is timely and effective and engages all participants in a useful and simple process

Pre-chapter questions

- As a student, what would you expect to see in a workshop devoted to helping you to develop and refine strategy?
- As a tutor, how would you organise a strategy development workshop? What would it contain? How would you structure it?

Key terms

- Affordances – the properties of an object or tool- its possibilities or constraints. (Jarzabkowski and Kaplan, 2015)
- Goal – unquantified and open-ended statement with no specified time for completion (Wheelen, 2012)

10.1 Introduction

This chapter offers the reader a simple model for undertaking a strategy workshop. It has been adapted from Ackermann and Eden's Strategic Options Development and Analysis model (SODA) (Ackermann et al., 1992; Eden, 1992; Bryson et al., 1995; Eden, 1995; Ackermann et al., 2010), with the addition of some classical tools and a modification of some elements. If you find this method appealing, we strongly recommend reading

DOI: 10.4324/9780429344305-15

further around Ackermann and Eden's work and exploring the Decision Explorer (Jones, 2002) software designed for the purpose. The process shown here is a simple and straightforward method for eliciting strategy that can work at any level within the organisation, from an organisational team or department through to higher corporate levels.

The approach demonstrated here has a number of advantages:

- It is fast and efficient.
- All participants will have their voices and insights heard and linked to the final outcomes.
- It is a democratic process where decisions and insights are collated jointly.
- The cognitive map itself is effective and simple way of expressing complexity.
- The process is fundamentally simple and relies on the insights of the participants to generate content.
- No special resources are required.
- The model is fairly open in nature (although it must be noted that all strategy tools have affordances and limitations).
- Participants can attend the workshop with no pre-existing work or preparation.

The following section details the mechanics and processes within a workshop. Participants will be asked to compile issues, core competence, goals, actions, and develop a summary statement. This is undertaken through the following process within the workshop.

10.2 Process overview

The strategy making workshop has five key elements: issues, distinctive competence, goals, actions, and statement of strategic intent.

1 What are the strategic issues facing the organisation?
2 Resources and distinctive (Core) competence?
3 What goals/aspirations emerge from this?
4 What actions would you commit to taking (to achieve goals in light of these issues, support by distinctive competence)?
5 What would be a strategy statement that summarised those actions?

The process is illustrated in Figure 10.1.

The elements of the workshop are framed and presented to participants as questions, which are then responded to either individually or as a group. As you can see from Figure 10.2 we start by exploring what strategic issues are facing the organisation. This is first undertaken by individuals with no particular guidance, just using their insights and observations. The second part of this issues generation utilises a range of classical strategy tools to elicit a broader range of issues and address a common concern in public sector organisations and smaller operational units that they can be too inward or operationally focused Issue generation is the longest element of the workshop and is followed by the participants' clustering and bringing together of ideas and issues that are linked or complementary. This is illustrated in Table 10.1.

There is no right or wrong way of forming clusters, as the participants themselves will understand the linkages and will relate and connect ideas that make sense to them from

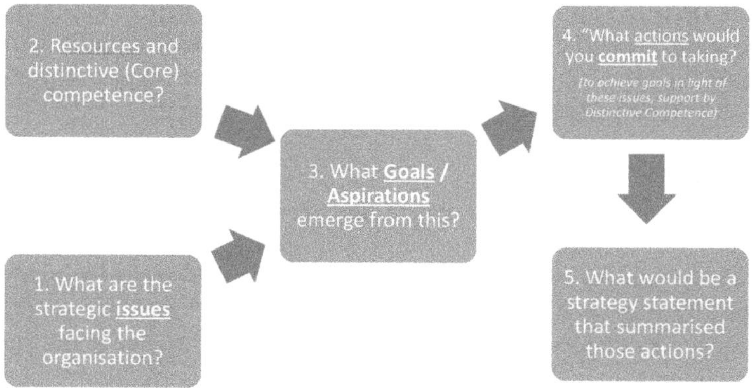

Figure 10.1 Strategy-making overview process

Figure 10.2 Professionals undertaking a strategy workshop

their perspective. The most effective way of restructuring the map is to let the participants do this themselves, moving issues/post-its around on the wall until they achieve a consensus. Once clusters are formed, the participants will be asked to title the clusters, thereby making sense of the more complex range of issues within the cluster.

The workshop will then turn to explore unique capability or core competence. The facilitator will introduce the nature of core competence and this tends to be one of the more difficult aspects of the workshop. Participants are asked to find capability that is unique and distinct, and workshops frequently draw a blank with no unique competence ideas generated. After a strict application of core competence the author has found it

Table 10.1 Strategy-making table of activities

Stage	*Question*	*Group or individual*	*Activity*	*Capture method*
1a	What are the strategic issues facing the organisation?	Individual	Write issues on colour-coded post-its.	Place colour-coded post-its on wall until individuals can no longer develop issues
1b			Develop further issues using a variety of standard strategy tools	
1c		Group	Group issues, with group consensus	Move issues into groups and title
2	Explore core competence	Individual and group	Brief clarification of definition of core competence by facilitator. Write and or debate	Produce colour-coded core competencies using post-its placed on wall
3a	What goals/ aspirations emerge from this?	Individual	Write goals on colour-coded post-its, linked to group issues	Place colour-coded post-its on wall above grouped issues
3b		Group	Discuss and refine goals to reach consensus	Modify goals, rewrite and finalise
3c			Link core competence to goal clusters	
4	What actions would you recommend the organisation takes	Group	Group discussion	Produce colour-coded post-its of actions and finalise actions with group consensus
5	Develop a strategy statement that summarises actions	Group	Group discussion	Written statements

beneficial to soften the theory and generate the capability that the participants feel is beneficial, which may not fit the strict definition of core competence.

At this point, we then ask the participants to explore goals or aspirations which emerge directly out of the original issue clusters. Is important at this stage that goals or strategic intent do not come from elsewhere (such as an existing strategic plan); the idea is to have the goals emerge causally from the issues generated. Again the range of goals can be clustered and labelled directly by the participants.

Participants are then asked to link any developed competence to the goals, asking: are any of the goal supported by any of the capability within the organisation? This can be interesting as some competence may no longer be useful to the goals stated, or there may be goals that do not have any competence or capability underpinning them.

Next, the participants are asked to develop specific actions that can be undertaken to meet the goals. This may be problematic in some settings as specific action setting may require higher level approvals; but actions for actions, such as establishing meetings to further discuss or seek approval for, may be appropriate at this stage.

Lastly the participants are asked to summarise their strategic intent. This could be through a mission statement or a summary of the session or even just an agenda for discussion at the next meeting. Frequently mission statements do not fit within some cultures within the public sector, and so other ways of summarising the strategic intent are appropriate. Figure 10.2 shows a group of students who are undertaking the exercise.

In Figure 10.3 we can see a model of the cognitive map and how it may piece together.

Figure 10.4 offers two images showing examples of working walls under development

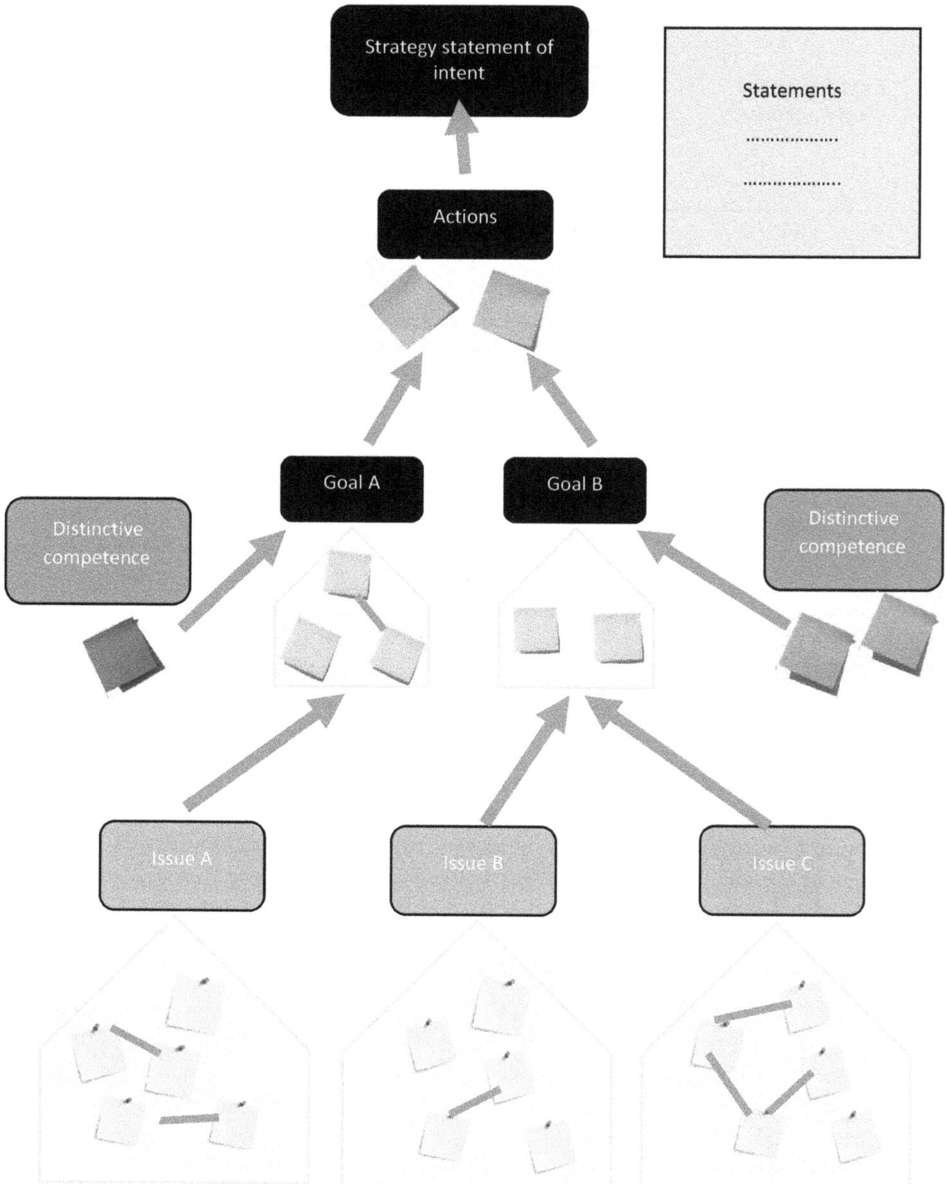

Figure 10.3 Cognitive map shape

Figure 10.4 a, b – Examples of working walls

10.3 General guidance

The following are some insights and tips for running a successful workshop. They are borne from our own experiences but, of course, these can be modified to suit the needs of the specific session.

Roles

The workshop requires at least one facilitator. This person can also be a part of the strategy-making process but is key to guiding the process,

- keeping the process to time
- ensuring
    - causal linkages,
    - generation of clusters
    - clarification of words/issues/content

Participant Numbers: workshops can be undertaken on individual basis through to large groups. The largest the author has undertaken was around 120 participants with the NHS. As a rule of thumb for a fast and effective group, 5 to 15 participants works well. But this is not absolute, and different group sizes can bring different dynamics and insights.

Time

Although the original SODA literature refers to numerous days for a strategy workshop (Eden, 1995), in the authors experience public sector organisations have limited time, and a single seven-hour-day is ideal. However, workshops can be successfully run in three to four hours. This may not be the preferred length but the only time available by colleagues and staff. This short time period is perfectly feasible but relies on the facilitator to keep the workshop moving and focused. Feedback from organisations has emphasised that they appreciate a timely and driven workshop, with the facilitator keeping the group to time and maintaining a fast but un-rushed pace. Other organisations appreciated a break halfway through the session, a natural breakpoint being after the core competency work. Other groups ran to time without significant time management by the facilitator, and the three- to four-hour time period seems to work well.

Focus

"Get it on the map!"

Given the collegiate and interactive nature of the workshop, the facilitator will frequently find conversations and debates taking place. This is fine and to be expected, but to avoid the session turning into the dreaded "talking shop", the facilitator must ensure that any insights content or observations are recorded on the cognitive map. If it is not on the map it is not recorded and, thereby, strategic insights will not be derived in a formal manner.

Location

An ideal location will be a room that would comfortably house 15 to 30 participants with a large whiteboard, an overhead projector linked to a computer and tables, and seating that can be formed into a conference layout (i.e. one large tabled area with participants facing each other). Figure 10.5 is taken from one of our own workshops. The majority of rooms used like this have plenty of space for the participants to move around and work with the wall without feeling cluttered or finding they are entering each other's personal space.

The working wall/'issues wall' should be a long flat vertical space where content – such that paper/post-it notes, etc. can easily be placed, positioned, and viewed by all participants. The key benefit of a cognitive map is that complexity can be displayed in a manner which encompasses all of the thoughts and insights of the group. So a wide vertical space which can be viewed as a whole is essential

All participants will work with the "issues wall"; this will be the wall located within the room within which all participants place issues and ideas onto a number of flipchart sheets which have been previously blue tacked to the wall. The flipchart sheets enable groups of

Figure 10.5 Workshop in progress

factors to be manoeuvred easily up or down on the wall, changing the focus of the wall as the session moves forward.

It is important that the participants can clearly see the generated issues/factors and their links and can easily gain access to the wall.

Resources

It is quite possible to undertake the cognitive mapping process via software and should you be interested in pursuing this the author recommends Decision Explorer as it has been designed specifically for this purpose. However, given that time may be limited and the added complexity of bringing technology into the process, we would advise a simple flipchart paper with a set of coloured post-it notes.

- coloured post-it notes
- flipchart paper
- blue tack
- marker pens – mainly black other colours are useful

The standard colour format that we use in our own workshops is:

- yellow post-it notes for issues
- green post-it notes for goals
- pink post-it notes for core competence
- orange post-it notes for actions
- blue post-it notes for statement of strategic intent

Given that more post-its will be used for issues than any other area, we use yellow for this activity simply because they seem to be the colour most commonly available. Keeping the cognitive map colour-coded also helps the participants view the shape and frame of the finished map and really does assist in making sense of the complexity.

We prefer marker pens over pens or pencils, as they force the writer to use larger text which can be seen from a distance. Text written with a normal pen cannot be seen from a distance, and again the benefits of the cognitive map is lost.

Writing the ideas or concepts

The participants within the workshops will frequently use single words for concepts such as "time" or "money". Following training on cognitive mapping, all participants will be asked to use verbs and actors; for example "time" would change to "more time required by tutors", thus giving analytical detail and context. This would also mitigate against misunderstanding of the participants meaning within their proposed idea. This is referred to as actor and action with a guide word count of no more than 10 words per post-it. This helps clarify the idea and limit complexity. Figure 10.6 shows students in discussion.

The participants will need to keep to one idea per post-it; this enables the group to move the post-its freely – clustering and causally relating to other concepts and ideas.

- the use of single words for concepts lacks detail for analysis, include verbs and actors; for example, "time" would change to "more time required by tutors"
- concepts/ideas = one idea per post-it note

Figure 10.6 a, b – Student discussions

Managing the physical content

One useful approach the facilitator can take is to start off by having flipchart paper at eye level whilst generating the issue's content. Once this section is complete and the issues have been clustered, the flipchart paper can be moved down to waist level. This leaves room for fresh flipchart paper above the issues to generate goals and actions. This gives the map a hierarchical structure and room to breathe during the session.

Causality and relationships

The causal nature of a cognitive map is a critical element in developing insights. Issues may link to other issues which then link up to and imply goals. The goals themselves may be causally underpinned by unique capability, and then goals will causally link up to actions and a strategy statement. It is the causality that binds the map together and ensures that all insights and the participants cognition is worked through. Looking at the finished map the cognitive links can imply which ideas or areas are critical or core to the thinking of the group, known as core constructs. If required, deeper analysis can also be undertaken by analysing the cognitive links and utilising software to further analyse the linkages and implied importance rankings of concepts

Pre-work

One of the benefits of this process is that participants can arrive without any formal preparation work. In many ways capturing the participants thoughts/cognitive schema is useful in understanding where priorities are and what is concerning participants.

Managing expectations

The overall process intends to explore and group issues facing the organisation, understand the unique capability the organisation may have, develop goals that emerge from the issues and capability, and then specify actions on the strategic intent. Within public sector organisations, the final specification of committed actions in a detailed and targeted manner may be difficult. Larger public sector organisations tend to have a complex hierarchy and approvals process. So committing to specific actions within the bounds of the developmental workshop might not be feasible; it may be more feasible to develop themes or areas for exploration or even actions to be considered by wider or more senior management. This is not a shortcoming just the nature of a large public sector organisation, and the workshop will assist in clarifying the strategic direction and focus of the organisation or department.

A further expectation is that all generated ideas and concepts will be causally linked across the map. Many of us would have participated in post-it note workshops where hundreds of post-its were developed, and perhaps it was not clear how they are related to or informed the final outcome of the workshop. Given the causal nature of this process, every post-it will be linked to a group, cluster, and subsequent goal, so that every participant's insight is in some way connected. The author has found that this is essential for engagement and legitimacy within the process and separates the process out from looser collaborative working approaches.

Photography

At various points during the session, it is worth recording the maps development with photography. Any camera is appropriate as long as the ideas and concepts are legible when zoomed in. A tip would be to take far more photographs than you think you require and to also photograph single flipchart sections, as well as taking photographs of the whole map, to get a feel for the wider causal relationships.

Our suggestion is that photographs be taken at the end of each stage, as the process of grouping and summarising issues can hide compiled stacks of physically mounted post-it notes containing the issues or factors. These can then be obscured and are then not captured with photographic evidence.

10.4 Worked example

This section shows how we conduct a typical workshop. We begin by getting students to highlight issues, and we work our way through the workshop outlining some of the key models that we have found to be effective from our experience.

Stage 1a – Issues

(Yellow post-it notes)

The facilitator directs participants to write issues that their organisation or department faces. The participants use marker pens and yellow post-it notes to avoid single words

Figure 10.7 – Stage 1a

and attempt to state actor and action. It is important that each post-it note contains a single issue. This activity continues until participants "dry up" and can no longer think of any new issues. Throughout this process the facilitator collects and roughly groups the ideas on the wall (Figure 10.7). We find that it is sometimes convenient to have draft titles at this stage just to assist in the initial grouping. Typically, this stage takes about 45 minutes.

Stage 1b – Issues, with models to prompt issue generation

(Yellow Post-it notes with directed models to support thinking and evaluation)

The facilitator introduces single slides or offers brief overviews of common strategy development tools. Following the brief explanation of the nature of the tool, participants individually explore any issues that may be prompted by these tools or perspectives. It may be the case that the tool does not generate any further issues. This is not an error nor is it a problem. It is merely an indicator that the tool did not inspire wider insight. It is not the intent at this stage to dwell excessively on individual strategic tools; it is a brief explanation and exploration of the tool to widen participant's perspectives and generate issues. Figure 10.8 shows some potential avenues for exploration.

Tool 1 market basics

This tool is a consideration of the market or the "sector" of the market. Participants may give consideration as to whether their particular sector or field is growing demand or size, how this compares to previous years, and the extent to which their organisation accommodates or shares the sector with other providers. The facilitator should explain market

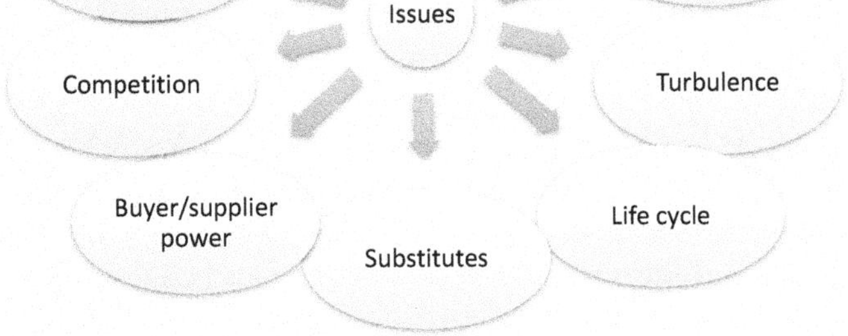

Figure 10.8 A sample of classical strategic management model insights

basics and then explore each one in order to elicit insight and issues from the participants of the workshop. Typical areas to explore might be:

- sector definition and size
    - What is the market/sector? (Scope of strategic opportunity)
    - What is its size? (annual sales)
- sector growth
    - Previous year? Patterns and trends? (linked to growth objectives)
- sector share
    - Is a large share beneficial? Is a small share a problem?

Tool 2 turbulence

This tool can assist participants in evaluating the future of their sector, how likely it is to change, and how predictable that change might be. The facilitator should explain the various aspects of the turbulence model (Lynch, 2021) and then explore each of the sections in order to elicit insight and issues from the participants of the workshop. Areas in Lynch's (2021) model to explore might be:

- Changeability
    - the degree to which the environment is likely to change
    - complexity *e.g. Information Technology changes the nature of work, changes lifestyles, alters consumer behaviour*
    - novelty (new situations)
- Predictability
    - the degree to which changes can be predicted
    - rate of change (of the environment)
    - visibility of the future

As Lynch (2021) observes, areas of high turbulence and/or hyper competition are difficult environments to study, and thus the facilitator may need to spend extra time in these situations.

Tool 3 the industry life-cycle model

The industry life-cycle model prompts participants to consider their industry or sector in terms of its life-cycle (Figure 10.9) Is the service or provision near the end of its life-cycle or in development, and if so, does this prompt any strategic issue generation? The facilitator should explain the various aspects of the industry life-cycle model and then explore each of the sections in order to elicit insight and issues from the participants of the workshop.

	Development	Growth	Shakeout	Maturity	Decline
Users/ buyers	Few: Early adopters	Growing adopters: Trial of product	Growing selectivity of purchase	Saturation Repeat purchase reliance	Drop-off in usage
Competitive conditions	Few competitors	Competitor entry Fight for share Undifferentiated	Many: Price-cutting Shakeout of weakest	Fight to maintain share Emphasis on low cost	Exit of some competitors

Figure 10.9 The industry life-cycle/portfolio matrix

Tool 4 FESTEL

The macro-economic environment can be brought into the analysis using PESTLE. Students need to consider how various aspects of the external environment impact on their own organisation:

- political
- economic
- sociocultural
- technological
- environmental
- legal

Within the public sector, we have found this one of the more useful tools as it can direct organisational and operational units to consider higher-level macro-economic drivers, thereby ensuring that participants have considered these drivers when considering strategy. The facilitator should explain the various aspects of the PESTLE analysis and then explore each of the sections in order to elicit insight and issues from the participants of the workshop.

There are many versions of PESTEL that might be explored at the discretion of the facilitator (such as PEST, PESTELE, SPECTACLES, LE PEST C, LONGPEST), and readers are encouraged to explore these for themselves.

Tool 5 Porter's five forces

Porter's five forces traditionally supports strategic analysis at the industry level. Interestingly, we have found that participants from the public sector who are perhaps in a contracting or commissioning role find the model exceptionally useful. Staff within a more operational setting within the public sector find the use of the model, in its true sense, difficult. However, consideration of the various forces can be beneficial and, although this would be a modified use of the model, some interesting strategic insight can be developed by its exploration during the workshop.

The facilitator should explain the premise of Porter's five forces analysis and then explore each of the forces in order to elicit insight and issues from the participants of the workshop. We have explored this model extensively earlier in the book.

Tool 6 value chain (especially support activities)

Value chain analysis can also be useful in mentally breaking organisational staff members out of their departmental unit or service and considering the wider value generating order tracking elements of their organisation. Although the standard diagram is based on manufacturing, explaining to participants the difference between primary and support activities has proved beneficial to public sector participants in considering the wider organisation and its impact on local or organisational level strategies. The facilitator should explain the nature of value chain analysis and then explore each relevant support activities, primary activities, and the wider value network in order to elicit insight and issues from the participants of the workshop. Again, we have explored this model earlier in the book

Tool 7 stakeholders of a large organisation

It is highly likely that participants have already considered a wide range of stakeholders when reviewing strategic issues. Figure 10.10 outlines a range of stakeholders which we have found useful as a prompt for participants to consider a wider range of organisational stakeholders and to use the power interest matrix to establish stakeholders of particular strategic importance.

The facilitator should direct participants to consider a wide range of stakeholders and evaluate their power and interest in order to elicit insight and issues.

Tool 8 SWOT

The final tool within this brief exploration of classical models is SWOT. Although seemingly a very straightforward strategy tool, our experience shows that this final sense checking activity can be useful in eliciting strategic issues. The very simplicity of the model can open up participants thinking and bring in issue ideas previously hidden. The facilitator should direct participants to consider each of the elements of SWOT – ensuring a focus on the internal aspects for strengths and weaknesses and external aspects for opportunities and threats in order to draw out insight and issues.

We have found it especially insightful to use a TOWS matrix to take the analysis to a deeper level. We ask students to draw a grid with threats and opportunities along the top and weaknesses and strengths down the side (Figure 10.11).

By doing this, students are encouraged to apply SWOT. How can an organisation use its strengths to exploit its opportunities? How can an organisation use its strengths to manage its threats? etc. In this way, we have found that the simple application of SWOT can produce a lot of rich discussion.

Figure 10.10 Range of stakeholders that might be considered in a strategy workshop

	Threats	*Opportunities*
Weaknesses		
Strengths		

Figure 10.11 TOWS matrix

Stage 1c – working with the issues

At this stage the facilitator/researcher may have roughly grouped some of the issues as they are produced. The participants are then asked to stand up and physically move issues into groups on the wall. Participants are directly asked to do this as the language, references, and aspects of the issues will only be clearly understood by the participants. As this process reaches completion the facilitator/researcher then goes through each grouping with the participants focusing on each group in turn, ensuring consensus and refining the groupings and reaching a consensus on the words/titles used. Figures 10.12 and 10.13 show the stages in action.

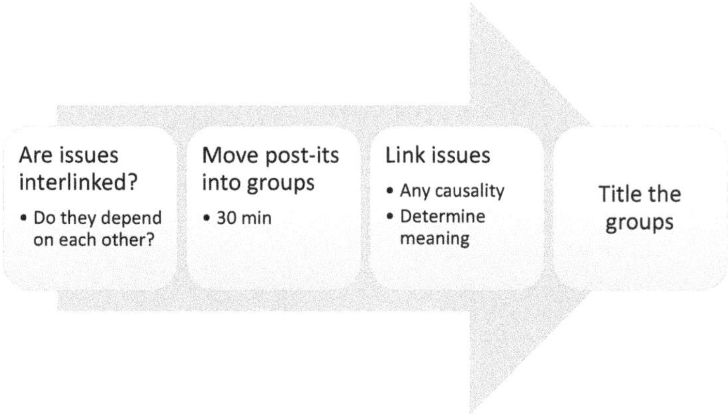

Figure 10.12 Working with issues

Figure 10.13 Students working with issues

Stage 2 core competency

(Pink post-it notes)

The facilitator/researcher gives a brief overview and explanation of core competence as defined by the strategy literature. This section tends to be difficult for the group as highlighting unique resource or competence, strictly to the academic definition, is difficult. As we can see in Figure 10.14, for a something to be classed as a unique or core competence it must meet a number of strict criteria. Although difficult, some factors are frequently produced and debated by the group.

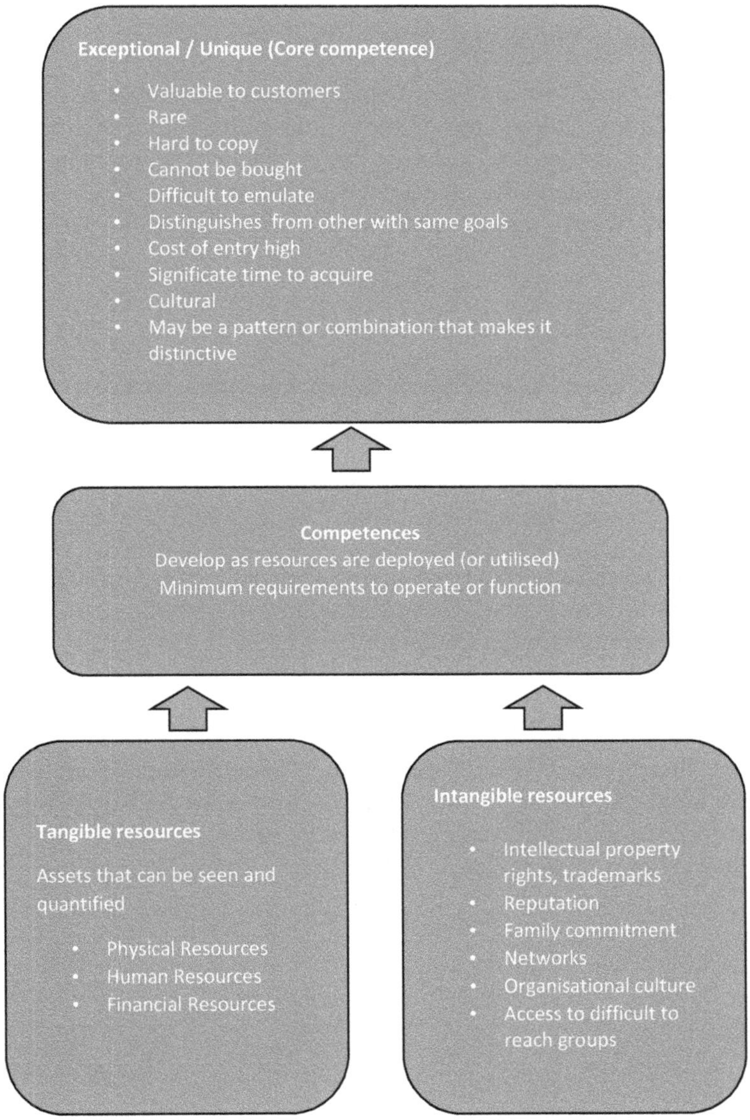

Figure 10.14 Describing and using core competence

One observation is that the focus in this section is on what unique core competence or unique resources the organisation may have; however, you may wish to allow the debate to explore lacking core competence or core competence that could be developed. This may be beneficial as it could give strong indications of actions and resources required for the future. A further element of this section is to "soften" the definition of core competence, thereby allowing participants to explore attributes or competencies that they feel are beneficial to their organisation, even if they do not meet the strict terms of the theory.

Stage 3a & b Goals

(Green post-it notes)

The facilitator individuals now guides participants to generate implied goals, linked to (and emerging from) the organised groups/clusters. At this point, the facilitator/researcher can move the flipchart sheets down to waist level to enable new flipchart sheets to be placed above the grouped issues, showing a natural link from issues up to goals. This works well, and the production of goals and the refinement of these goals into groups is generally straightforward.

Sense check

Before we move to the next activity, it can be beneficial to undertake a sense check.

The facilitator should ask the participants:

- If these goals drove you organisation, does this make sense?
- Is there anything missing?

This activity may produce nothing but is useful in redirecting the participants to the strategic nature of the activity and give a sense of how they would respond if these goals became the organisations strategic direction.

Stage 3c linking competences to goals

This is where the map starts to really take shape. The facilitator will ask participants to link the core competence clusters to relevant goals, thereby finding a supporting core competence for each goal. This can be achieved by physically moving the core competence clustered notes next to the goals or by drawing a causal line using between them (Figure 10.15).

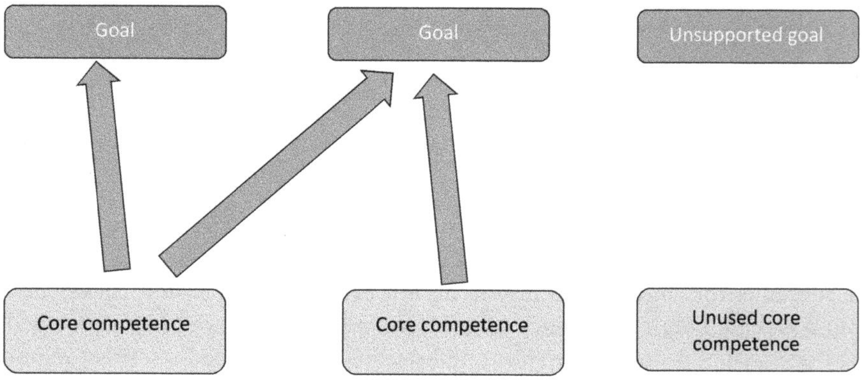

Figure 10.15 Linking competence clusters to goals

Stage 4 moving towards actions

(Orange post-it notes)

The facilitator asks participants to develop actions either individually or in groups that emerge directly from the goals. Is worth directing the participants to consider the supporting core competence or any lacking core competence for the desired goal as this may imply strategic action. Actions should lean towards a SMART-targeted approach, but the group may encounter some difficulty at this stage, in particular if working with a large public sector organisation. Where participants feel that specific actions can only be developed or approved with higher-level authority, the facilitator could direct participants to develop desired actions or actions which initiate the development of further activities; for example, by establishing working groups or undertaking discussions with relevant teams or staff.

Once participants have developed a number of ideas that are drying up, it can be worthwhile introducing the following guidance model (Figure 10.16). The intent here is to specifically ask questions relating goals and core competence and giving prompts that may support a generation of further strategic actions. The facilitator should work through the list exploring the broad strategic actions and develop new actions as a whole group.

Stage 5 summarising

(Blue post-it notes)

The final stage of the strategy workshop is to consider and develop a statement of strategic intent. Traditionally, this would be formed within a mission statement, but any statement that encompasses a summary of the business model or even the development of a draft

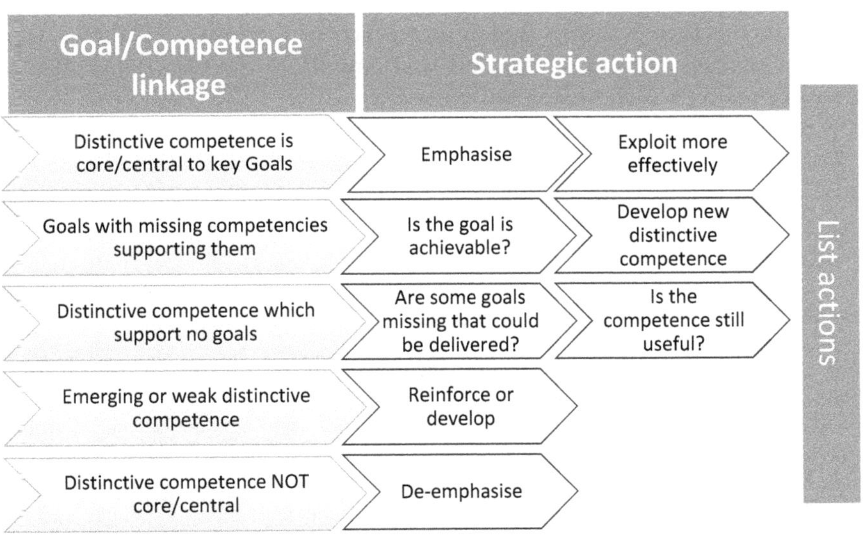

Figure 10.16 Linking competences to actions

agenda or specific actions for the next meeting could also be appropriate. The form of this final section is very dependent on the culture and nature of the organisation, but having an endpoint to the session, which encapsulates the broad strategic direction or broad themes established within the workshop, can very much round-out the work and give a more complete sense of having identified and expressed a strategy.

10.5 Chapter summary

We hope that the instructions and guidance given in this chapter will give you a good starting point for undertaking a strategy workshop with your colleagues or team. The addition of the classical models to Ackermann and Eden's standard strategy-making approach will hopefully broaden out participant's thinking, perhaps taking them into the macro- or industry-level environment. One reason for including these models is their ability to direct thinking outside of normal patterns or approaches, so they may be beneficial. Do remember that if participants do not produce ideas or issues, move on; the process is very much qualitative and dependent on the insights, thoughts, concerns, and priorities of the participating actors. If the group "dries up", keep moving.

Some final tips: establish how long the participants have available for the session and then keep the session moving to a fairly rigid clock. The issues section will be the most complex and generate the most information with subsequent sessions becoming faster and more focused. One thing to watch out for is the session turning into a discussion. Frequently participants have not had a formal opportunity to discuss strategy and so topics and issues will start to be debated in the group; a balance must be reached between allowing useful insightful debate and getting through the session. So having the constant mantra of "put it on the wall" will ensure that any conversations or insights undertaken by the group are logged and recorded within the cognitive map and are adding to the broader strategic insight, rather than just being lost in a talking shop.

A certain enthusiasm is always useful, as a much better map is produced when the facilitator encourages participants to move and coordinate the map rather than use the facilitator as a proxy; it is also faster and more fun.

Lastly, the maps will always start off looking complex, confused, and relatively cluttered. The process of grouping and reducing overlaps really does clean the map up; and no matter the number of issues or ideas generated, the map will distil down into some key important thematic areas which participants will recognise.

References

Ackermann, F., Eden, C. & Brown, I. (2010). *The Practice of Making Strategy: A Step-by-Step Guide*. London: Sage.

Ackermann, F., Eden, C. & Cropper, S. (1992). *Getting Started with Cognitive Mapping*. Cumbria, UK: Banxia Software.

Bryson, J., Ackermann, F., Eden, C. & Finn, C. (1995). *Using the 'Oval Mapping Process' to Identify Strategic Issues and Formulate Effective Strategies*. In: J.M. Bryson. Strategic planning for public and nonprofit organisations. San Francisco, CA: Jossey Bass, pp. 257–275.

Eden, C. (1992). On the nature of cognitive maps. *Journal of Management Studies*, 29, 261–265.
Eden, C. (1995). *Strategic Options Development and Analysis (Soda).*
Jarzabkowski, P. & Kaplan, S. (2015). Strategy tools-in-use: A framework for understanding "technologies of rationality" in practice. *Strategic Management Journal*, 36, 537–558.
Jones, M. (2002). *Decision Explorer User's Guide Version 3.2.3.2 Ed.* Kendal: Branxia Software Ltd.
Lynch, R. (2021). *Strategic Management.* London: Sage Publications.
Wheelen, T. L. (2012). *Concepts in Strategic Management and Business Policy: Toward Global Sustainability Plus New* [Place of publication not identified]. Harlow: Prentice Hall.

Chapter 11

Case studies and insights from public sector strategy sessions

Learning outcomes

After reading this chapter you should be able to:

- identify potential challenges when developing public sector strategies
- observe institutional tensions and actor perceptions in strategy development
- gain insight into undertaking and evaluating strategy workshops
- be aware of value disconnections

Pre-chapter questions

- Is a business unit held back by their local legitimacy, or are the higher order fields lacking perception about the unit's attributes or values?
- Does a business unit and the higher order stakeholders share the same values or objectives? Is the purpose of the organisation clear?
- What is the scope of a strategy session? Do participants include or exclude aspects of their profession?

Key terms

- Allied Health Professions (AHP) - a wide range of health professions, distinct from nursing and pharmacy, including occupational therapy, physical therapy, speech and language, etc.
- University Technical College (UTC) – a form of UK schools linked to an industry frequently focusing on technical or STEM subjects.

11.1 Introduction

This chapter builds upon the previous chapter which showed how a workshop might be run. In this chapter we present worked examples to show what can be achieved in these

DOI: 10.4324/9780429344305-16

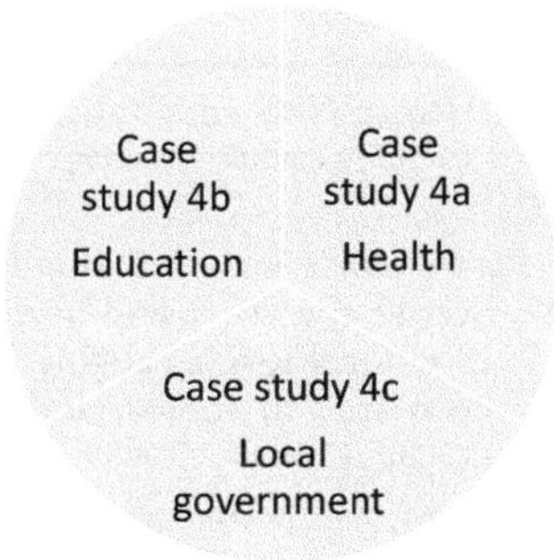

Figure 11.1 Case study sectors explored in this chapter

workshops and the level of understanding that can be gained. The purpose of this chapter is to examine a number of public sector strategy case studies and draw insights and guidance on the type of barriers, thinking, and approaches encountered when exploring strategy. The insights are not definitive, and the authors would caution against assuming universality of the analysis, but this exploration may give the reader a starting point for meta-theoretical thinking when undertaking organisational strategy; that is, thinking about the underlying assumptions or nature of the reality experienced by the participants within the public sector. The case studies were all undertaken using the strategy-making (Eden and Ackermann, 1998; Ackermann et al., 2005; Ackermann et al., 2010) approach outlined in Chapter 10 and analysed using Decision Explorer (Jones, 2002; di Gregorio, 2006) software with themes emerging following Braun and Clarke's (2006) thematic analysis principles.

The chapter explores three separate organisations: a profession within the UK National Health Service, a department within local government, and a new form of school. This is illustrated conceptually in Figure 11.1.

Each organisation and each sector is facing its own challenges but, as we will see, there are some interesting overlaps within legitimacy, organisational fields, and expectations of value.

Each case study describes the nature of the organisation, the numbers present in the workshop, the "apparent" organisational field (the use of this term will become clear during the case studies), the numbers of factors or ideas generated, a graphic of the map produced, the core constructs and their causation, and finally insights and summaries. The maps key themes are summarised within the table of core constructs and causation, and then each area is described; this is followed by an overview discussion. Please note that what is shown here is a summary and that brief overview analysis, specific details, and reports from decision explorer are omitted. The authors are happy to discuss the details further with interested parties.

11.2 Case study 4a health sector

Introduction to organisation

This workshop was undertaken for a single Mental Health NHS Foundation Trust within England. Participants came from a broad set of professions referred to as allied health

Table 11.1 Introduction to health workshop

Mental health professionals Mental Health NHS Foundation Trust Session details	
Participant numbers	10
Broad description of range of participants	Participants included allied health professional leads across the trust and interested clinicians from a variety of clinical levels ranging from band 6 to 7. These consisted of senior clinical staff and professional leads.
Organisational field and dimensions	• health • large, but made up of a broad range of partner organisations within health and public services • public • heavily regulated • localised to a region in England, UK
Workshop Revealed cognitive causal mapping details	Ideas generated: • issues 119 • goals 89 • core competence 1 • actions 6 • statement of strategic action NA Total: 215

professions or AHPs. This is a diverse range of professions including occupational therapists, physiotherapists, radiologists, paramedics, etc. (England, 2020). The workshop took place over two full days, and the participants chose not to undertake the final stage, the statement of strategic action. The work was developed into a published strategy and is currently in operation (Newbury, 2020). Table 11.1 provides information about the workshop

The organisation, situated within the Health Sector of the UN's National Health Service, is large and publicly owned.

In Figure 11.2, we can see a cognitive causal map as developed by the participants.

Although this diagram is difficult to read, we discuss the key elements in the coming pages. We did briefly consider presenting an extract of the diagram, but that might have led the reading into getting bogged down in the detail of each box rather than seeing the big picture. What is important for the purposes of this chapter is the general impression that the diagram reveals. Figure 11.2 clearly shows how ideas are structured and grouped, how common themes emerge, and how ideas link to other ideas. In this way, it becomes possible to identify relationships that may otherwise have remained hidden. In this particular case study, a number of interesting insights were obtained. Figure 11.3 is a thematic analysis of the cognitive map and summarises key core constructs and their causation.

Figure 11.4 shows the authors' interpretation of the detailed cognitive map. We have analysed the map alongside a centrality and domain analysis from Decision Explorer (as discussed in the preceding chapters), and we have then condensed our thoughts into the diagram.

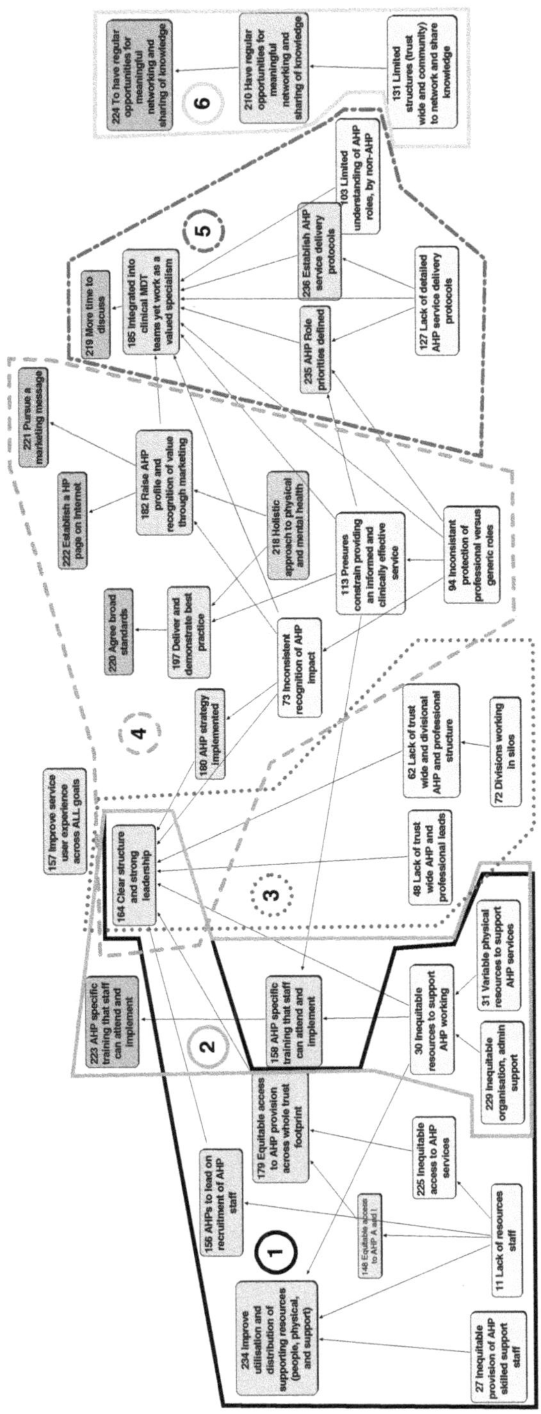

Figure 11.2 Revealed causal cognitive map: health sector

Causation	*Core constructs*
Improve access and equity of AHP provision across the trust, including recruitment, *lack of structure, and professional leads*	Legitimacy/value Clear structure and strong leadership
Barriers to training, research, practice, and measurement constraining an informed and clinically effective service. *A perception that AHP has low value, is dispensable, and it is difficult to express its value* *Conflicts and protection of professional role versus generic roles.* *Holistic approach to physical and mental health*	Legitimacy/value Demonstrating best practice and communicating this through marketing
Lack of detailed AHP service delivery protocols, pathways, and standards. *Limited understanding of AHP roles, by non-AHP practitioners*	Legitimacy/value Integration and recognition as a specialism supported by defined role and service protocols
Inequity of administration and physical resources *Improve, people and physical resources to assist in mitigating any inequality in provision*	Clear structure and strong leadership for resource and support
Inequity of administration and physical resources	AHP-specific training
The geographical and structural difficulties in interacting, networking, and sharing knowledge.	Establishment of meaningful networking and knowledge-sharing opportunities.

Figure 11.3 Key summary of core constructs and causation: health

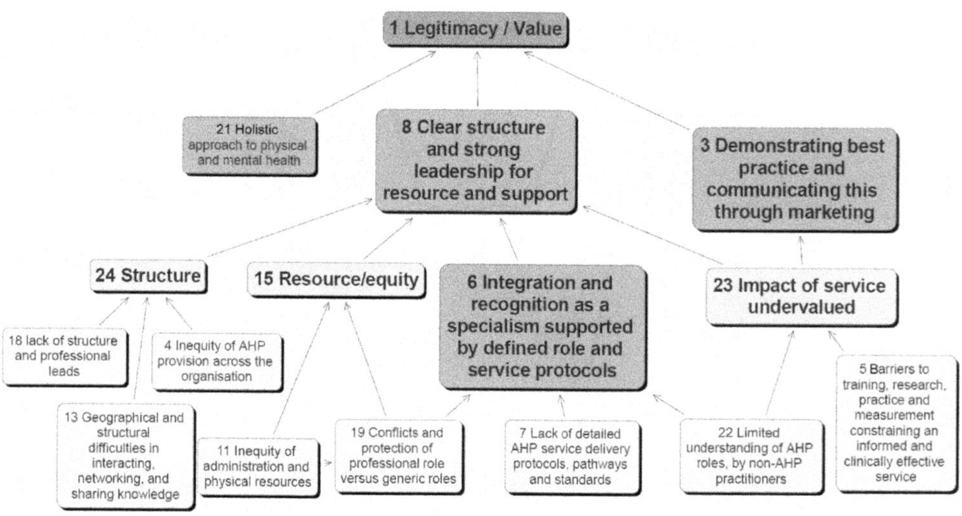

Figure 11.4 causal cognitive summary of analysis: health

Summary

Legitimacy/Value

A key element that is apparent through a centrality analysis is the group's need for legitimacy. This is articulated through issue areas, such as inconsistent recognition, comments on being a valued specialism, and the need to demonstrate best practice. Furthermore, participants stated the need to champion their unique approach to health care.

Leadership

This focus on legitimacy crosses over into the group's interest in improved leadership. Issues are raised on the nature and strength of the leadership and ensuring that the leaders of the wider organisation retain a focus on their field, which is currently viewed as overlooked.

Resource/equity

Leadership and legitimacy relate across to resource allocation and a lack of perceived equity in resource allocation both within the broad AHP's field and across differing AHP groups. In response to this the group looked to have more direct control over recruitment and training and the utilisation and distribution of supporting resources.

Structure

The resource and leadership themes also aligned with concerns of a lack of organisational structure within their field, this effecting promotion and career development.

Clarity of the offer: marketing

Many of the key areas of concern were seen to be addressed or linked to marketing and relationship marketing. In particular other parts of the organisation not understanding the AHP role or recognising its value linked to legitimacy drivers. Marketing, in its broadest sense, was key in the workshop as the solution to many of the above issues.

Overview discussion

The overarching key construct within this causal map is the notion of legitimacy or value. For example, the idea with the highest domain and centrality ranking, which also features in 4 of the 6 clusters, is the goal of *clear structure and strong leadership* (this can be seen in the map as having the most connected elements). An interpretation of the map is that the lack of value, recognition, and understanding of the Allied Health Professions could be resolved through strong leadership, clear structure, and marketing the nature and values of the profession to the wider institution. The causal argument within the map is that this very lack of structure and leadership has resulted in pressures on structure and resource equity. The participants feel that their service is institutionally undervalued, resulting from a lack of understanding of what that service is and can do. This lack of understanding and value has resulted in an impact on resources. Participants are highly focused on raising the perception of their service within the main organisation, with the majority of ideas produced focusing on equity, distribution of resources (seen as unequal), recognition, lack of understanding of the service, profile, etc.

The institutional and organisational field attributes are interesting. This case study is framed as one field within the health sector, but this definition seems to be problematic. The participants are part of the allied health professionals, a sub-group of professions that is underrepresented or misunderstood. The case under study would better described as allied health professionals. Notions of legitimacy and interaction within the wider institutions then become clearer to understand and analyse.

Our participants express the lack of the AHP field's legitimacy as a key strategic issue within their wider organisational setting. Those within this organisational field state that their service is institutionally undervalued, resulting from a lack of understanding of what that service is and can do. The group feels that they receive inconsistent recognition and are an undervalued specialism within the health sector. This lack of value and legitimacy is underpinned by a limited understanding by non-AHP practitioners of the nature of the sector's specialisms and roles. Participants also state that it is difficult to express the value of the service/sector. Overall this contributes to a perception that the field has low value and is dispensable. Other parts of the organisation are then perceived to not understand the specialist's role or recognise its value. This lack of understanding and value has resulted in an impact on resources

Participants relate the lack of value, recognition, and understanding of the allied health professions directly to a lack of representative leadership and organisational structure. Participants describe the limited number of senior leaders from their operational area and link this to the perception of a lack of legitimacy and value. In short, as the leadership is not from the profession, they do not understand the benefits or impacts of the profession and, therefore, do not value it. The causal argument within the map is that this very lack of structure and leadership has resulted in pressures on profession and resource equity. This lack of value and recognition is expected to be resolved through the securing of representative leadership and an organisational structure that incorporates professionals from the sector in the hierarchy.

This lack of legitimacy and value within the sector is addressed through marketing actions. The assumption being that communicating and expressing the value of their offer through broader marketing methods would counter perceptions and educate the wider institution. This includes a desire to demonstrate and communicate best practice and champion their unique approach to health care. Many of the key areas of concern within the map were addressed or resolved via marketing and relationship marketing actions. Marketing, in its broadest sense, was key in the workshop as the solution to the lack of legitimacy. This is supported by the need to demonstrate the impact of the profession through comparative evaluation of impact, via benchmarking activities. The purpose of which is to demonstrate value, which is in turn used to inform marketing activities. Participants believe that through evidencing and benchmarking impact, the organisation will attract resources. This differs somewhat from a traditional neo-institutional view of isomorphic alignment with the institution (Dimaggio and Powell, 1983). The field does not fit with the institution and rather than adapt, they hope that by marketing and educating the higher-level institution they can gain institutional legitimacy, a subtle but distinct difference.

A fascinating observation of this workshop is that although the workshop is about a health profession situated within the health sector, the actual practice itself and the production and any mention of the patient are missing. The service, production, or activities of the profession are not explored; it is a given, and the actual nature of the service is not reviewed. Further to this, a search for the terms "customer", "patient" or "service user" all result in minimal findings.

An interesting observation is that the participants did not focus on the end user or customer within this strategic workshop. For example, out of over 200 ideas raised:

- the term "service user" appears three times with one or fewer links
  - a common abbreviation for Service User is "SU" = zero
- the term "patient" appears three times with one or less links
  - common abbreviation for "patient" is PT = zero
- Client appears 0 times
- Customer appears 0 times

These results are highly relevant to this textbook. We have repeatedly emphasised throughout the book that the notion of value creation is key to public sector strategy and that fundamental to this is the organisational impact on society, and vice versa. Our results suggest that not everyone shares this view, and we would be interested in discovering the reader's observations and thoughts on these findings. What do you think?

11.3 Case study 4b education sector

Introduction to organisation

This one-day workshop was undertaken for the new university technical college (UTC) in England. UTC's are for students aged 14 to 19 and focus on a specialism – in this case

Table 11.2 Introduction to education workshop

University technical college session details	
Participant numbers	10
Broad description of range of participants	Board of governors, comprising of industry partners (Engineering) and teaching staff.
Organisational field and dimensions	• education • small 50–5 • independent organisations – regulated and financed through government funding, UK-based
Workshop Revealed Cognitive Causal Mapping details	Ideas generated • issues 111 • goals 43 • core competence 2 • actions; the organisation paused the session after goals. Statement of strategic action, NA Total: 156

energy and engineering. The UTC is sponsored by a university, and various engineering companies sponsor and support the school. The workshop involved the schools board of governors, comprising of industry partners (Engineering) school managers and teaching staff. Table 11.2 provides information about the workshop.

In Figure 11.5, we can see a cognitive causal map as developed by the participants

Again this diagram is difficult to read, and again we do not want the reader to worry about this. Once more, we wanted to demonstrate the big picture, and we present the diagram to show that the techniques we discussed in the preceding chapters are directly applicable in real situations. In this case, rather than present the "raw" causal map as we did in the previous case study, here we have begun the process of analysis; the numbers 1–7 are clusters. The reader will remember from Chapter 10 that clusters are the first stage of the analysis, and they explore distance or similarity in the data.

Figure 11.6 is a thematic analysis of the cognitive map – and summarises key core constructs and their causation.

Instead of showing our interpretation of a detailed cognitive map as we did in the previous case study, because we have already begun the process of clustering, we are able to consider each of the clusters and hone our analysis in that way. This is what we do next in the summary.

Summary

The map contains two particularly strong clusters: **culture and performance of staff** and **high-performance through values**

Culture and performance of staff

Cluster 1 is focused on the performance of staff underpinned by significant high rankings of ideas within centrality and domain particularly around culture. A positive culture with the aligned motivation and morale plus appropriate recruitment and staff capacity is viewed as causally critical to high-performance.

High-performance through values

Cluster 3 in some ways extends this notion into an underpinning set of values. The inference being that high-performance will be achieved through the distinct values and offering of the organisation. Performance can be measured and values that move across staff and students.

Clusters 1 and 3 occupy large areas the map and include the majority of the high level centrality and domain ideas.

Marketing/collaboration to counter negative perceptions by stakeholders

Cluster 2 can be viewed as causally underpinned by a range of negative perceptions by stakeholders. On one hand causal goals are developed to demonstrate value through marketing and communication. The second approach is for wider collaboration with sector stakeholders.

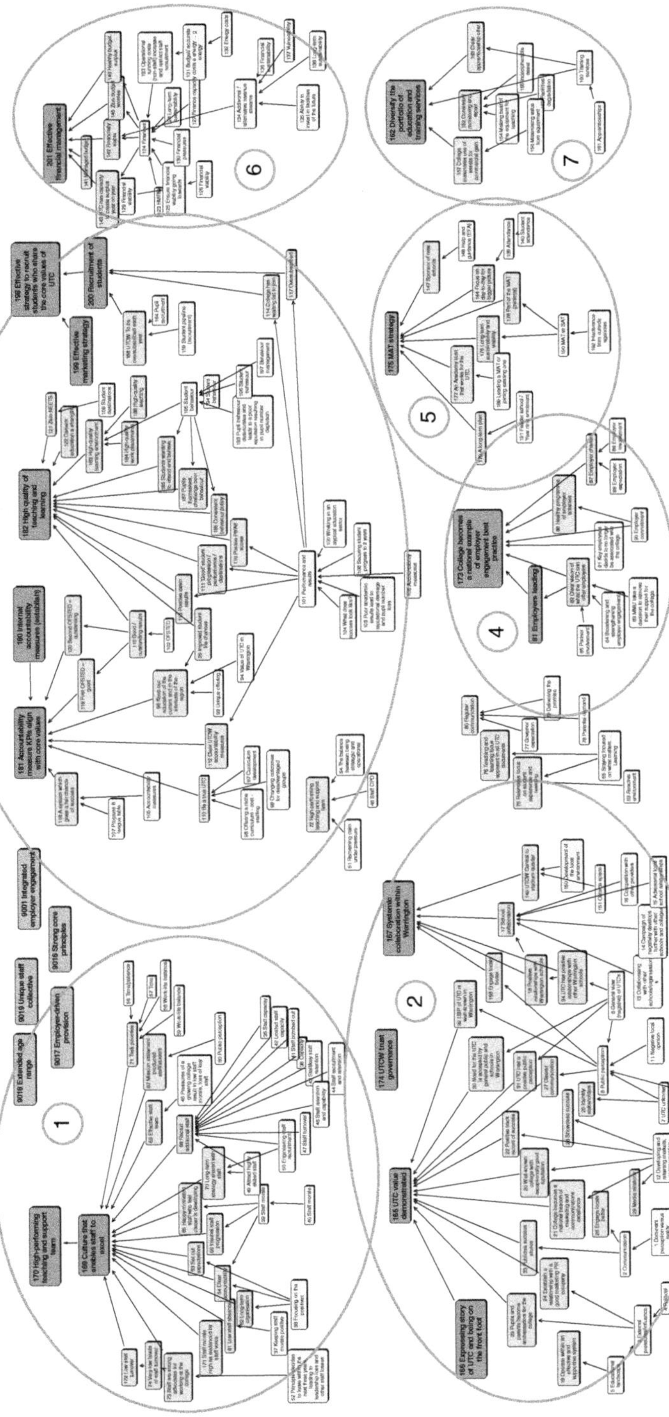

Figure 11.5 Revealed causal cognitive map: Education sector

Causation	*Core constructs*
The causal underpinning of a high performing team is causally underpinned by staff culture, capacity (recruitment), motivation, and morale	High performance within staff
Mitigation of negative perception through marketing and communication will succeed in demonstrating value	Demonstration of value
Negative perceptions of local sector to be resolved through collaboration and relationships	Collaboration with sector
High performance against metrics causally underpinned by leveraging the unique value offer of the organisation. *This value-driving performance of the organisation, its students, and recruitment*	High performance through distinctive values driven offering
The risks and benefits of stakeholder/employer partners in support of establishing the value offer.	Stakeholder (employers) central to offer and quality
Long-term considerations may align to strategic partnerships	MAT strategy, externally driven strategic options
Financial stability through budget management and additional revenue streams	Financial management and financial sustainability
Potential diversification causally underpinned by potential headroom within resources	Use of assets for diversification

Figure 11.6 Key summary of core constructs and causation: Education

Cluster 4, although a separate island, further explores employer stakeholders to widen and reaffirm the value offer.

External support/quality mechanisms

Cluster 5 refers to a specific approach to partnership (MAT strategy -Multi-academy trusts [2020]) but perhaps is more interestingly viewed as external initiatives which could support long-term sustainability.

Financial management

Cluster 6 refers to financial management., and again is a separate island cluster linking financial probity to stability.

Internal unused resources

Cluster 7 is a small cluster exploring the possibility of leveraging unused resources.

Overview discussion

The UTC is a new and different type of school very much supported by employers and organisations but seen as competition and undervalued by the local education sector. This differentiation somewhat separates the school from the mainstream. The impact of this on the strategic thinking of the actors is that the organisation has a need to demonstrate and express their value to stakeholders and the wider community. "Vying for legitimacy with the established sector (education)" is effectively raised as the main area of strategic attention and cognition for the organisation. The organisational actors focus on the demonstration of value, not by creating new value but by expressing the value that they perceive they already have in an attempt to be legitimised by the wider organisational field.

This perception of value is also seen critical in the development of performance and culture Values can be seen as driving performance and recruitment. The issue of lack of perceived value was also seen to be resolved via marketing activities, thereby not changing the organisation to meet homogeneous institutional norms, as per the isomorphism argument of neo-institutionalism, but by attempting to change the institutional norms. The actors here displaying significant agency in championing their position and values.

One observation from the actual delivery of the workshop was a stalling point over a future external funding initiative. This particular governmental scheme was required to be responded to within the forthcoming year. The strategy session effectively stalled over this strategic issue and, in some ways, the group found it difficult to think past this. Longer term and more important issues where side-lined. This was eventually reconciled but it served as a reminder that strategic thinking (the long-term direction and scope of an organisation) can easily be deflected with pressing environmental or operational challenges.

These issues can be brought more into focus by the use of tools such as the balanced scorecard (chapter 2.2), which allows the various competing objectives to be explored collectively so that the overall aims of the organisation can be delivered. This can help to address short-term variations and ensure that the strategy is not buffeted by extraneous factors.

11.4 Case study 4c local government sector

Introduction to organisation

This workshop was undertaken for the transport and highways department within a local council. This department is a public-facing operational department and is responsible for all transport and highways areas across the entirety of the council's duties and geographical footprint. Although all staff are members of the local council, a number of them are also qualified engineers. Indeed, many of the team self- identify as engineers first and local government employees second, and this was seen to have a significant influence on their perceptions. Table 11.3 provides information about the workshop.

In Figure 11.7, we can see a cognitive causal map as developed by the participants.

As before, the fact that this diagram is difficult to read is not important – far more important is that, once more, the techniques we discussed earlier in the book are directly applicable in real situations. For convenience, rather than present the initial causal map, we have again begun the process of analysis – this time, there are nine clusters, not seven as in the previous case study. This shows that there is no "right" number of clusters. There may be three clusters, eight clusters, or 27 clusters. What matters is that the analysis needs to be followed wherever it leads, and it would be a mistake to force data into a predetermined number of clusters.

Table 11.3 Introduction to local government workshop

Transportation and Highways session details	
Participant numbers	5
Broad description of range of participants	Support staff, engineers and managers from within the Local Council
Organisational field and dimensions	• public sector • large • societal/governmental • UK-based • (Engineers present)
Workshop revealed cognitive causal mapping details	Ideas generated: • issues 181 • goals 29 • core competence 36 • actions 46 • statement of intent 4 Total: 296

As we did above, we summarise our findings in Figure 11.8, which is a thematic analysis that summarises key core constructs and their causation.

Summary

Manage expectations of stakeholders via education and communication

The most significant of the core constructs can broadly be described as the management of expectations. This is causally underpinned, firstly by issues highlighting the range of stakeholders, in this case councillors, the public, and organisational management; Secondly, because the expectations of these parties are unrealistic. These unrealistic expectations include workload, demands on resources, and budgets. The actors within the workshop perceive that the management of these expectations can be addressed by educating and communicating the expertise and role of the department to the stakeholders. The assumption is that training of stakeholders and communicating capability will mitigate the strategic issue. The ability to undertake education and communication is underpinned by their core competence of capability and knowledge. Reviewing domain and centrality analysis, it can be seen that these issues within this map constitute some of the most significant concepts.

Express and communicate expertise and role

Within this cluster the two dominant core constructs are *respect of technical experts* and *communicating up*. These have a number of causal attributes:

1 The technical experts are not respected or valued.
2 The expertise that the technical experts (perceive) they have needs to be communicated the organisation's hierarchy.
3 A demonstration of this lack of respect is that training and recruitment is constrained.

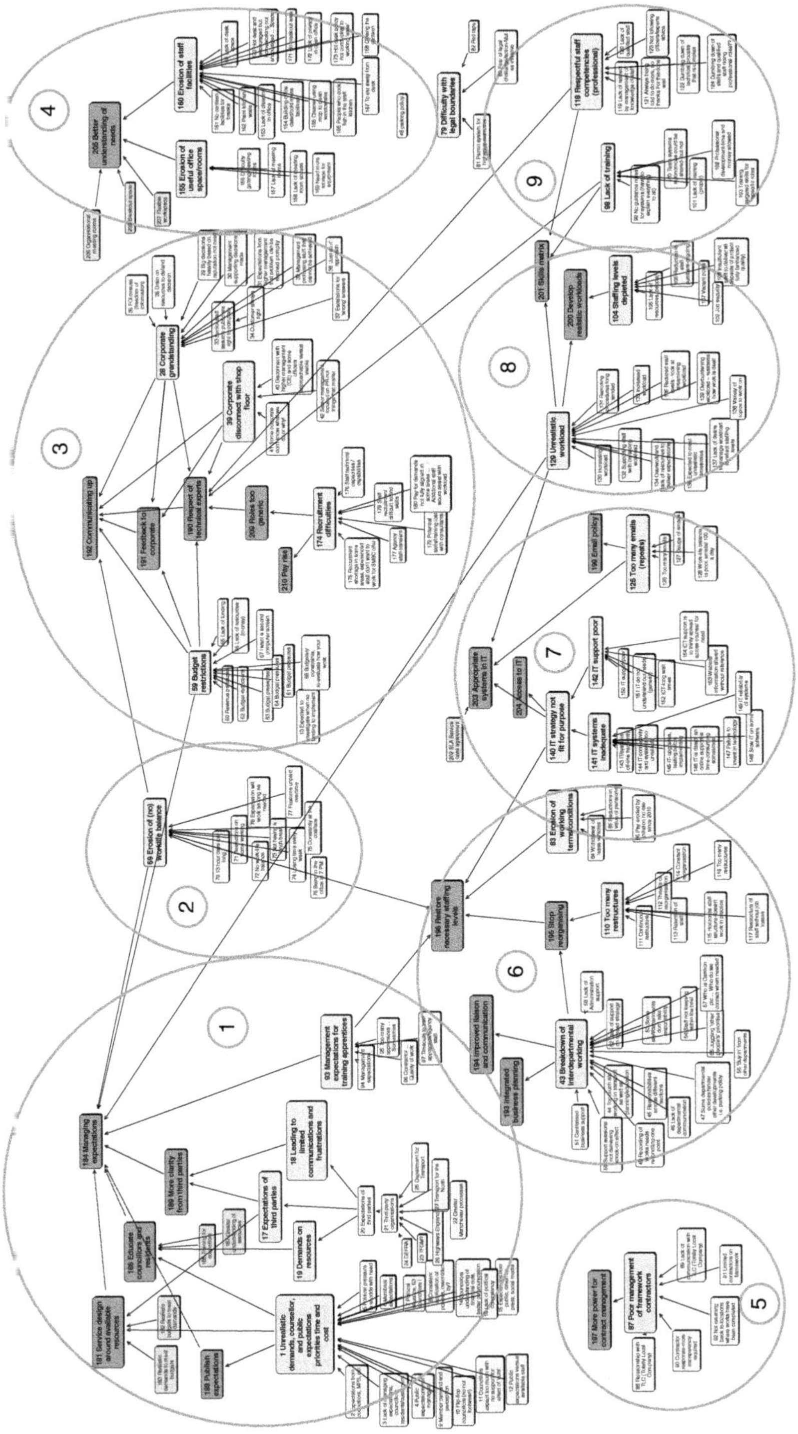

Figure 11.7 Revealed causal cognitive map: local government sector

Causation	*Core constructs*
Unrealistic expectations of stakeholders; knowledge capability and approach of team	Training and communication to manage expectations
Staff expertise not valued; training and recruitment constrained	*Express and communicate expertise and role*
An erosion of facilities and space	*Clarify office environment resource needs*
Limitations of current contract management and the ability of the team to deliver alongside their legal powers	*Clarify contract issues and control*
A breakdown of interdepartmental working	*Continued work on integrating and communication between departments*
Too many emails; IT systems and support inadequate; depleted staff levels impact on workload	*Change expectations on communication policy*

Figure 11.8 Key summary of core constructs and causation: local government

The goals and actions emerging from these issues revolve around the expression, communication, and training of actors up the hierarchy and across the organisation.

Clarify and communicate office environment resource needs

Clarify office environment resource needs, causally underpinned by an erosion of facilities and space.

Cluster 4 is a relatively isolated island focusing on the physical facilities and space available for staff. The detailed issues linking to *erosion of staff facilities* include decorating, cleaning, temperature, food preparation, and other day-to-day impacts of this erosion of facilities. The hierarchical conclusion of this is that senior management do not understand the needs of staff. The actions developed from this insight focus on the raising of senior management team's understanding of staff needs, with better communication and consultation in developing the facilities. This is the second broad area of interest that the participants believe can be resolved through better communication and education.

Clarify and empower actors within contract issues and control

The second aspect of cluster 4 is causally underpinned by the actor's perception of poor management of framework contracting. This has a goal of enabling the transport team to have more power and use their unique legal powers to ensure contract compliance of residents and organisations.

Continued work on integrating and communication between departments

This cluster explores a breakdown of interdepartmental working alongside an erosion of working conditions and work-life balance. Participants relate this to the number of restructures occurring within the organisation. Communication is again seen as critical for mitigating this breakdown of communication. Similarly, communication via consultation is seen as an action to enable a better understanding of needs for the department and to counter some of these issues. Education and communication through consultation are both again prevalent within this cluster and viewed as a solution to issues within inter-departmental working and work-life balance. Communication is viewed as an essential conduit for improving efficiency coordination and integration.

Change expectations on communication policy

Cluster 7 also explores communication in relation to workload, email overload, IT systems, and staffing levels. Solutions being suggested include policies improvements in policies and IT systems alongside staffing levels and realistic workloads.

Missing areas

Throughout the strategic map there is no mention or consideration of the core product/service or functioning aspects of the department. The expertise and quality of the service is taken as a given and not questioned.

Overview discussion

The Transport and Highways Department strategy session resulted in a clear focus on a number of issues encountered by the team. The most significant being the high expectations of stakeholders regarding the teams capability and approach, and that the participants perceive that their technical expertise is neither respected nor valued. The insight being that stakeholders do not have realistic expectations of the team, this runs alongside a perception that their (the transport team) expertise is not valued or senior management does not understand the team's needs, resulting in a lack of basic facilities. These areas are (perceived to be) resolved by communication and education of the stakeholders to manage expectations and express the nature and skills of the team. Of interest is that participants do not question the nature of the service, its quality, and its value to the organisation is a given. The nature of value is solely judged by actors within the organisational field. Further to this, the actual activity or production and the work undertaken by the team is not discussed or evaluated; it is a given. The session did not focus on improvements to that provision or on efficiencies or new ways of working; the actual production aspect of the departmental unit was excluded as a strategic area of concern.

11.5 Summary insights on the three cases

The local government strategy session has a significant focus on the value as perceived by the actors within the department versus their understanding of what their perceived value is from senior management teams and stakeholders. From their (the departmental actor's) perspective they have significant expertise, local knowledge, and capability which, from their viewpoint, appears to be undervalued, underused, and poorly understood. This is similar to the health case study, where the lack of value, recognition, and understanding of the profession could be resolved through strong leadership, clear structure, and marketing the nature and values of the profession to the wider institution. The causal argument within the map is that this very lack of structure and leadership has resulted in pressures

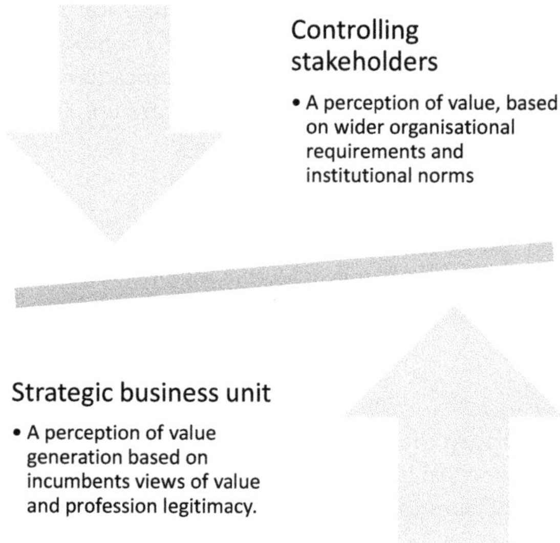

Figure 11.9 Value disconnect with strategic business unit in the public sector

on structure and resource equity. The school also establishes a lack of perceived value by local stakeholders as a critical issue to be resolved; the actual value of the offer or product is assumed to be of high value – just not understood.

In all cases, the participants believe that influential stakeholders are not informed or clear on the capability and expertise within the organisation. This may be a perception on the actor's behalf, but it raises the question of how value is evaluated and by whom. This could be referred to as a ***value disconnect*** (Figure 11.9).

The legitimacy drivers and socially constructed (Berger and Luckmann, 1966) perception of the business unit's offer is not shared by wider stakeholders or management. In fact, it could be argued that the "other" (management/stakeholders) have an entirely different institutionally driven or socially constructed view of what is valuable.

Our participants believe that by communicating their needs, expertise, circumstances, and insights, this will change how they are managed and resourced. They lean towards marketing activities as a way to resolve this disconnection. This makes an assumption that their perception of reality is potentially shared by stakeholders and that, subject to the stakeholders having the same information, they will come to the same conclusion. Although this could be correct, the actors under study do not appear to consider that their socially constructed reality or institutional drivers may be different. In fact, the perception of reality by the various actors may be entirely different and come to entirely different solutions or conclusions, regardless of the accuracy or content of any training or communication.

The institutional and organisational field (Dimaggio and Powell, 1983) attributes are also interesting. These case studies appear easily definable as one field each, but this "surface level" delineation seems limiting. The participants across all of the cases are part of a higher-level organisational field but also a part of a sub-group of professions or type that they clearly feel is underrepresented or misunderstood. The actors under study all have their own institutionally defined field with its specific legitimacy drivers, but they are also positioned within a larger field with differing legitimacy drivers and homogeneity.

The school is a new and different type, very much supported by employers and organisations but seen as competition and undervalued by the sector. Allied health professions are again a newer form of health and feel separate from mainstream medicine. The engineers within the council have different background, professions, and priorities. They all demonstrate a need to express their value to stakeholders and the wider community. The institutional norms and accepted legitimacy of established sector forms seems to show as a key area of strategic attention and cognition for organisations/departments that do not fit neatly into institutional norms.

The case studies all express the lack of a field's legitimacy as a key strategic issue within their wider organisational setting. These "sub" organisational fields appear institutionally undervalued, resulting from a lack of understanding of what that service is and can do. The group feels that they receive inconsistent recognition and are an underrated specialism within the sector. As the higher-level field owns or controls resource allocation, the actors are left with a problem. The strategic response to this is to attempt to change the perceptions and value judgment of the higher-level field, although marketing and communicating the benefits and value of the lower-level field. The organisations then focus on the demonstration of value, not by creating new value but by expressing the value that they already have.

Overall the actors under study are generally positive in their analysis of their value regardless of wider organisational perceptions. If we consider a classical view of strategic analysis, for example the resource-based view or value chain, an assumption is made that the benefits, competence, and value-adding activities of an organisational unit can be established. This focus on the internal, more managerial aspects aligns with the classical value chain analysis. However, each case misses core operational activities/professional attributes and, critically, the value of activities is very much evaluated by the participants not by the buyer; in this case by the part of the organisation with control of resources. Value then is proffered by the actors within the operational unit but not evaluated against the value as perceived by the buyers of the service. A value chain approach would have a different insight on this, where value is generated and evaluated on the buyer's perception of value. Within these examples we can observe that there is a disconnect between the value as perceived by the actors within the organisational unit and how they perceive the wider stakeholders evaluate them. Although we have only reviewed three case studies, it does raise some interesting insight into how value is perceived and by whom.

A fascinating observation of the health workshop (and similarly within the local government example) is that, the actual health practice itself – and any mention of the patient – is missing. The service, production, or activities of the profession are not explored; it is a given, and the actual nature of the service is not reviewed. Further to this a search for the terms "customer", "patient", or "service user" all result in minimal findings. One interpretation may be that participants view their hands on activities, i.e. the health aspect of their work, as linked to a professional standard or professional body. A physiotherapist or occupational therapist will turn to that professional body or sector for guidance, insight, and development regarding the nature and development of their practice. In effect, the actual production of the service and the recipients of the care are considered to exist in a separate strategic space to that of the management of the organisation. Strategy activity then may be viewed by actors as the management of business or people, and health practice is not included as it is accommodated in a separate mental space. This is not a deliberate delineation of two worlds, but it does remind the strategy practitioner that an individual's perception of what they do may not be the same as the organisational perception. The participants can all be considered diligent, highly productive, and invested, but a strategy workshop just may not be seen as a place where health care practice and function is discussed. This could be seen as an affordance (Jarzabkowski and Kaplan, 2015) of the format of a strategy workshop within the sector. The very nature of a strategy workshop could effectively direct health care practitioners to focus on business/organisational aspects not on service or production; potentially this is either a limit on organisational actor's understanding of strategy or a limitation within the nature and form of the strategy workshop. Either way, ensuring that participants engage with the full range of strategic activity with a workshop would be beneficial and potentially improve the insights and outcomes.

11.6 Chapter summary

For this chapter summary, we offer something different. We present our summary in the form of a few questions and sub-questions. In this way, we pose some thoughts that people may wish to think about when they are trying to address our case study insights in their own practices.

- Is the business unit held back by their local legitimacy, or are the higher-order fields lacking perception about the unit's attributes or values?
- Would perhaps establishing the neo-institutional legitimacy aspects of a field would clarify the isomorphic drivers and add insight to any discussion or developments?
- Do the business unit and the higher order stakeholders share the same values or objectives? Is the purpose of the organisation clear?
- At surface level, the organisational purpose and the nature of the generated value may appear self-evident; exploring this in more depth may reveal some subtlety and insights.
- What is the scope of a strategy session? Will participants include or exclude aspects of their profession?
- Will participants just explore what they perceive as "management", or will the profession or service be included? If not, where is this developed and how does this link in?

References

Ackermann, F., Eden, C. & Brown, I. (2005). *The Practice of Making Strategy: A Step-by-Step Guide*. London: Sage.

Ackermann, F., Eden, C. & Brown, I. (2010). *The Practice of Making Strategy: A Step-by-Step Guide*. London: Sage.

Berger, P. L. & Luckmann, T. (1966). *The Social Construction of Reality; A Treatise in the Sociology of Knowledge*. Garden City, NY: Doubleday.

Braun, V. & Clarke, V. (2006). Using thematic analysis in psychology. *Qualitative Research in Psychology*, 3, 77–101.

Di Gregorio, S. (2006). *Introduction to Decision Explorer*. A short course note. Retrieved August 8, 2018, from https://banxia.com/pdf/de/DEIntro1.pdf.

Dimaggio, P. J. & Powell, W. W. (1983). The iron cage revisited – institutional isomorphism and collective rationality in organizational fields. *American Sociological Review*, 48, 147–160.

Eden, C. & Ackermann, F. (1998). *Making Strategy: The Journey of Strategic Management*. Thousand Oaks, CA, London: Sage.

Education, D. F. (2020). *Multi-Academy Trusts: Establishing and Developing Your Trust*. London: Department for Education. Multi-academy trusts: establishing and developing your trust – GOV.UK (www.gov.uk)

England, N. H. S. (2020). *"NHS England" the 14 Allied Health Professions*. NHS England: The 14 allied health professions.

Jarzabkowski, P. & Kaplan, S. (2015). Strategy tools-in-use: A framework for understanding "technologies of rationality" in practice. *Strategic Management Journal*, 36, 537–558.

Jones, M. (2002). *Decision Explorer User's Guide Version 3.2.3.2 Ed*. Kendal: Branxia Software Ltd.

Newbury, G. (2020). *Trust Strategies*. www.gmmh.nhs.uk/trust-strategies.

Section 5

Summary

Chapter 12

Summary and conclusions

12.1 Introduction

Public sector management is largely sidelined in the literature. Despite the fact that public sector organisations employ many thousands of people, despite the enormity of public sector budgets, and despite the impact of public sector decisions on all of us, it is still seen by many as less important than the private sector. Nowhere is this more true than in the field of strategy. Public sector strategy is fundamentally different from that of the private sector, focusing on value for its stakeholders rather than on profitability and competitive advantage. And yet, it is neglected by scholars and is often overlooked by lecturers in the classroom.

This book has been a labour of love from the authors. In our teaching practice, we frequently come upon students from the public sector who bemoan the traditional focus on private sector management theories. We undertake consultancy work with organisations from the public sector, and we sometimes have to search long and hard to identify practical case studies to draw upon. There is a clear gap in the market for a strategy textbook that meets the needs of this large and important sector of society. Moreover, most academic strategy texts focus on theory and high-level strategic planning but few explore how strategy is actually practiced, delivered, and implemented, especially in the public sector. As we have seen throughout this book, managers do not simply roll out the strategy that has been developed. Instead, the reality is more nuanced, and public sector managers need to think for themselves and react to rapidly changing situations.

This book has been designed to furnish readers with the key knowledge from the traditional private sector perspectives on strategic management, but we also show how this needs to be modified and adapted for the public sector. By interweaving theory with practical cases, we have sought to equip managers with practical tools and insights for use in the workplace.

12.2 Summary of the key chapters in the book

The book is divided into four key sections, each of which is subdivided into separate chapters. Each chapter builds upon the last, and the nature of public sector strategy unfolds logically and consistently. Theory and practice are interspersed so that students can become familiar with how concepts are applied in the "real world" and gain an understanding that strategy in the public sector is not some abstract theory that is never used; rather, it has significant practical applications.

DOI: 10.4324/9780429344305-18

Section 1 introduces the public sector. It sets the scene for the book and provides the context for the rest of the book. It contains a single chapter that gives a sense of the enormity and complexity of the sector. We show that the "public sector" is hard to define and its precise role, scale, and function varies considerably across the globe. The public sector is, therefore, made up of a range of organisations with a wide remit of functions; but despite the diverse nature of these bodies, public sector organisations have a number of common characteristics and operate according to general rules and procedures. Fundamental to this is the notion of value creation. This is the underlying principle behind public sector strategy, and we return to this theme repeatedly throughout this book.

Section 2 provides much of the theoretical underpinning for the book and outlines key theoretical frameworks which are fundamental to students and managers' understanding of strategy.

Chapter 2 explores the history of public sector management, and we show that there has been an increasing trend towards the introduction of private sector management techniques. We explore three lenses through which public sector strategy can be viewed – traditional public administration, new public management, and network governance – and we show that the move towards managerialism has impacted widely across the sector.

The second chapter is a large one. This chapter is where the reader will find Porter's five forces model. This chapter is where the reader will find VRIO and the value chain. This chapter is, therefore, what many readers will expect to see in a strategy textbook – and with good reason. These are tried and tested models and theories with an extensive pedigree, and they have been developed by some of the biggest names in the field. Although they were developed with the private sector in mind, they contain much that is relevant for the public sector. It is, therefore, important that they are given the attention they deserve. However, because of the unique nature of the public sector and its focus on value creation, it is necessary to modify and adapt some of these approaches. Building on the concept of "shared value" and shareholder and stakeholder perspectives on value, we discuss how value creation within the public sector requires a clear understanding of how value is perceived and captured for different stakeholders. Finally, drawing on earlier discussions and building on key theories of value creation within the field of strategy, we review and discuss the important public value frameworks that take into account the public and the business requirements that many government organisations experience.

Section 3 offers something different and is something that most strategy textbooks completely overlook. In this section, we explore how strategy is developed and how managers create and refine strategy for their organisations.

The first two chapters begin to consider how people are not as logical and independent as they might think they are. The first chapter demonstrates that, whatever we like to think of our own impartiality and ability to avoid being influenced, we are all affected by intrinsic and extrinsic factors. These can skew our thought processes and can impair the quality of the strategic decisions we make. This chapter should, therefore, have proved to be helpful in allowing readers to become more aware of what they do and why they do it. The second chapter builds on this by exploring how neo-institutional theory underpins much of strategic thinking and strategy development in the public sector, and in this chapter we lay bare how unconscious assumptions can arise, and we explore how these can impact the strategic decisions that management makes.

The next two chapters use psychology theory to get inside the minds of strategists to understand how people make strategic decisions in the real world. In the first of these, we get to the root of what a "strategic decision" actually is, and we offer a theoretical framework for understanding these types of decision. Normative decision-making uses logical and rational approaches to undertake a series of steps to consider and evaluate the various options that present themselves and, in doing so, produces a final decision that is underpinned by robust analysis. However, behavioural decision-making uses experience and gut instinct to cut through the mass of data that managers are often confronted with, and the resulting decisions are fast but may be skewed by bias or other factors. We demonstrate that, even though we think we are using a normative approach (five forces, value chain, VRIO etc), in practice strategy is often based on a series of non-rational steps. The final chapter in this section builds upon the first three chapters. It again takes a psychology-based approach to examine the use of cognitive heuristics when developing strategy. Cognitive heuristics are shortcuts, or rules of thumb, that are inherent within us all, and they can be used to make decisions. We show, with worked examples, that although public sector managers think they are being logical, in fact, the strategic decisions they make are guided as much by instinct and intuition as they are by facts and figures.

Section 4 is again something that most strategy textbooks completely overlook. In this section, we explore the *practice* of strategy. We build upon the earlier parts of the book – especially Section 2 – and we apply the theoretical underpinnings in a range of natural situations.

In the first chapter, we argue that some traditional theories are somewhat mechanistic: if you plug in some facts and figures into a model, then a good solution will emerge. Strategy As practice challenges this idea. Strategy is a social practice which pays attention to how strategy practitioners act and interact. We introduce the idea of causal cognitive mapping to break down strategists' thinking and lay bare the thought processes behind these. We argue that strategy as practice moves strategy away from being the preserve of the senior manager and incorporates the wider range of actors and influencers.

The second chapter builds on these ideas to explore a practical example. We use our own empirical research to explore an application of the causal cognitive mapping process detailed in the previous chapter. This leads into a discussion of how a strategy workshop can be developed. This will be particularly useful for prospective managers and those who train them. Borne from our own experiences, we suggest ways in which a workshop, or a series of workshops, might be run. We explore ways in which facilitators can gather ideas and harness thoughts and then work with the participants to refine and develop these further into a plan of action.

The next chapter is a practical guide for running a strategy workshop. Again, drawn from our own experiences, we offer a worked example of the previous chapter's ideas. The process shown in this chapter is a simple and straightforward method for eliciting strategy that can work at any level within the organisation, from an organisational team or department through to higher corporate levels.

The final chapter in this section builds upon the previous one. In that chapter, we show how workshops might be conducted, but in this chapter we provide worked examples to show what can be achieved in these workshops. This chapter examines three public sector strategy case studies and draws insights and guidance on the type of barriers, thinking, and approaches encountered when exploring strategy. The chapter explores three separate organisations: a profession within the UK National Health Service, a department within local government, and a new form of school.

12.3 Concluding thoughts

We have aimed this book at business and management students who are employed in the public sector or who are aiming for a career in the public sector, and who are in the final year of their degrees or are undertaking master's level studies. It will also be of benefit for public sector managers, consultants, and private sector organisations who wish to interact with the public sector. By exploring the psychology behind strategic decision-making, this book will offer a new approach to text books in this field. It will explore "how" managers make their decisions. In this way, it will offer guidance that improves clarity by helping managers to refine their thinking and will, thereby, improve students' strategic decision-making and give students key knowledge and practical tools that they can apply in their own workplaces.

Public sector strategy is a significantly under-researched area, but it is both vibrant and essential, with budgets of several 100 million dollars and strategic choices that are literally life-and-death decisions. Therefore, it is important that students and managers understand how it works: both to improve their own decision-making but also to better integrate the public and private sectors at a senior level.

We hope you have found this book informative and useful, and we would genuinely be interested in your thoughts and ideas for further development of the book in future editions.

Index

Page numbers in *italics* indicate a figure and page numbers in **bold** indicate a table on the corresponding page.

Milton Keynes UK
Ingram Content Group UK Ltd.
UKHW031946130923
428633UK00006B/32

9 780367 361754